DISRUPTIVE WOMEN

The Untold Story of Nova Scotia's Pioneers of Peace and Suffrage

Sharon M. H. MacDonald

NIMBUS PUBLISHING
NIMBUS.CA

To disruptive women everywhere

but especially

in loving memory of

Marguerite Andersen, Muriel Duckworth,

and Marta Robertson-Smyth.

Copyright © 2025, Sharon M. H. MacDonald

All rights reserved. No part of this book may be reproduced, stored in a retrieval system or transmitted in any form or by any means without the prior written permission from the publisher, or, in the case of photocopying or other reprographic copying, permission from Access Copyright, 1 Yonge Street, Suite 1900, Toronto, Ontario M5E 1E5.

Nimbus Publishing Limited
3660 Strawberry Hill Street, Halifax, NS, B3K 5A9
(902) 455-4286 nimbus.ca

Nimbus Publishing is based in Kjipuktuk, Mi'kma'ki, the traditional territory of the Mi'kmaq People.

No part of this book may be used in the training of generative artificial intelligence technologies or systems.

Printed and bound in Canada
NB1729

Editor: Marianne Ward
Editor for the press: Angela Mombourquette
Cover & Interior Design: Bee Stanton

Library and Archives Canada Cataloguing in Publication

Title: Disruptive women : the untold story of Nova Scotia's pioneers of peace and suffrage / Sharon M.H. MacDonald.
Names: MacDonald, Sharon, 1948-author
Description: Includes bibliographical references and index.
Identifiers: Canadiana (print) 20240491505 | Canadiana (ebook) 20240492617 | ISBN 9781774714331 (softcover) | ISBN 9781774714348 (EPUB)
Subjects: LCSH: Suffragists—Nova Scotia—Biography. | LCSH: Women pacifists—Nova Scotia—Biography. | LCSH: Pacifists—Nova Scotia—Biography. | LCSH: Women—Nova Scotia—Biography. | LCGFT: Biographies.
Classification: LCC HQ1455.A3 M33 2025 | DDC 324.6/230922716—dc23

Nimbus Publishing acknowledges the financial support for its publishing activities from the Government of Canada, the Canada Council for the Arts, and from the Province of Nova Scotia. We are pleased to work in partnership with the Province of Nova Scotia to develop and promote our creative industries for the benefit of all Nova Scotians.

Table of Contents

	Preface	vii
	Introduction	xiii
Chapter 1	Shaking the Family Tree	1
Chapter 2	Political Involvement During the Last Decade of the Nineteenth Century	19
Chapter 3	The Beginning of a New Century	33
Chapter 4	War, Peace Advocacy, and Suffrage Work	49
Chapter 5	Polly's International Studies and Adventures	71
Chapter 6	Mary Chesley's Final Days and Polly's Emergence as an Activist	113
Chapter 7	A Canadian Activist in England	155
Chapter 8	Voluntary Poverty in India	167
Chapter 9	Celebrating Voices of Dissent	227
	Acknowledgements	233
	Appendix I	235
	Appendix II	237
	Endnotes	239
	Bibliography	246
	Index	249

PREFACE
Searching for the Chesleys

I FIRST ENCOUNTERED THE NAME OF MARY RUSSELL CHESLEY while carrying out research at the Nova Scotia Archives, looking at the papers of various women's organizations for evidence of wartime relief work in the province. While the Woman's Christian Temperance Union (WCTU) participated in relief work, what captured my attention were the WCTU's Department of Peace and Arbitration reports, written by Chesley. Already a major figure in the WCTU for her suffrage activism as superintendent of the Department of Franchise, Chesley noted in her first report, in 1908, "At our convention last year it was decided to take up again the work of Peace and Arbitration, and I became Superintendent. I accepted the appointment with the hope that a younger woman would take charge of the Franchise work. Now I find myself in a similar position to that of a young lady who is undecided between two suitors, captivated with number two before free from number one, the earliest and first love. I trust some solution of this difficult position may be found."[1]

Chesley courted the two suitors for the rest of her life. In 1918, the year property-owning Nova Scotian women who were British subjects got the vote, the Department of Franchise became the Department of Christian Citizenship, and Chesley worked tirelessly to inform women of the issues and ensure they voted. She also maintained unwavering passion for the peace cause until her death in 1923.

In the 1990s, I was writing a thesis on Nova Scotian women's wartime relief efforts, and Chesley's reports on peace and arbitration resonated with me. As someone averse to war, I was intrigued by Chesley's cogent political writings. Despite having been written one hundred years earlier, her reports seemed remarkably contemporary. Chesley's Peace and Arbitration work became the main subject of a thesis chapter.[2]

The outbreak of the First World War caused division among suffragists. Some believed that supporting the war effort would prove that women deserved the vote. Among pacifist suffragists, some changed their position, particularly when sons enlisted. Any public display of pacifist conviction during wartime was deemed unpatriotic; however, pacifists considered their own position to be patriotic. Canadian pacifists Ada May Brown Courtice and Andrew Cory Courtice believed that to educate the public toward pacifism, "the negative forces of nationalism and militarism [should be replaced] with the positive virtues of patriotism and humanitarianism."[3] Laura Hughes, a pacifist and labour activist, in writing to fellow pacifist Violet McNaughton concerning reading material on international arms, secret diplomacy, and war profiteering, declared, "If you can get a group studying these books you will be doing good patriotic work, for the truth is always patriotic."

It was only later that I researched Chesley's role as a pioneer suffragist. Going beyond the WCTU records, I found biographical profiles and newspaper accounts of her activities as well as her articles and letters to editors. As I uncovered more information on Chesley and her family, surprising and dramatic personal events emerged. The Chesleys were no strangers to tragedy, of which more will be said. In attempting to trace family papers, I searched for the only surviving child of Mary and her husband, Samuel, Mary Albee Chesley (known familiarly as Polly), who had moved to England and, in the mid- to late 1920s, ran a small private school (Anthorne) in Potters Bar, just outside of London. I discovered that Polly had joined the Religious Society of Friends (the Quakers) in England. Like her mother, she had been an activist, involved with a number of pacifist and leftist political and social groups, so I hoped the Chesley papers might have been preserved somewhere. My queries began with the Library of the Society of Friends in London, which held the Quaker archives.

The archives contained two surprising references to Polly Chesley: one in Marjorie Sykes's historical account of Quakers in India; the other a memorial notice in Britain's Quaker journal *The Friend*, dated June 26, 1936, announcing Polly's death in India, with effusive praise from none other than Mohandas Karamchand Gandhi, better known as Mahatma Gandhi.[4] Among other things, he said, "In [Chesley's] love for India's villages she was not to be excelled by anybody. There was nothing of the patron about her. She would serve anybody with the greatest zeal."

Oh, the temptation! The unexpected discovery of Polly's friendship with Gandhi threatened derailment from the primary goal of completing my thesis. I wanted to rush off on another tangent and find out more about this young woman from Lunenburg (Polly was only forty-four when she died) whose life had intersected with one of the most famous figures in global history. I made forays to discover more about Polly but knew that any project concerning her would have to wait. Polly did, however, become the seed for my next writing project. In my research on Polly in India, I found other like-minded Western women who also supported Indian independence and Gandhi's village uplift movement. The result of that research was a collective biography in the form of a dissertation.

In the years since discovering the Chesleys, I have had other projects; however, the family has remained of compelling interest. This narrative is not only a story of their lives, but also a story of my own journey to track down the Chesley history. As will become evident, the Chesleys had an intense interest in social and political issues, both local and international in scope. In their day, both Mary and her daughter Polly held prominence in activist causes, yet they have largely disappeared from the historical record.

What do we remember of the past efforts of humankind? We tend to honour those who rule, those who make war, the occasional scientist who makes a breakthrough discovery, and we seem to be curious about dastardly criminals. Even in huge cataclysmic events such as revolutions or social change of any sort, only the perceived leaders are remembered. We often forget that countless individuals and collectivities help pave the way for historical shifts. So, this account sheds light on two women who participated in movements that influenced major changes in their day.

The Chesley family line ended with Polly in 1936, so there were no descendants to help keep alive memory of the Chesleys. In spite of Mary Chesley's pioneer role in Nova Scotia suffrage, I believe that because she lived outside the metropolis of Halifax and died soon after suffrage was granted, she dropped off the historical radar. Catherine Cleverdon, who in 1950 published her work on suffrage in Canada, had no opportunity to meet and interview her. She relied heavily on the oral testimony of Ella Murray, who, according to some, was not well disposed toward Mary.[5] Cleverdon's work established the base upon which other suffrage history has relied, so Chesley, as well as other suffragists in the province who did not live in the Halifax metropolis, received short shrift.

I have generally shied away from the mystical or inexplicable; nevertheless, I confess that throughout my long years of searching for the Chesleys, I have sometimes felt that I had been appointed the task of bringing to light these forgotten figures. During the times when clues dried up and I felt at an impasse, serendipity or synchronicity would open a new door that would convince me I was supposed to carry on. It is years since I accepted this task as somehow inevitable.

In large part, the Chesleys (mother and daughter) have been inspirational—physically long dead but very much alive in my imagination. I have come to see that my "appointed" task is to ensure that their lives are brought out from the shadows of obscurity.

This might be considered out of step with current research directions; the early suffrage movement participants were largely white, middle-class women. Is their history still relevant at this time when important work is being carried out to bring forth stories of forgotten Black, Indigenous, and other communities? My hope is that one avenue does not cancel out the other. There are missing pieces to the story of suffrage and peace activism in the late nineteenth and early twentieth centuries, and this is an attempt to fill in one small part.

The task of scanning miles of microfilm has been both tedious and exhilarating. There is nothing better for a historian than to stumble upon a gold nugget of information when the mining has been predicated on pure hope that something *might* turn up. Such discoveries make up for hours of research yielding nothing. In this book, I quote liberally from the primary source documents (in abbreviated form), because I believe the phrasing allows the reader to experience the voices of the past and the sentiments and ideas of the period and of the persons quoted. I am the medium, providing the channel through which these women can make themselves known.

The two Marys have taken me on fantastic adventures. For the reader and, perhaps, the aspiring historian, my hope is to provide a window into the process and sometimes thrilling enterprise of research. Meticulous sleuthing is part of the work, but it takes a certain stubbornness and wild hope to carry one forward in the dry spells. The following narrative is the result.

INTRODUCTION
Me and the Chesleys

MARY RUSSELL CHESLEY LIVED HER ADULT LIFE IN LUNENBURG, Nova Scotia, during the late nineteenth and early twentieth centuries; I had lived in Lunenburg from 1979 to 1987 but had never heard of her. Indeed, when I lived in Lunenburg, I would not have imagined the town spawning Mary Russell Chesley's radical voice. Before moving to town, I had lived in various rural spots in Lunenburg County. I had joined the Lunenburg County Women's Group (LCWG), an organization mainly comprising women who, like me, were "from away." We threw our energies into establishing continuing education classes, well-women's clinics, and other services that did not exist in the county. Our mission to improve the lives of rural women was both altruistic and self-serving. Largely ex-urbanites, the majority of us were also young mothers who felt the isolation of living far from amenities such as universities, cultural opportunities, and, perhaps of equal importance, city playgrounds where one could meet others going through a similar phase of life. Spread out across the county, we isolated women found that the LCWG provided opportunities to get together for both meaningful community activism and good times.

I now realize that I had far more in common with Mary Russell Chesley than I had previously imagined. Chesley's trajectory was very much like my own. She came from a larger metropolis: Dartmouth/Halifax. The organization to which she dedicated her energy, the Woman's Christian Temperance Union, had more in common with the Lunenburg County Women's Group than I would have owned up to. After all, the idea of temperance in the late twentieth century seemed old-fashioned and prudish to my youthful self. Unbeknownst to me at that time, scholars were beginning to reassess the temperance movement and recognize that it was not an unreasonable response to a significant social problem.

Founded in 1874 and led by American Frances Willard, the WCTU's impetus was a desire to fight the liquor trade, which was destroying many families. But Willard had broader interests. She set up the organization so individual unions could take on other causes if they chose to do so. Willard's "Do everything" motto allowed the freedom to remain focused on temperance only, or groups could consider other issues. Not surprisingly, women saw the vote as a tool in the fight for temperance legislation. In Nova Scotia, the most active leadership for women's suffrage came out of the WCTU. Their interests also expanded to other areas of social reform.

Almost one hundred years later, a parallel situation happened with the Lunenburg County Women's Group. Although members had certain common interests, there were individuals who espoused particular causes. I can now recognize that the LCWG had a certain "Do everything" aspect to it. Within our group, individuals took up various social and environmental issues and would write letters to politicians or prepare briefs for commissions. Often the handiwork of individuals, letters and briefs would carry the endorsement of our organization. In truth, we were a relatively small group, but our impact was felt, and we were both bemused and amused that politicians and governmental organizations saw us as a much larger force than we really were.

I have "lived" with Mary Russell Chesley for years and am only now realizing our common ground. In the past, I assumed that some of the odd common threads I shared with daughter Polly were the more compelling reasons why I was attached to the Chesleys. For example, in the 1960s I dropped out of university to pursue dance. In 1986, my second child was in school, and I was in need of intellectual stimulation, so I returned to university part-time. Because Lunenburg had no post-secondary institutions, I commuted to Halifax to attend Mount Saint Vincent University. In that first year, I took a course in creative writing, and an instructor recommended that I submit one of my stories to the annual competition of the Nova Scotia Writers' Federation. One had to choose a pen name so that there was no danger of the judges favouring a person they knew. I chose the last name of Behn, having discovered in one of my courses the writer Aphra Behn (1640–1689), the first woman to live by her pen in Britain during the Restoration period. I was taken with her story and wrote a number of essays concerning her work. When I learned of Polly's life in India, I discovered that she had acquired the name Tara (meaning "star") and that she also carried the honorific Behn (sometimes spelled Ben or Behen), meaning "Sister"—the custom for addressing unmarried women in India. Tara Behn, the Quaker formerly from Lunenburg (I, too, had an association with Quakers), spoke to me across the years.

This book was conceived as an attempt to share with readers what I know of these remarkable women and my own voyage of discovery.

Without further introduction, the story begins.

CHAPTER 1
Shaking the Family Tree

HOW AND WHY THE CHESLEYS BECAME THE PEOPLE THEY WERE cannot be explained by either nature or nurture; however, both Mary Rebecca Russell and her future husband, Samuel Ainsley Chesley, had antecedents that helped to form them.

Mary Rebecca Russell, born September 4, 1847, in Dartmouth, Nova Scotia, was the third of six children born to Nathaniel and Agnes (Bissett) Russell. Mary's grandfather, also named Nathaniel, had come to Nova Scotia from Boston in 1776 and, according to Mary's brother Benjamin, was "compelled by conscientious scruples against the taking up of arms, more than he was prompted by want of sympathy with the Revolutionary cause."[6] In other words, he was more of a pacifist than a British Loyalist.

According to one account, Nathaniel was born in 1746 and married by 1768 to a Mary Hibbert in Boston.[7] Eight years later they were living in Dartmouth and, by the 1790s, had two adolescent daughters, Mary (known as Polly)[8] and Rebecca.[9] Polly was in her late teens in 1798 when a jealous suitor (Thomas Bembridge, a British soldier) stabbed her to death (Bembridge was subsequently hanged for his crime).[10] Sadly, Polly's mother and her younger sister Rebecca both died soon after, circa 1800.

In 1808, the widowed Nathaniel Russell married the widowed Mrs. Alma (Jonathan) Elliot, whose father had been a Quaker preacher who came to Dartmouth from New England. While the Russells were not Quakers, they had friends and neighbours who were part of the migration of Quaker whalers from Nantucket, Massachusetts, who first settled in Dartmouth in 1785. After the American Revolution (or War of Independence), Britain imposed heavy tariffs upon the whaling industry. For this reason, along with not wishing to take sides in a war, Nantucket whaling families moved to Nova Scotia.[11] The fact that Nathaniel's two daughters from his first marriage, Mary (Polly) and Rebecca Russell, are listed as witnesses to a Quaker marriage that took place in Dartmouth in 1795 also speaks to the Russell family's connections with the Quaker community.[12]

Nathaniel and his new wife had one son, also named Nathaniel, born in 1809 and married in 1835 to Agnes Davidson Bissett. They had six children, Mary Rebecca Russell and her five siblings. Mary's parents named her after the two children of her grandfather's first marriage, the young girls who had died. The sad fate of Nathaniel's first family must have been part of the descendants' consciousness at some level and, along with their pacifist leanings, may have had some influence on the continuing anti-violence sentiments within the family. Nathaniel the younger was an active member of the Methodist church; however, the Quaker connection continued to carry some meaning and importance in the family. Traditionally, Quakers hold what is called the Peace Testimony. The Religious Society of Friends is known for conscientious objection to war. In various biographical references, Mary Chesley is referred to as being "of Quaker descent," which would have come through her paternal grandmother, Alma, whose father had been a Quaker minister.

Mary Rebecca had two older sisters, Alma and Agnes, and three younger brothers, Benjamin, John, and Howard. We know very little about Mary's youth, other than brief mention of her in her brother Benjamin's autobiography. Less than two years apart in age, the little evidence we have would indicate that they were close, and her brother, who became a well-known judge and political representative of Nova Scotia, regarded his older sister with respect and affection. Benjamin was not without a sense of humour, and it would seem that this trait ran in the family. In his autobiography, Benjamin speaks of his father's kindness and sense of humour and recalled how Nathaniel, a tinsmith, owned the only hand-cart in the town, excepting the one in which groceries were delivered from the store. The vehicle was frequently borrowed and no reasonable application was refused. The Sermon on the Mount was a rule of conduct for my father. One day a merry Irish blacksmith borrowed the hand-cart and brought it home suffering from the ordeal to which it had been subjected. "There," said he, "is your hand-cart, Uncle Nat, and I would advise you to have the thing mended before you lend it again." My father enjoyed the joke greatly. It was a source of merriment in the home circle.[13]

Another incident Benjamin recalls concerns Mary and gives a hint of their family life in the 1850s and '60s:

My sister Mary and myself used to visit a farmhouse about two miles from Dartmouth, sometimes to bring back greens for the dinner table. On one of these occasions we were carrying such a burden home and the weight was not fairly distributed between us. To readjust the load seemed too commonplace a solution. I found a stone of suitable size and weight, and added it to the load in the basket, thus distributing the burden evenly between us. I cannot remember that my sister objected. I fancy that she thought the proceeding must be all right or I would not have adopted it. I was a boy and she was only a girl. If these were the feelings that lay at the base of her submission, she lived to outgrow them and became a most strenuous and persistent and widely recognized advocate of woman's rights.[14]

By the time of Benjamin's recounting, his sister Mary was not alive to tell her side of the story, though the last part, that she would become an advocate of women's rights, was accurate. I believe her active involvement in the suffrage movement and her peace advocacy had an influence on her brother. Benjamin would become a well-regarded judge and Member of Parliament and was noted in his obituary as being very active in raising funds for homeless Belgian and French children during the First World War.[15] He would also become the chair of the Nova Scotia Committee for Relief of German Children in the postwar period, a cause his niece Polly spearheaded.

When the whalers eventually left Dartmouth, the Quaker meetings more or less died out. Quakers remaining in Nova Scotia were absorbed most commonly into Methodism. Mary's father, Nathaniel, was a pillar of the Methodist Church in Dartmouth, and it seems that his Christian faith was not merely ornamental. Mary's mother also must have played a large part in the formation of her children. Regrettably, Benjamin makes no mention of her in his autobiography. Experience leads me to believe that good mothers, taken for granted, write themselves out of history; it is only when a woman is not a good mother that we hear of it.

As will be evidenced by other clues, the Russell family, in spite of financial ups and downs and personal losses, seemed to have had the capacity for enjoyment and were, in spite of being teetotallers, not necessarily straight-laced. For example, when Mary's sister Alma Russell died in 1924 at the age of eighty-three, her niece Polly wrote the following in *The Wesleyan,* November 12, 1924:

> She was a member of the choir, collected for every good cause, a Sunday School teacher and class leader. To list her activities however does not tell the tale, for it was not what she did but what she was—so full of fun, even to her last year, the life of every party—a mingling of the purest humor and the richest love. To nearly all who knew her she was "Aunt Am." She was always humble, the tenderness of her ready sympathy, her love of nature and outdoor sport—in bathing in her eighty-second year and boating within two months of her death—and that wonderful sense of humor which enabled her to rise above the vexations of life and enabled her to meet sickness and death itself with a smile.

Polly's effusive praise for her beloved aunt might be somewhat hyperbolic, but it does give a sense of a vibrant and intelligent spirit, a strain that seemed to run through the family. Born in 1841, Alma had never married and for over thirty years lived with Mary and family in Lunenburg. As someone who enriched the lives of her niece and others with whom she came in contact, "Aunt Am" was every bit the person Polly described, according to Natalie Corkum of Lunenburg who was born in 1915, the daughter of Polly's close friend Lena (the Bachmans and the Chesleys shared a cottage at Princes Inlet, on the outskirts of Lunenburg).

Mary's oldest sister, Agnes, married William Forbes in 1872. He died in 1876 when their only son, Edgar William (Will), would have been two years old. (An older cousin to Polly, Will features later in this story.) On August 12, 1896, the Halifax *Morning Chronicle* reported that "The death occurred yesterday of Mrs. Agnes T. Forbes, after a long and protracted illness."

Apart from Benjamin, little is known about Mary's other younger brothers. John and his family lived for a time in Lunenburg but moved back to Dartmouth where he became involved in the family business. John had three daughters who all remained single. Mary's youngest brother, Howard, was unmarried and followed in his father's footsteps as a tinsmith. He drowned in 1901 when only in his forties.[16]

According to the Mount Allison records, Mary Russell spent a term at the Mount Allison Ladies' Academy in 1868, just a few years before Mount Allison became the first university in the British Empire to grant degrees to women. That Mary was given this early educational opportunity gives a strong indication that her parents recognized her intelligence. Benjamin indicated in his autobiography that his own attendance at university, begun in 1864, represented a financial burden for his father, so it is revealing that the Russell parents supported their daughter's post-secondary education. She was the youngest girl in the family and the only one given this opportunity. The other boys in the family did not go to university. That Mary would become an advocate of rights for women surely had much to do with family support for her higher education. School records indicate that Mary's mother, Agnes, attended school at least until the age of fifteen, so she likely played a role in encouraging Mary.[17]

I have found no other records of Mary's life before her marriage in 1874 to Samuel Ainsley Chesley.

Robert Ainsley Chesley, father of Samuel and grandfather of Polly. [LOCAL HISTORIES COLLECTION (CU16080885), LIBRARIES AND CULTURAL RESOURCES DIGITAL COLLECTIONS, UNIVERSITY OF CALGARY]

Samuel was born in Petitcodiac, New Brunswick, on August 14, 1849, the son of Robert Ainsley Chesley and Hannah Elizabeth Albee.[18] His grandfather and great-grandfather served as justices of the peace in the Annapolis Valley. In both the Russell and Chesley families, vocations in law and ministry prevailed. Mary's father, Nathaniel, instrumental in the establishment of Grace Methodist Church in Dartmouth, served as a circuit steward, a Sunday school superintendent, a class leader, and a lay preacher. Mary's husband, Samuel, was a lawyer, then a probate judge. Her brother Benjamin followed in the same profession and eventually became a Supreme Court judge. Mary's oldest sister, Agnes, married a minister (Rev. Forbes), and their only son, Will Forbes, also went into the Methodist ministry, eventually becoming a United Church minister after Church Union of Methodists, Congregationalists, and some Presbyterians in 1925. Although a lawyer, Samuel was an active layperson in the Methodist, then the United Church, serving on boards and also as the superintendent of Sunday school (like his father-in-law) throughout most of his adult life.

When Samuel was only seven years old, his father, the Reverend Robert A. Chesley, died during a typhus epidemic, months after taking on a new pastoral charge in St. John's, Newfoundland. Robert, who was only forty when he died in 1856, left behind his pregnant wife, Hannah, and four small children. The fifth child, John Beecham, born only a couple of weeks after his father's death, also succumbed, and the father and son were buried in the same grave.

According to colleagues who wrote memorials in the *Provincial Wesleyan*, January 22, 1857, Robert was considered a compassionate man and a beloved minister. A Rev. T. Harris wrote, "[I] found that our lamented Bro. Chesley had during his brief sojourn in St. John's gained the affection and sincere regard of all classes of the community" and said, "A subscription list was opened for [Robert's widow's] benefit and about three hundred pounds have already been subscribed." This was a not inconsiderable amount raised to help support the family. Samuel, at age seven, was the oldest child, his brother James Albee was less than two years younger, and the last two were only toddlers.

In 1859, the two youngest children died of "putrid sore throat." Thus, only Samuel and his brother James lived into adulthood. In the 1861 census, Hannah and her surviving sons are listed in Digby County; however, Samuel, aged twelve, is also listed in the same census as living in Sackville, New Brunswick, and attending the Mount Allison Academy. He received his BA in 1866 when only seventeen years old.

Mary's brother Benjamin and Samuel Chesley met at Mount Allison. After receiving his BA, Samuel taught at the Wesleyan Academy in St. John's, Newfoundland, and later at the Mount Allison Academy. At some point, Samuel moved to Dartmouth, for the 1871 census places him there, living with Mary's brothers Benjamin and John. Samuel and Benjamin are listed as law students and John as a bookkeeper. In 1872, when Mary's sister Agnes married William Forbes, Samuel served as a witness. The following year, he was witness to the marriage of Mary's younger brother John, so Samuel's relationship with the Russell family was firmly established by the time he and Mary married in 1874.

Admitted to the bar in 1873, Samuel also completed an MA in 1876. A vigorous and multitalented person, in addition to practicing law he was an official reporter for the House of Assembly from 1873 onward into the twentieth century and, in association with his brother-in-law, Benjamin, worked as co-editor of the *N.S. Law Reports* and co-authored the nine volumes of *The Nova Scotia Reports, Vol. 40: Containing Reports of Cases Argued and Determined in the Supreme Court of Nova Scotia*. Active with Methodist church affairs as the superintendent of the Sunday school in Lunenburg for many years, Samuel also served on the national church board and as treasurer of the missions board.

Samuel and Mary lived in Dartmouth in the early years of their marriage. In 1879, Samuel (age thirty) and Mary (thirty-two) moved to Lunenburg with their children, Robert (four) and Agnes (three). A third child, Mary Albee (Polly), was born in 1891. Samuel opened a law practice; he was appointed Judge of Probate Court in 1882 and later Recorder and Stipendiary Magistrate.

As mentioned, I discovered Mary through her annual reports in the WCTU records. Little is known about the early years of Mary's married life; however, by the time she had her last child, she had already begun her political activism.

Mary Chesley's involvement in the WCTU and her writings and advocacy for suffrage threw her into the public spotlight on a national and international level. In the September 1896 issue of *Catholic World*, Thomas O'Hagan wrote of Mary in "Some Canadian Women Writers":

> "As a writer of strong and vigorous articles in support of the demands of women for enfranchisement, Mary Russell Chesley, of Lunenburg, Nova Scotia, stands at the head of Canadian women. Mrs. Chesley is of Quaker descent and possesses all a Quaker's unbending resolve and high sense of freedom and equality. This clever controversialist in defence of her views has broken a lance with some of the leading minds of the United States and Canada, and in every instance has done credit to her sex and the cause she has espoused."[19]

Rather than using the name Mrs. Samuel Chesley, the typical appellation for a married woman, she always signed her articles using Mary Russell Chesley or M. R. Chesley, an indicator of her feminism.

Henry James Morgan's 1898 publication *The Canadian Men and Women of the Time* carried profiles of prominent public figures—the Canadian equivalent of *Who's Who in America*—and has an entry for Mary that borrows somewhat from O'Hagan's words but elaborates more on her franchise work.

CHESLEY, Mrs. Mary Russell, controversialist, is the dau. of Nathaniel Russell, by his wife, Agnes Bissett, and is of Quaker and French Huguenot descent. B. at Dartmouth, N.S., Sept. 4, 1847, and m. Saml. A. Chesley, barrister. It is only within a period of 4 yrs. that she has taken interest in public questions. At the time mentioned the W.C.T.U. of N.S. petitioned the Legislature for the enfranchisement of women. Mrs. C. has worked and written for the promotion of the "cause." Perhaps her reply to Atty.- Genl. Longley's elaborate address in opposition to the Bill, has received the widest notice. Mrs. C. is Predt. of the W.C.T.U. of N.S. She is an adherent of the Meth. Ch., but in the matter of belief holds herself free. She believes that "no nation or state has its foundations in righteousness which excludes half of its citizens from a voice in its Govt." She also believes in the "single tax," the prohibition of the liquor traffic, the settlement of national difficulties by arbitration, and in co-operation as opposed to competition. –Lunenburg, N.S.

Mary would subsequently be written up in Morgan's 1912 edition of *Canadian Men and Women of the Time*, and she was included in the 1914–15 edition of *Women's Who's Who in America*.

The acknowledgement that Mary was of Quaker descent indicates that she herself must have attached importance to this fact. And while she grew up in the Methodist Church, "in the matter of belief [she held] herself free." This hints at her independence of thought, a trait more likely to be found among Methodists and Quakers. Morgan's entry confirms that Mary's interest in peace and arbitration was firmly established long before she took on responsibility for the WCTU Department of Peace and Arbitration.

Chesley's response to Longley to which Morgan refers occurred in the spring of 1895, following the defeat of the Franchise Bill. In chapter 2, I deal with this huge disappointment for Chesley and the pro-women's lobby for the vote.

Significant as this disappointment was, a far greater personal tragedy for the Chesley family occurred later that same year when Mary and Samuel suffered the devastating loss of their two older children, Robert and Agnes, who were in their late teens.

The following, published in the *Halifax Herald* on October 12, 1895, under the title "The Lunenburg Drowning Tragedy" first appeared in the *Lunenburg Progress Enterprise*. Fortunately, it was reprinted in the Halifax paper, for there is not a full run of the Lunenburg paper in existence on microfilm, and the day in question is no longer accessible.

> The Lunenburg Progress has the following regarding the sad drowning accident at Lunenburg on Tuesday [October 8]: Shortly after ten o'clock Robert and Agnes Chesley, only son and oldest daughter of Stipendiary Chesley, boarded a sail boat at Young's wharf and headed for [Feltzen] South. On arriving at the fishing stage of Israel Spindler, Miss Chesley proceeded to Ritcey's Cove to teach piano pupils while her brother remained at South with friends. At five o'clock they boarded the boat, put up jib and large mainsail and belayed everything hard and fast. At this juncture the wind was blowing fiercely. Samuel Whynacht, of Corkum's Island, saw the boat when half way home, sail dragging in the water. The Knickle boys of Battery Point, after watching, lost their attention to something on shore, but when they again looked, no sail was visible. About 4:30 Wednesday morning, while gathering sea grass at the rear of the Peter Corkum property, Wm. Anderson found the lifeless form of a female. He aroused Capt. S. Silver and Mr. Benj. Morash. They sent for Dr. DesBrisay, believing him to be the coroner. One glance showed him that the features were those of Miss Chesley. The body was removed to the store of Austin Young, where it remained [until] Undertaker Hopps took charge. A gaff-topsail and the cap worn by Robert were also found at the rear of the Corkum property, thus showing that the boat sank and both occupants perished. Robert was 20 and his sister 18 years of age.

The *Halifax Acadian Recorder* also reprinted this article, with a slightly different intro and the following closing paragraph: "A gentleman who came from Lunenburg yesterday says the accident happened about three-quarters mile from the shore. Miss Chesley was a good swimmer, and as she did not have her underskirts on when found, it is thought she divested herself of these and swam to the shore, and that when she almost reached there she was so exhausted, and thus perished after having made such a brave struggle."[20]

Neither the boat nor Robert had been found when Agnes's body was discovered, so the story unfolded in the newspapers over the course of the next few days. The *Halifax Acadian Recorder*'s first report fills in a few personal details about Robert and Agnes not mentioned in other accounts and is suggestive of the family's significance in their community: "Robert will be well remembered by his long connection with the City Engineer's office, where he studied for some time. Miss Chesley attended Sackville Academy."

Almost nothing is known about Robert beyond this. I found a single mention to him in the *Lunenburg County Times* of July 29, 1885, when Robert was a child: "Last, and least in size, on Monday of this week, two very young gentlemen, Master William Forbes, aged 11, and Master Robert Chesley, aged 9, travelled to Mahone Bay and back on tricycles, feeling quite independent as they pedalled off alone, and feeling quite proud as they pedalled back home, where they arrived about half-past six in the evening, apparently little tired after their fourteen miles journey."[21] This gives us a further hint about the kind of independence the Chesleys fostered in their children and that the family was open to adventures.

Discrepancies appear in the various accounts regarding the ages of Robert and Agnes when they died. Born on October 30, 1875, and November 25, 1876, respectively, they were nineteen and eighteen when they died, with Robert only a few weeks short of turning twenty. From the Saturday, October 12 issue of the *Morning Chronicle*:

> Lunenburg: Oct. 11 – The body of Robert Chesley was found a few feet from where the boat was found yesterday. It is supposed that Chesley went down with the boat, tangled in rope, and that the body fell out while the boat was being raised. The funeral of both sister and brother took place this afternoon and was a melancholy sight. Rev. Mr. Day officiated, assisted by Reverends

McGillivray, Haslam, Rafkin, Archibald and Grunland [*sic*], all representing different denominations. Robert Chesley's body was drawn by the members of the fire department in one of their wagons. The deceased was a member of the company. The hearse containing Agnes Chesley followed. The funeral was largely attended. The catastrophe has cast a gloom over the town and everybody is awestricken at the termination of the lives of two young, bright and promising children.

One month after the accident, the Methodist newspaper *The Wesleyan* published a letter to the editor with a message addressed to the children's father, Samuel, as well as further information surrounding the event. Samuel was active on both the local and national levels of the Methodist Church. In fact, the *Daily Echo* (October 9, 1895) reported that he had been attending the board of the Methodist conference in Montreal when he was called home at the time of the drowning. The letter to the editor in *The Wesleyan* provides more evidence of the impact of this tragedy on all concerned.

> Dear Mr. Editor:
> At a special meeting of the Lunenburg Methodist Quarterly Board held on Nov. 2nd, the following resolution was passed:
> Resolved: That we the official representatives of the Lunenburg Methodist Church, take this first opportunity since our pastor's return to express our deep, heart-felt sympathy for you during these dark days, consequent upon the terrible bereavement and we ask that you will kindly convey the same to Mrs. Chesley and Miss Russell [Aunt Am], in our name.
> We beg to remain
> Affectionately yours.
> [Signed by the Chairman and all the members of the Quarterly Board.]

Never had Lunenburg Co. been more deeply stirred than by this tragic event. Robert and Agnes were two of the most popular young people in town. As assistant engineer of the new water works in Lunenburg, Robert had not only won the esteem and confidence of the management, but every man under him regarded him as his friend.

Agnes Chesley's name has always stood in this town as synonymous with all that is good and sweet.

All places of business were closed on the day of the funeral.

The S. School children over whom Mr. Chesley has been superintendent, marched before the procession and then dividing at the cemetery gates sang, "Safe in the Arms of Jesus" as the caskets were borne to the grave. Not only all the town people but hundreds from the surrounding country, made part of the largest funeral cortege ever seen in Lunenburg.[22]

Students and staff at the Ladies' College at Mount Allison in Sackville, where Agnes had spent three years, also expressed their grief through their school newspaper.

Died at Lunenburg, N.S., Oct. 8th, Agnes Davison Chesley aged 18 years, daughter of Samuel A. and Mary R. Chesley.

> I sometimes hold it half a sin
> To put in words the grief I feel;
> For words, like nature, half reveal
> And half conceal the Soul within.

It was with a feeling akin to this, that teachers and students assembled to pay a loving tribute to Agnes Chesley. We felt that a young life, full of promise had suddenly gone out. Miss Alcorn spoke of Agnes' life among the girls and voiced the feeling of all who knew Miss Chesley when she said, "we had a friend worth loving, and we loved her, and we told her that we loved her, and the words spoken in loving remembrance, are only the echoes of those spoken to her, while she was with us."[23]

The article included further religious sentiment and poetry. As well, in the following month, an "In Memoriam" poem appeared, dedicated to Agnes, likely written by one of her friends. The first and last verse, included here, indicate that Agnes was known for her music:

> The music of a life we heard,
> The purer breathing of whose song
> Made us forget earth's woe and wrong,
> And life to nobler action stirred.
> …
> Farewell, sweet singer, at His call
> Thou'rt gone to rest in that bright home
> To which God's faithful children come
> Where life is love and Christ is all.
> – M.M.L.

Agnes Chesley (inset and above, front row right, black dress, looking up), daughter of Mary and Samuel, at Mount Allison Ladies College. [MOUNT ALLISON UNIVERSITY ARCHIVES, 2007.07/14 AND 2007.07/1348]

It was on Agnes's return from giving piano lessons to children at Feltzen South that she and her brother perished, and this memorial poem provides an indication that she may also have been gifted as a singer.

An online history of the Chesley family gives Samuel's recounting of the drowning in a letter written to Israel Chesley, a cousin in the United States. It only hints at the shock and grief that Samuel and Mary must have experienced. As religious people, they had to trust that their children were in God's hands: "I can tell you very little about the drowning. They were both strong, athletic young persons, good swimmers, accustomed to the water and to boats.... They were lovely and pleasant in their lives, and in death they were not divided. God is keeping them for us." [24]

The headstone marking the grave of Robert and Agnes Chesley in the Hillcrest Cemetery, Lunenburg, repeats the phrase "Lovely and pleasant in their lives and in death they were not divided." I imagine the Chesleys had to dig deep in the well of faith to deal with their loss. Perhaps they found some comfort in the idea that the two children were together. Apart from the excerpt of Samuel's letter to a cousin, we have no other personal account. Did Mary write to anyone about her loss? Did she keep a journal? We will likely never know; from the grave comes only silence.

Although we cannot know how the Chesleys dealt with their loss and grief, it is likely that having a four-year-old child helped to keep them going. Mary would have been almost forty-four when Polly was born in 1891, and based on Polly's activities as a young woman, one can imagine that she was a lively child, full of energy. Children live very much in the present, and for her parents to address their surviving child's needs, they would have had to give themselves over to the present as well. From the evidence of Polly's development, it would seem that Mary and Samuel provided good parenting, giving Polly love and support and yet allowing her the freedom to explore the world in her own way. Other parents might have tried to curb such an adventurous spirit, afraid of losing their only surviving child.

In the Lunenburg WCTU minutes for October/November 1901, it is noted that ten-year-old Polly gave a recitation of "The Elf Child" at

Polly Chesley, c. 1900. [Audrey Chesley Oldershaw].

a Parlor Meeting. It was likely "Little Orphan Annie," an 1885 poem by James Whitcomb Riley, first titled "The Elf Child," a poem written to be recited.[25] At a Parlor Meeting in February 1903, Polly is noted as having given another recitation. A December 2, 1903, entry in *The Wesleyan* provides a further hint of young Polly's personality: "At the invitation of Judge S. A. Chesley, of Lunenburg, teachers of the Sunday School met at his residence on the evening of the 12th ult. After [business] was discussed and voted upon, refreshments were served, a solo was sung by Miss Elma Smith and a humorous reading was well rendered by Miss Chesley."

These small items, combined with later evidence of Polly's personality and activities, led me to conclude two things: that she developed a penchant for public speaking early on; and the tragic loss in the family did not overshadow Polly's childhood. Her natural exuberance was given free rein by her parents. A postcard photograph (shown here on page 17), dated December 25, 1905, gives us a clue in that regard.

Hugh Corkum of Lunenburg (son of Natalie Corkum, mentioned earlier, whose mother was a good friend of Polly's) shared this image with me. Hugh is a collector of Lunenburg memorabilia, and by sheer chance, he found this postcard during his collecting travels. Addressed by Mary R. Chesley to her brother John and family in Dartmouth, she wrote on the back of the photo: "with love and Xmas greetings to John

Chesley house, 119 Lawrence St., Lunenburg. Mary, Samuel, and Polly Chesley, 1905. This image appeared on a postcard sent by Mary R. Chesley to her brother John and his family in Dartmouth, NS. [HUGH CORKUM, LUNENBURG]

and Alice. Look thro' a magnifying glass." Indeed, a magnifying glass was needed to make out the figures in front of the house.

Only when I had the photo blown up did Samuel, Mary, and Polly become visible. The photo is revealing. In this picture, Polly would have been about fourteen years of age. Sitting on the fence, she looks like the tomboy that she probably was. Polly's location in the photo says much about Samuel and Mary as parents. They did not force her to pose with them in a polite, ladylike way. She established her independence but with her parents' tacit consent. After all, this is a picture that Mary was sending with the family's Christmas greetings. As the only record I have of the Chesleys during this period, this photo speaks the thousand words I cannot find or fabricate.

The following chapters, organized by decades, are gleaned largely from impersonal and archival sources. While mostly a record of activities and ideas, personal information does filter through at times. What I did discover, particularly in reference to Polly, were letters by and about her published in newspapers, and I am forever indebted to small-town papers for their social reportage. Fortunately I found a few individuals who had known the Chesleys. Considering that Mary, Samuel, and Polly, respectively, died in 1923, 1930, and 1936, it was fortuitous that I was able to interview anyone with first-hand knowledge. All informants have subsequently died.

The 1890s were pivotal to the Chesley family both personally and publicly. Chapter 2 addresses Mary Chesley's political activities in the 1890s, and chapter 3 covers the first decade of the twentieth century—a time of quiet persistence after the disillusionment of failure to see the franchise bill pass in 1895. As well, we see the evolution and sophistication of Mary's peace and arbitration thinking and analysis. Polly went off to university during this period, and I rely on the Mount Allison records to follow her progress. The second decade of the new century was a time of continuing activism on the part of Mary and emerging activism and adventure on the part of Polly. This decade is broken up into two chapters, dealing first with Mary's activities and second with Polly's experiences. While Samuel is not the focus of this study, his activities are worthy of mention because they flesh out in a minor way his diverse interests and reveal his support for women's empowerment and the peace movement, the passionate interests of both his wife and daughter. The 1920s chapter begins on a hopeful note, but Mary dies in 1923. The bulk of the chapter is devoted to Polly's activities both in North America and England where she eventually settled in her teaching profession while also increasingly engaging in political/social activism. Samuel joins Polly in England for a few years, and his death in 1930 ushers in the chapters covering the 1930s up until Polly's untimely death in 1936, the aftermath of her death, and concluding observations.

In recounting the story of these remarkable women, I share something of my research process. Researching and writing history is part slog, part wonderment of discovery, and part reimagining lives that we can go only so far to know. Mary Rebecca (Russell) Chesley and Mary Albee (Polly) Chesley played roles, if largely forgotten, in pivotal political and social organizations during the late nineteenth and early twentieth centuries. This is an attempt to tell their story.

CHAPTER 2
Political Involvement During the Last Decade of the Nineteenth Century

WHILE LUNENBURG FIRST ESTABLISHED ITS WOMAN'S Christian Temperance Union in 1890, surviving minute books for the Lunenburg union only begin in February 1892. Mary and her sister Alma (Polly's Aunt Am) were members at this time, although Mary rarely attended meetings in that year. She would have been busy with a baby—her youngest child, Polly, who was born less than a year earlier. Nevertheless, by December 1892, Mary became Recording Secretary, and the following month, she also became Superintendent of Franchise. Additional mentions of Mary in subsequent years include the minutes of March 27, 1893: "Mrs. Chesley reported having received communication from the Maritime Supt. of Franchise, also copies of petitions for circulation through town and members were asked for their signatures."[26] And the following year, the minutes recorded that Maria Angwin, an active member of the WCTU, read Mary R. Chesley's paper on "Ways and Means to Secure the Ballot." [27]

During this period, unions in Nova Scotia were under the umbrella of the Maritime WCTU. With the dissolution of the Maritime body in September 1895, Nova Scotia established its own union. Edith

Archibald of Halifax was slated to become the first president of the provincial organization; for some reason she was unable to take on the role, so Chesley became the first president.

Although suffrage would be the chief focus of Mary's energies, it would be remiss not to acknowledge that the WCTU was initiated to fight the liquor trade. There were many temperance organizations in the nineteenth century, but the WCTU was the first women's only organization. For women, the devastation wrought by alcoholic husbands in families dependent solely on a man's income was terrible and terrifying. Lacking the vote, women could only register their desire to restrict liquor trade through petitions.

The WCTU's "Do Everything" motto inspired some groups to take on a spectrum of social activism. In Lunenburg, the early WCTU records provide a glimpse of the multipronged concerns of the women and the numerous social services they offered in the community before the existence of a public social safety net. References are made to providing food for the infirm, and one entry in the minutes referred to Miss Russell (Aunt Am) telling the group of her intention to visit "a Miss Backman who was suffering from temporary insanity." As this girl was limited to prison fare, Alma suggested it "would be as well for the members of the Union to send any delicacies they had." The union arranged an adoption for an orphan and sought a position for "Old Mrs. Curl, who is in need of employment suited to her age and failing strength." Moreover, the group maintained an ongoing interest in the welfare of prisoners.[28]

Considerable reassessment has occurred in more recent years regarding the WCTU's significance in the suffrage cause. Earlier historians, writing of the suffrage movement in Canada, made the assumption that Nova Scotians were not particularly active because of the paucity of organizations exclusively involved in the franchise question. The strongest action on the suffrage front came from the WCTU, with Mary Chesley taking the lead, along with well-known Halifax activists such as Edith Archibald, Eliza Ritchie, and others. Mary has tended to be forgotten over time. References to Mary's involvement in the suffrage movement are almost entirely restricted to occasional footnotes.[29]

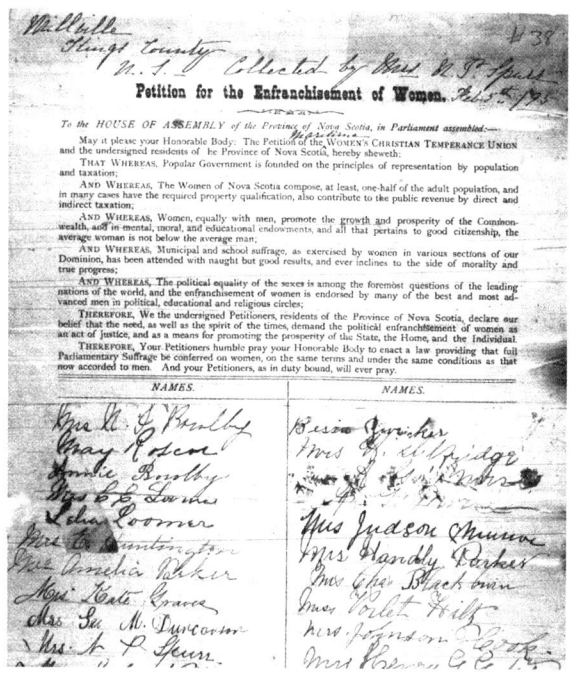

An 1895 petition to the Nova Scotia Legislature for Women's Franchise. [NOVA SCOTIA ARCHIVES]

If Mary could speak now, how would she describe the tumultuous events of 1895? The year began with high hopes with regard to women closing in on the right to vote. In February of that year, the WCTU was still under the Maritime umbrella, and this body, under Mary Chesley's leadership, was actively petitioning for the vote with hopes that the bill would pass in the provincial legislature. Petitioning afforded women one of the only avenues for political expression, aside from writing to the newspapers. At least eleven thousand men and women across the province signed the Petition for the Enfranchisement of Women that year.[30] In the spring of 1895, the world was full of promise. Women believed that the vote was within their grasp.

Pro-suffrage forces had good reason to feel optimistic. In the previous year, the bill for the enfranchisement of women had failed to pass by only one vote. What had not been anticipated was the powerful mobilization in the legislature by the bill's opponents, under the leadership of Attorney General James Wilberforce Longley, well known for his persuasive oratory. The following article appeared in

POLITICAL INVOLVEMENT 21

the *Daily Echo* of March 16, 1895. Written by "Silent Observer," it gives an idea of how some men responded to the question of suffrage.

> The dear old girls who filled the house of assembly on Wednesday afternoon when Attorney General Longley was speaking received a terrible roasting. The ladies stamped their feet and shook their canes (women suffragists all carry canes: they will smoke next). But nothing came of it and they started for home. Many a man went without his supper and many a child was put to bed that evening without saying its little prayer, all because the dear wife and mother wanted to see the great emancipation measure carry in the house. But the vote [was] twenty-one to twelve! That should convince the suffragists that they had better settle down to domestic affairs for a few years more.

The last sentence is telling. Though anti-suffragist, the writer must have known that the move toward the franchise for women was inevitable. Being able to put it off "a few years more" was within men's power, but perhaps those same men were aware of the injustice of such a position.

Longley's speech, which lasted hours, did not impress Mary or her colleagues. Mary's four-thousand-word rebuttal to Longley's speech, published in the *Halifax Herald* on March 23, made front-page headlines. Mary's article gives readers an opportunity to observe her passionate advocacy, and unlike her adversary, she correctly backed up her facts.

> To the Editor of the Halifax Herald:
>
> SIR, As Mr. Longley has taken the task of chief spokesman for the party in our legislature which is opposed to woman suffrage, a resume of his address may not be unprofitable, for, while it is calculated to convince the unconvinced and so convert the unconverted, its many sophistries may beguile the unwary. With the solemn air of having made a new and important discovery, Mr. Longley tells us that men and women were created different.

By what process of reasoning Mr. Longley has made the discovery that suffrage would deprive woman of the "exercise of her natural functions and destroy those softer and finer qualities which constitute her chief value in the world," he does not condescend to explain. In the absence of such explanation it is safe to go back to Wyoming—the only place where complete woman suffrage has had a fair trial—and ascertain whether it has had the dire effects from which Mr. Longley would fain guard us. [A US senator] passing through Wyoming a few years before, made particular enquiries of all the leading men he met and heard nothing but praises of it. But Mr. Longley wishes to dwell upon "the real function and true ideal of woman."

As this is a subject upon which the hon. gentleman, from his known popularity with the fair sex, is qualified to speak, his remarks are worthy of consideration. His ideal and ours have several points in common [but] we do not share his admiration for the "weak and confiding," nor have we yet become convinced that it is one of woman's principal duties "to charm men." Our observation has been, the "weak and confiding" do not fare as well as their strong-minded sisters. Mr. Longley says, "What the world wants more than anything else is more spiritual life, more elevation of aim and purpose."

It is gratifying to find Nova Scotia's second leading statesman holding such lofty views, but is not Mr. Longley too magnanimous when he wishes to relieve us of all participation in the affairs of state in order that we may be free for the exercise of the "higher functions" pertaining to the spiritual life?

With due gratitude to Mr. Longley for his chivalrous desire to save us from self-destruction, we will take the risk of the strain upon our delicate "moral fibre" of depositing a ballot once in four years. Mr. Longley, however, told the crowd of enthusiastic ladies in the galleries that he suspected that the secret of their interest in this government was their lack of "personal charm." This discourtesy to the ladies of Halifax, I fear will not strengthen his position among supporters in his own county.

Mr. Longley says: "Fathers have not the exclusive control over their children, as the law now empowers a judge of the supreme court to give the custody of the children to the mother when ever desirable."

In only six of the United States does the law give mothers and fathers equal guardianship of their children.

As regards this class of law in our own dominion, I cannot better refute Mr. Longley's statement than by recalling in an article on "The legal disabilities of women,"

> "A husband, even if himself a minor, can, in the event of his death beforehand, leave his unborn child to the guardianship of any one whom, without even telling his wife, he may select. This awful thing was done six years ago. A husband, not twenty-one, conceiving a grudge against his wife, did will away his coming child, and at its birth it was carried off and she never knew what became of it."

This law will be found in the revised statutes, Chapter 96, Section 1. But we are gradually emerging from the condition of semi civilization, for I find by an act passed less than two years ago, that, in the event of the father's death, the mother may be guardian, singly or jointly, with one appointed by her husband.

With regard to property, while theoretically endowed with all our husbands' worldly goods, all that we could claim as widows (in the event of no will) is a life interest of one-third of the landed property. On the other hand, if the wife dies, if she leaves a child, the husband has a right to the whole of her landed property as long as he lives. By this arrangement, which illustrates the chivalrous spirit of our legislators it is possible for a man to marry a wealthy widow with children and upon her death, if he so chooses, turn her children, or their children (when of age) adrift without a penny. It is that provision, by which the stalwart sons of this Dominion are protected from the wily machinations of a most dangerous class—young girls of fourteen, fifteen, sixteen and upward. [I]t can never be charged that our Canadian law for the protection of girls is "based upon sentimentality." It has for the foundation the sound, healthy principle, that man's first duty is self-protection.

A study of the laws relating to the protection of girls all over this continent, even after frequent efforts at improvement on the part of the W.C.T.U. and other societies, would lead any of Mr. Longley's intelligent readers to the conclusion that however competent men may be to legislate with regard to sugar, codfish, lumber, etc., they are not, unaided, capable of regulating the morals of a community.

The editor of the Woman's Journal says: "There could hardly be more instructive reading for any woman who believes that women and girls are already adequately protected and that women do not need to vote."

Mr. Longley's rhetoric to the contrary, it is ballots, not "personal charms" that count with politicians. Having paid his addresses to the ladies who were present, Mr. Longley extends his compliments to the large class of respectable wage-earning women all over the province, women who, as starchers, seamstresses, sales women, etc., are earning an honest and independent income. It is in this class, I suppose—that the "large class of vicious women" so greatly to be dreaded, is to be found. As a result of Mr. Longley's remarks, the woman suffragists of Nova Scotia will in the future find no lack of ready canvassers among the large and important class of wage-earning women all over the province.

Mrs. Lillie Devereaux Blake, in the Woman's Journal (Boston) says: "Some of the papers have been trying to give an impression that the movement for suffrage was confined to the wealthier classes, but this is untrue. We have received endorsement from a long list of labor organizations. I will mention only a few. The united joiners, 1,000 strong sent in their ratification. The federation of labor, over the signature of Samuel Gompers, the president, has declared itself in favor; the trade, labor and reform conference, numbering over twenty different bodies, has also signed the petition. The shoemakers union, the bakers union, the millers and millwrights union, the cigar makers, the Swiss embroidery makers and the typographers are only a few of the long list of unions which have endorsed our movement."

Mr. Longley says: "There is no justification for saying that this movement has the support of the clergy."

I claim that I can speak from larger experience. The suffrage petition has been circulated in this town three times and through the county twice. In '93 we received the ready signatures of all the clergymen then residing in the town but one. In both the last canvasses of the county our principal aid has come from clergymen and their wives. It was through their help that this county more than doubled the number of signatures sent up last year. My impression is that the W.C.T. unions all through the province have been supported in this movement by the clergy, and will declare Mr. Longley's [statement] without foundation.

Mr. Longley says that he feels bound, as a representative of Nova Scotia, to do all in his power to prevent woman suffrage "from coming." NEVERTHELESS IT WILL COME.

Notwithstanding Mr. Longley's chivalrous efforts, the women of Nova Scotia will not have to wait much longer for enfranchisement. When my children were younger I used to watch with interest their sport as across a certain tide-filled stream they built a dam of mud and sticks and stones. As I noted the steady rise of the flowing tide I smiled at their pleasure over a construction that was destined so soon to perish. The opposition of the legislature of our province seems no more significant than the temporary resistance to the inflowing tide of the children's dissolving mud dam.

M. R. Chesley, Lunenburg, March 20th

Mary's willingness and ability to rebut such a powerful politician says much about her intense belief in the suffrage cause. It would have taken courage and conviction to go head-to-head with a man such as Longley. While he had his supporters, there were also members of the public who supported Mary, and the letters that were subsequently published in the paper in response reveal as much.

An articulate E. J. Willis wrote to the *Evening Mail* (March 30, 1895) in response to Longley's speech and Chesley's rebuttal:

Let me assure Mr. Longley that the time has passed when manly men sneer at "old maids," but is it the case that only those with "no power to charm men," viz., the ugly, old and crabbed, favor this movement? No, some of the most charming women I have ever met lead the movement in Halifax, women who are not only "charming" to men, but who take the trouble to be pleasant to their own sex.

It is strange how those who oppose woman's suffrage harp on the one string, namely, that of home. To hear Mr. Longley speak of the sacrifice of "home duties," is to see in mind a picture of women wildly uprooting the home, breaking the furniture and rushing madly into the streets, there to tramp up and down for four years until the time for voting comes. Before men's minds arises an awful vision of unrocked cradles, undarned stockings, piles and piles of buttonless shirts, uncooked dinners, and such horrors. Women can vote at municipal elections now, and no such reign of terror has taken place; why will voting for members of parliament bring about such terrible effects? Far from wishing to "uproot" the home, it is for protection of home that women want the franchise. But Mr. Longley's ideal of women seems to be not the queens of "home" but of "fashion," those women in society who make pleasure their aim. Mr. Longley is afraid the power to vote will cause women to desert their home duties, but how do many society women attend to their homes? How many leave their children to the care of servants, while they are away on their nightly rounds of gaiety and pleasure "charming men" by their sweet smiles and winning graces?

Mr. Longley must remember that every woman cannot stay at home to be the object of some man's devotion, to be "weak and confiding" to be loved and cherished. The necessity of earning their bread and helping their families drives them into the world to work at anything they can get to do. If women want the franchise for one thing more than another it is for fair pay in wages. In no employment are they paid as well as men. Yet Mr.

Longley stands before an intelligent people and calmly says that equal and just rights are given to women as to men.

A gentleman made the remark to me after reading Mrs. Chesley's reply to Mr. Longley's speech that "she had better have stayed at home." I assured him that she probably had not gone into the yard or the street to write it, and neither has the writer of this.

There were other letters supporting Mary Chesley's position; however, the newspapers often included anti-suffrage opinions and were quite preoccupied with the question of woman's proper place in the world. Over the course of that year, several poems or limericks were published concerning the "new woman," or suffragist. The odd one took a sympathetic look at the question of the changing role for women, but in general the suffragist or "new woman" became a target of ridicule.

In the *Acadian Recorder* of March 26, 1895, the following appeared on the front page:

WOMAN SUFFRAGE

There's been a mighty change of late
In my dear little wife,
And since that change has come about
I've had a dreadful life,
She ain't the lamb she used to be,
And all of Home's delights
Have turned to troubles since dear Sue
Had heard of Women's Rights.
She's read somewhere that women-folk
Will rule things by and by,
And now I'd give the world to know
If she's the man, or I!

If I a button choose to lose,
Or get my trousers torn,

And ask my wife to right the wrong
I only get her scorn!
And when I'm forced to sit me down
The damage to repair,
She brings her frocks for me to mend
And vows "It's only fair!"
And if I dare to make complaint –
Lord! How her tongue does fly!
And ere she stops I'm all in doubt
If She's the man, or I!

I used to like an evening's fun
Down at the club or lodge,
But when I now would venture out
I have a club to dodge!
"Your lodge be blowed!" my wife declares
"I'll make you ride the goat!
You can't come that game on me now
Since woman's got a vote!"
And when I set me down, suppressed,
To wonder and to sigh,
She talks and talks till I can't tell
If Sue's the man, or I!

Three days later, on March 29, the same newspaper published a rare positive poem on the new woman. However, in the *Herald* a day later, the concern men had over their loss of someone to sew on their lost buttons resurfaced:

THE SUFFRAGIST

She abandons her feminine ways:
She changes that elegant phrase
Which marked her relation to man
Beyond a shadow of doubt;
For now, in the civic shocks

> When it comes to the regular knocks
> She turns on the lords of creation,
> and threatens to knock them out!
>
> She may not handle the sword:
> But a brighter triumph is scored—
> She can put three million stitches
> (or any number you like)
> With her needle plunged to the hilt
> In the minister's crazy quilt,
> But the tyrant who wears the suspenders
> Must button them with a spike!
> – Sporus

There is no doubt as to the meaning of this doggerel; the choice of the pen name is revealing. In Roman history, Sporus was a beautiful youth, castrated and taken as a "wife" by Nero. Using this pen name perhaps suggested that men would feel emasculated by women if both sexes shared equal rights.

The rhymes were invariably penned anonymously. The insults levelled and the way in which the newspapers took aim at and made fun of women who wished to have a part in public life clearly indicate how threatened men felt at the notion of gender equity.

In 1895, victory for the suffrage side seemed within women's grasp. Newspaper coverage on the suffrage debate in the spring was impassioned on both sides. The issue was not going to go away, but the topic went somewhat flat in the news over the next few years. In her annual Department of Franchise reports, Mary Chesley continued to urge the WCT unions in the province to be active on suffrage, occasionally penning articles for newspapers. Additionally, under the banner of the WCTU, the *Lunenburg Progress Enterprise* printed franchise news from elsewhere.

As already mentioned, the autumn of 1895 brought personal tragedy to Mary Chesley and her family with the drowning deaths of her two older children. Only weeks before the accident, Mary had become the first president of the newly formed Nova Scotia WCTU, with the dissolution of the Maritime body. The annual reports in those early years are sparse, but there's little indication in the records that Mary allowed herself to step back from her organizational responsibilities and the franchise issue after the deaths of her children. Individual responses to grief are vastly different. One can only assume that, for Mary, burying herself in work helped to assuage the pain of loss.

Mary's husband, Samuel, was more open-minded than the majority of men of the time. Samuel went one step further, though, working for the inclusion of women as fully participating members of the Methodist Church, and he was acknowledged for this. The 1895 annual report for the Maritime WCTU carried the following note: "It was unanimously resolved that the members of this Convention express their sincere appreciation of Judge Chesley's efforts at the last General conference of Methodist Church in Canada in behalf of the ecclesiastical enfranchisement of Women."

As the nineteenth century winds down, so does information on the Chesley family. What follows in the next decade, along with Mary's continuing suffrage work, is her increasing interest in international peace and arbitration, which she proclaimed with her powerful analytic voice; Samuel's coinciding as well as divergent interests; and Polly's entrance into university life.

CHAPTER 3
The Beginning of a New Century

AFTER THE FAILURE OF THE FRANCHISE BILL IN 1895, THE women's movement for the vote became more muted; however, Mary Russell never abandoned the mission and continued to stir up the embers of the franchise fire, and not without her dry wit. In 1900, she wrote:

> I have small patience with those who object that women are not sufficiently educated to vote—that we are not ready for the ballot. Those who use this argument overlook the fact that the ballot is an educator. We would not think of saying to a strong-limbed child, "No, you would not be able to use the skates properly if you had them. You must learn about the construction of skates and be informed in regard to the laws of motion and then you will be able to use the skates." We would simply give her the skates knowing that she would soon learn to use them.[31]

Mary was relentless in her struggle to educate members of the WCTU and the general public as to the importance and necessity of the women's vote. She tried to be positive and encouraging; however, her disappointment in how little interest some unions had in the topic crept into her reports. Encouraged by what was happening elsewhere in the world, in 1907 she wrote:

> The most important victory for Woman Suffrage during the past year has been the Enfranchisement of the women of Finland. Let us rejoice in this victory.
>
> Next in importance to this victory was the granting of Suffrage to all women of Norway who possessed the Municipal ballot. This measure will give full suffrage to 300,000 Norwegian women, enough to ensure the extension of full suffrage to all the other women of Norway.
>
> Advance has also been made in Great Britain by the measure passed by British Parliament, which makes women eligible to seats on borough, town, and county councils. This concession is doubtless the result of the vigorous agitation which has been carried on by the newly organized society, the Woman's [sic] Social and Political Union.[32]

The members of the Women's Social and Political Union (WSPU) would eventually become known as suffragettes, and their actions would raise controversy even among suffragists. Mary's endorsement of the more radical approach of the WSPU is interesting and will be discussed further as the group established more extreme tactics over time.

In Mary's 1907 report, the final sentence hints at her feeling that her efforts were not adequate to the task: "In closing this meagre report, I can only express the hope that the work of this, 'the most important department in our Union,' will pass into abler hands." This did not happen. During the rest of Mary's life, no one stepped up to take on the leadership. Mary continued to work for suffrage but added to her labours another field of interest, that of peace and arbitration. At the turn of the twentieth century, there were people convinced that civilization was advanced enough to settle international differences at the arbitration table rather than on the battlefields. The Chesleys held such a belief and acted upon this.

While Mary did not take up the position of Superintendent of the Department of Peace and Arbitration until 1908, based on Morgan's biographical entry in *The Canadian Men and Women of the Time*, we know that she believed in "the settlement of national difficulties by arbitration, and in co-operation as opposed to competition" at least as early as 1898 and likely earlier. She was not the first WCTU member in Nova Scotia to head up this department. Margaret B. McKay of Pictou wrote Peace and Arbitration reports as early as 1895, and like Mary's later reports, McKay's reports struck a chord with my own concerns.[33]

I became a mother in the mid-1970s. Through the previous decade, I had been involved in civil rights activism and had supported conscientious objectors from the US who had arrived in Canada; the Vietnam War remained fresh in our memories. In 1895, McKay wrote that she had written a letter to the local papers regarding "the impropriety of giving children toy guns and swords to play with"—a sentiment I and many of my contemporaries endorsed. Of course, my antipathy to guns was not universally shared. My young son, initially deprived of a toy gun, did what many children do. He created imaginary weapons out of sticks. His father eventually relented and made him a leather holster to house a toy pistol. To my relief, he outgrew his interest in weaponry. I am not sure whether the desire to "play at war" or "good guys/bad guys" is built into human (male?) genetics, but based on lack of success in preventing cadet training in schools, neither Margaret McKay nor Mary Chesley was any more successful than I in banning weapons, whether toy or real.

The provincial WCTU annual reports and the Dominion WCTU monthly newsletter, the *White Ribbon Bulletin*, offer a trove of evidence of Mary's commitment to the role as Superintendent of Peace and Arbitration.

An impassioned article in *The Wesleyan* dated November 18, 1908, gives a clear indication of how strongly Mary opposed any form of war-making. Evidently a reprint of a presentation made at the WCTU convention, the article also reveals the depth of her intellect and the breadth of her reading. An excerpt from that article highlighting some of the salient points illustrates just how radical a position she held. Mary's faith was grounded in the teachings of Jesus Christ. Her understanding of how Christ's teachings were perverted is revealed in her review of early Christianity:

The spirit and practice of war is so opposed to that gospel, the essential element and fundamental principle of which is love, that we may ask how it is that nations called by the name of Christ have, for centuries, settled their differences by shedding each other's blood. Those who lived nearest to the time of Christ and had more of the mind that was in him, did not engage in war. Tatian and Justin Martyr, ecclesiastical writers of the second century, speak of soldiers and Christians as distinct classes, and Tatian says that Christians "declined military commands." About the end of the second century Celsus, one of the opponents of Christianity, charged the Christians with refusing to bear arms. Even after Christianity had spread over almost the whole of the known world, Tertullian, in speaking of a part of the Roman armies said that "not a Christian could be found among them, that war is irreconcilable with Christianity." Irenaeus, who lived about the year 180, affirms that the prophecy of Isaiah that men would turn their swords into plough shares and their spears into pruning-hooks had been fulfilled in his time. Later Constantine finally united Church and State by declaring the Christian religion the official religion of the Empire.

No man can really serve two opposed masters—we "cannot serve God and Mammon." When the early church came under the protection of Constantine—a man who was not only a warrior, but a murderer, having killed his father-in-law, his nephew, and his own son, and finally, his wife—when the church came under this ruler's protection, and was constituted the state church of Rome, it was freed from persecution, but it also forfeited its independence. It grew worldly and corrupt. [What] succeeded [was] that long period of moral and intellectual depression known as the Dark Ages.

Mary went on at length, quoting the apostles as well as referring to radical thinkers such as Leo Tolstoy and John Bright. She was very clear in her understanding that the established Church had become far removed from Christian principles and that the marriage of church and state was problematic: "How can you expect a church whose bishops are appointed and salaried by the Crown and whose church edifices are largely maintained at the expense of the government—how can you expect such a Church to take an independent attitude in regard to any great question?"

Mary suggested that those outside organized Christianity better understood Jesus's peace testimony.

> A great movement against war has been going on in England during the past few years. Among its leaders are Frederic Harrison, the positivist, Herbert Spencer, the agnostic, and John Mosley, the atheist, but nearly the whole bench of bishops has been on the side of bloodshed. In France the Church gave its unanimous support to the military conspiracy against Dreyfus and left it to the free-thinking Zola to show "What Jesus would do." In Germany and Russia the Church is the mainstay of military despotism.
>
> It would be easy to denounce the military method of settling national disputes because of its immense monetary cost. Forty thousand millions of dollars [four billion] is a sum so vast that the imagination fails to grasp it, yet this is about what the European nations spent in war during a single century—from 1796, the beginning of the Napoleonic wars, to 1896.
>
> To this must be added the destruction of property and the loss of life. A very low estimate of this loss, during the nineteenth century, places it at 14,000,000 men. The moral damage that is done by war and the destruction of soul life is its most awful effect.
>
> Rudyard Kipling—styled by one writer the poet laureate of brute force—in his poem on the "Torpedo" speaks of "the hate that backs the hand" that sends the missile of destruction. And in his "Drums of the Fore and Aft" he says, "you must employ either gentlemen or blackguards to do butchers' work with efficiency." We wonder just what Kipling's ideal of a "gentleman" is. It is impossible to conceive of a gentleman doing such butchers' work. [To quote] an excerpt from the letter of an English officer

engaged in the Boer war: "After the enemy was driven out, one of our squadron pursued and most excellent pig-sticking (a bayonet charge) ensued." Another of these "gentlemen"—General Baden Powell, in his book on "Scouting," said "man-hunting is a better game than football." From the autobiographical "Story of a Soldier's Life" by one who seems to consider himself a Christian I quote the following: "It is only through experience of the sensation that we learn how intense is the rapture-giving delight which an attack upon the enemy affords. I cannot analyze or weigh, nor can I justify the feeling. But once really experienced, all other subsequent sensations are but as the tinkling of a door-bell in comparison with the throbbing of Big Ben. That war is a horrible thing 'tis a very nice heading in a schoolgirl's copybook, but I confess that I thoroughly enjoy it."

But General Gordon, in his diary while in command in the Sudan, wrote, "It is not climate, not natives, but the soldiery that is my horror. It is organized murder, pillage and cruelty. Some write to me about 'noble work.' I have stopped their writing by acknowledging ourselves to be a pillaging horde of brigands." A war correspondent said, "War raises the worst passions and vices of men, and whoever expects soldiers—whether they be English, French, German, or Boers, to act in the heart of battle as a gentleman has very little knowledge of the ferocity latent in human nature. When life and death are the stakes, chivalry and mercy are easily forgotten. We condemn arson, adultery, murder, burglary, lying, theft. War includes them all."

Mary addressed the problems of maintaining a military force, referring to "the temptations to vice that result in enforced idleness and the unnatural lives that the soldiers of a standing army are obliged to live during the periods of peace" and referred to the way women become the "slaves of soldiers' passions."

In her concluding remarks, Mary left no doubt about where she believed the WCTU should stand on this issue: "I submit, Madame President and co-workers in the W.C.T.U. that there is but one attitude for us to take—that of active opposition."

Mary's first peace and arbitration report at the 1908 annual convention revealed her strong aversion to military cadet training:

> I read a notice to the effect that "Sir Frederick Borden's scheme for military training in the public schools" was to be put in operation for all boys. Teachers were also to be trained—those who became instructors were to receive a bonus.
>
> I consulted the Journal of Education and was surprised to find that Rifle Cadets already existed in three schools, those of Halifax, Middleton and Yarmouth; that in 1906 the strength of these Rifle Cadet Companies was reported at 290, and that since that date additional companies had been formed. So you see the militarization of the schools is already well begun.
>
> The militia expenses of the Dominion have grown from $2,000,000 to $6,000,000 within the last twelve years; the well salaried officials of the Department of Militia have increased from 8 to 23. One would suppose that in this country it was more useful to train boys in the knowledge of farming, cattle-raising, etc., and the other arts of peace; but we find that for every dollar spent in connection with agriculture, twelve dollars are spent on the militia. Why?[34]

Mary circulated a leaflet on "Military Drill in Schools" and urged WCTU members to get their ministers to preach peace sermons. Mary also recommended that unions subscribe to *Advocate of Peace* to circulate among ministers in town and copies of *Lay Down Your Arms* by Baroness Bertha von Suttner and *The Moral Damage of War* by Reverend Walter Walsh for circulation within their unions, and afterward "loan them to friends outside the Union."

As in her 1908 report, Mary's continued awareness of the budgetary investment in armaments is evident. Now, over one hundred years later, her report of 1909 sounds eerily familiar:

> The fever of militarism seems to have taken possession of the nations.

> Since the keel of the first Dreadnought was laid four years ago, there has been a race between the nations for supremacy in the size and number of battleships.
>
> The army—always jealous of the navy—clamors for its share of the people's money. Lord Roberts has been urging Compulsory Military Service.
>
> A speaker at the national Peace Congress of the United States, which met in Chicago last May, stated that "the annual expenses of the United States, Great Britain, Germany and France in preparation for war, or, as it is claimed, that war may be prevented, are today greater than the annual expenses of any of these nations during any foreign war in which it has ever engaged. In fact these expenditures have become so great, causing enormous deficits in their current revenues and necessitation of new sources of taxation to meet the demands in the construction of armaments."
>
> England is spending $300,000,000 a year on her army and navy as against $82,000,000 on education, science and art. Germany has increased her national debt from $18,000,000 to over $1,000,000,000, chiefly by expenditures on her army and navy. Russia is planning a billion dollar navy and is spending $200,000,000 a year as against $20,000,000 on education and the military expenditures of the United States increased 300 per cent while its population has increased but 10 per cent.
>
> In the meantime it is evident to any one who reads or thinks, *that the real enemies against which the nations need to defend themselves are poverty, ignorance, vice, graft, greed and oppression* [emphasis added]. What is any government doing to lessen these enemies?[35]

Samuel's concerns during this decade sometimes dovetailed with his wife's, but he had some independent projects that reveal a man of diverse interests.

Samuel's interest in peace is reflected in his becoming a charter member of the Canadian Peace and Arbitration Society in 1905; Mary's brother Benjamin Russell is also listed as a member by 1906, an indication of shared family interest. The society did not survive once the First World War broke out.[36]

Samuel was also an active member of the Independent Order of Odd Fellows (IOOF) and responsible for the construction of the Lunenburg Opera House (the IOOF hall was on the upper floor of the building). The Opera House (also known as the Capitol Theatre) opened its doors in 1908 and has been used over the intervening years for live concerts, theatre productions, and as a movie house.[37] Having survived harder times, the building is now restored and recently moved from private hands to ownership by the Lunenburg Folk Harbour Society. Samuel Chesley's initiation of this project reflects his significant contribution to the cultural life of the town. Like Mary's pioneer work for suffrage in Nova Scotia, Samuel's efforts also have been forgotten over time.

And what of Polly's life in the first decade of the twentieth century? Apart from the brief mentions of her rendering literary pieces at meetings held at her parents' home, we know very little about her, although we can assume that she was a precocious child. She was fifteen when she entered university, and it is through the Mount Allison records that we are able to paint a more detailed portrait of Polly. The main sources of information about Polly's university years are the Mount Allison paper *The Argosy* and the *Allisonia*, a shorter-lived publication put out by the Ladies' College. Because the brief biographical portrait of Polly written upon her graduation is so evocative, I will begin with this entry from October 1910 and work backward through other issues of *The Argosy* that cover the years when Polly attended Mount Allison.

> In September 1906, MARY ALBEE CHESLEY, a mere child, with short skirts and hair flying over her shoulders, found her way to Mount Allison, entering College—the youngest member of the Freshman class.[38]
>
> Classes at the University were not all the ambitious Polly had fancied, so she turned to the Ladies' College for subjects to fill up her spare periods, registering for drawing and vocal. Later that year, however, she became interested in Honor Courses and

gave up her Ladies' College work in favor of Honor Science and Mathematics.

It was then that Polly's powers as a student were discovered, and she maintained the high standard she set for herself in her Freshman days. She proved herself to be not only a thorough student, but a clear thinker. More than once her finer thoughts found expression in verse of no little merit.

But it was not only as a student that Polly distinguished herself. She was fond of every sport. It was largely owing to her efforts that a University girls' hockey team formed, and with Polly as Captain, warmly contested games were played with the Ladies' College team. Polly was also a member of the University Basket Ball team, always ready for any game.

In Alpha Beta also, Polly was a power. From her Freshman days on, she was considered one of the best debaters. She was a strong supporter of the cause of Woman's Rights, and was at her best when refuting arguments brought forward against Woman Suffrage. At a senior Oration she read a strongly written paper on this subject.

The Mount Allison University Women's Hockey Team. Polly, captain of the team, is at centre. [MOUNT ALLISON UNIVERSITY ARCHIVES, Argosy (MAY 1910)]

During her senior year Polly occupied the Chair as president of Alpha Beta. In her sophomore year she was vice-president of her class.

At present she is in Truro studying "A" work at the Normal School. The best wishes of her many friends will follow her there and on into the world, where in all probability Mary Chesley will make a name for herself.

Alpha Beta was a women's debating society. Coming upon this passage on Polly was pure gold. Years before, I had visited the Mount Allison archives and had looked up the indexed references to the Chesleys in *The Argosy* and *Allisonia*. This entry had not been indexed.

As fate would have it, while going through the Methodist newspaper *The Wesleyan*, I happened to stumble upon a poem by Polly, published in the January 13, 1909, issue of that weekly, with a note that it had previously appeared in the November 1908 issue of *The Argosy*. This item had not been indexed, which led me to suspect that other entries had been missed. I returned to the reels of microfilm, went through the years of interest, and found additional items, this graduation entry being the most evocative and colourful of all. The sentence "More than once her finer thoughts found expression in verse of no little merit" suggests that Polly may have been known for her poetry. The only extant example found is the following, written when she was seventeen:

Polly (Mary) Chesley, president of Alpha Beta, c. 1909. [MOUNT ALLISON UNIVERSITY ARCHIVES, 2007.07/26]

QUODLIBET

There is a Brook of purling rills, that chatters as it flows,
'Mid pasturefields where far and near,
With waters tumbling far and near,
Like chiming bells so silvery clear;
This Brook is Joy.

There is a River strong and deep, which surges on with angry roar:
The fields around are vast and drear;
The swimmer strives in mortal fear,
And sees the shore, but cannot near;
This Stream is Grief.

There is a Lake where sunbeams dance, and light a shimmering way;
There all is calm, with waters clear—
The waters of this inland mere,
Which mirror back God's upper air;
This Lake is Peace.

There is a Sea where men may sail, and never strand their bark:
Where white-capped waves run free and fair,
And ripples play and frolic there,
'Mid sunbeams shot through purest air;
This Sea is Love.

And Brook, and River, Lake and Sea,
Flow on in finest melody;
The major and the minor key
Make cadence through Eternity—
Forever.

– MARY CHESLEY

What struck me is the passage in the second verse, "The swimmer strives in mortal fear, And sees the shore, but cannot near; This Stream is Grief." This is the only indication of the mark that the drowning deaths of her sister and brother must have left on the young Polly; for that reason alone, the poem was a revealing find.

Many of the entries in the university journal have to do with Polly's athletic activities. As early as April 1907, she held the position of rover on the "All-Comers" team, which may have consisted of both university and college girls and possibly others from Sackville. By the following year, there were two teams, the university varsity team and the Ladies' College team, and throughout Polly's years at Mount Allison, these two teams played against each other.

In the February 1908 issue of *The Argosy*, the following item appeared: "A few days ago at a meeting of the Alpha Beta Society, Miss Polly Chesley was elected captain of the hockey team," a position she held throughout her time at Mount Allison. An entry from April 1909 indicates that Polly was a consequential player: "A large number of students gathered in the Sackville rink on the afternoon of March 19th to witness the girls' hockey match—Ladies' College vs. University girls. Miss Chesley, the captain of the University team, played an excellent game, shooting three goals for her side." The final score: 4–1.

There are also references to Polly playing basketball, and one *Allisonia* entry (June 1909) refers to Polly playing in a mixed doubles set in a tennis match. The writer of the sports report provided a graphic account of the weather that day: "The weatherman did not smile at closing this year. In the afternoon the track sports were witnessed at the peril of wet feet and ruined millinery. Also Tuesday afternoon, when the tennis tournament was in order, the weather was so cold that the onlookers sought the sunny side of the courts with chattering teeth, and looked askance at the ice cream."

As indicated in her graduation profile, Polly did not restrict her interests to sport. When she was a sophomore, her class hosted a dinner in honour of graduating theology and engineering students, and she responded to a toast (undoubtedly non-alcoholic!) made "to the ladies." The presence of "ladies" still held an air of novelty.

The Mount Allison University Women's Basketball team. [MOUNT ALLISON UNIVERSITY ARCHIVES, 2007.07/2004, 2007.07/8]

"The dining hall had been decorated for the event and the lady members of the class of 1910 lent an unwonted brightness to the place."[39]

Women at this time still had not achieved the vote or other forms of civil rights. Even though Mount Allison had been in the vanguard in offering degrees to women, there was still ambivalence on campuses about women's rightful place in society. Scanning newspapers from the 1890s throughout the 1910s, one finds that woman's suffrage remained a hot topic for university debating teams.

Unsurprisingly, Polly was a staunch supporter of woman's rights. Twice in the years when she was at Mount Allison, Polly is referred to obliquely in "Sackvilliana," a regular column in *The Argosy*. Obviously

Mount Allison Graduation, 1910. Polly is at far left, seated in second row.
[MOUNT ALLISON UNIVERSITY ARCHIVES, 5501/9/2/4/17]

meant to be funny, the column contained a series of university in-jokes. The first reference teased Polly about her position on suffrage. The second reference probably had to do with Polly's stand on temperance. While the jokes are almost completely incomprehensible today, they do not appear to be intentionally cruel. It is likely that the authors felt Polly was capable of taking a joke.

There is a general sense that Polly was well integrated into university life. Along with her leadership role in the Alpha Beta Society and serving as treasurer for the YWCA cabinet, she also had a part in a drama that the seniors put on for their graduation recital.

All these extracurricular activities did not get in the way of her studies. The January 6, 1909, issue of *The Wesleyan* published a list of the courses Polly was taking at the time: Logic, Latin, Roman

History, Evidence of Christianity, Ethics, Statics, Mathematics (Trig.), Advanced English, French, and one other course that is no longer readable on the microfilm copy. This seems like a considerable course load, but based on Polly's graduation bio, she liked intellectual challenges as much as physical ones.

Polly graduated from Mount Allison in 1910 and subsequently entered the Normal School in Truro. Thus, at the beginning of the new decade, Polly was embarking on the next stage of her education and subsequent work as a teacher. Always adventurous and ambitious intellectually, her travels were just beginning.

CHAPTER 4
War, Peace Advocacy, and Suffrage Work

BY 1910, MARY AND SAMUEL CHESLEY WERE IN THEIR SIXTIES. Mary's interest and Samuel's support in suffrage and peace issues continued unabated. On the surface, franchise activism was more muted, but Mary never lost sight of her mission. For the next few years she would continue with her forceful advocating and writing. With the exception of occasional holiday visits from their daughter, Mary and Samuel were on their own, although they kept in touch with Polly through correspondence. A collection of letters from Polly to her parents (discussed in the next chapter) indicates how closely their interests were aligned.

Based on evidence from newspapers and WCTU reports, Mary Chesley was the most outspoken voice for franchise in Nova Scotia. If anyone matched her dedication to suffrage promotion, it was Fanny Musgrave, who lived in the Annapolis Valley. Born in Antigua in 1850 to a distinguished family of colonial administrators, Fanny was close in age to Mary Chesley, and, like Mary, she had parents who believed in education. The family moved to Nova Scotia when Fanny was young. After her parents died, she managed the family farm, Holmwood, in Auburn, and for a time she and her sister Amy ran a private school for girls there. Fanny had one novel published,

Gabrielle Amethyst, in 1908.[40] She and her sister were active WCTU members and suffragists. In 1910 Fanny prepared a paper on suffrage for the WCTU. Mary Chesley's WCTU Department of Franchise report for that year is full of praise for Fanny Musgrave's work: "The publication in the Halifax Herald and the distribution of it to the local Unions, may be considered the best provincial work that has been done in this department."

Fanny Musgrave's nineteen-page paper, "The Dark Side and Bright Side of Woman's Franchise," was subsequently printed for wider distribution.[41] Like Mary Chesley, Fanny Musgrave was well-read, and they shared similar political and social views. In her address, Musgrave cited the words of a number of famous male pro-suffrage writers and political figures. Like Mary, she admired the work of the suffragettes and believed their extremist tactics were justified because Britain's parliamentarian intransigence prevented ratification of the vote. Fanny's list of the four great legalized evils—injustice to women, intemperance, militarism, and capital punishment—is another indication that she and Mary Chesley held common views.

Fanny Musgrave. [CLARA DENNIS, NOVA SCOTIA ARCHIVES, 1983-468 NUMBER 73]

Again, I am reminded of the assumption of earlier historians that radical political views radiated out from the city.[42] This notion is belied by the forceful writings of Mary Chesley and Fanny Musgrave, women from rural and small-town Nova Scotia.[43] Both women's views were strongly informed by their Christian faith—not a dry or rote faith in doctrine but one based on the radical teachings of Christ. In her paper, Musgrave's closing poem presents a utopian vision for the world, one that implies harmony and equality across gender, race, and class:

> God make the world one state
> All nations small and great
> One civic whole:
> Self-rules each people be
> All peoples linked and free,
> Glorious in unity
> From pole to pole:
>
> One world, one destiny,
> One race, one family,
> One God above!
> All states upheld in one.
> All laws excelled in one.
> All lives impelled by one,
> One life, one love!

It must have been inspiring for Mary to know that there were others, like Fanny, who held a vision similar to her own. Her work of educating the broader WCTU membership about the importance of the vote must, at times, have felt like an endless struggle.

Based on her 1912 report, Mary was doing all in her power to make Fanny's pamphlet available widely. She reported that she had written three letters to national newspapers, the *Montreal Witness* and the *Christian Guardian*, in defence of the suffragettes' militancy. In the midst of some bad press given to the suffragettes because of vandalism in London, Mary wrote to the *Montreal Witness*:

[Concerning an article] from the *Montreal Star*, under the heading "Suffragette Insanity," the writer says, "The uncultured miners conduct their strike with exemplary restraint and good nature; the cultured suffragettes conduct themselves by breaking plate glass windows."

The writer appears to forget that the miners have the ballot.

We would like to be told which weapon of the dazzling arsenal possessed by women has not been used by English suffragists during the past forty-five years. They have used tongue and pen, have held meetings and circulated literature, have petitioned and lobbied and succeeded in educating public sentiment.

With regards to the recent window-breaking raid, many, not unfriendly to the cause, will probably say "they have gone too far." I would not venture such an opinion. It seems to me that there should be some expression of resentment of the insult the government has offered them. *Neither am I so much concerned about the question of property rights. Human rights are of so much greater importance. If the rights of property must be ignored in order to procure all other rights, let the property go; it is of minor importance.* [emphasis added]

More "suffragette insanity," yes. Similar to that of Osawatomie Brown, whose soul went "marching on" till every dark-skinned brother of the Southern States was proclaimed free, but I prefer to apply the term to those British bureaucrats and lesser authorities who imagine that ideas can be killed by incarceration and principles beaten out with bludgeons.

M. R. CHESLEY
Lunenburg, N.S., March 26, 1912[44]

Mary's defence of suffragette tactics must have been made knowing full well that it would be unpopular. Also remarkable, considering her adherence to peace and arbitration principles, is Mary's defence of John "Osawatomie" Brown, who used violence in his attempts to rid the South of slavery.

I have italicized what I believe is key to understanding Mary's thinking. For her, human rights trumped other considerations. Even today, the privileging of property rights over human rights in courts of law is not uncommon. Stealing or destroying property is treated more harshly than the abuse and defiling of human beings; victims of abuse and sexual crimes are often revictimized by the legal system and the media, and the perpetrators of these crimes are treated more leniently than if they had robbed a bank.

While Mary continued her franchise work, a large part of her energy focused on peace and arbitration. In the years leading up to the First World War, her prescient reports reveal how much study she gave to international issues.

Mary's 1910 report held certain optimism, notwithstanding her comment that nations were piling up yet more munitions of war. She was pinning her hopes on a resolution passed in the US Congress: "Resolved, by the Senate and House of Representatives that a commission be appointed by the President to consider utilizing international agencies for the purpose of limiting armaments and of constituting the combined navies of the world for the preservation of universal peace, and also to diminish expenditures for military purposes, and to lessen the probabilities of war."

What Mary perceived as the other beacon of hope for the promotion of peace reveals her willingness to entertain more radical thinking: "Perhaps the most effective check to the increase of armaments and the outbreak of war is the growth of Socialism. Over 100,000 Socialists met recently in Berlin to protest against the German policy in connection with Morocco because it tended to provoke war with France.

"It was the policy of Napoleon to engage in foreign wars in order to divert the people from disturbances at home. Governments today are less likely to embroil themselves in war when one of the results is likely to be disturbances at home."[45]

The 1912 annual report of the WCTU's Department of Peace and Arbitration contained both disappointment and optimism. Dashed were hopes of the United States Senate approving arbitration treaties. Partisan politics got in the way; sadly, partisanship still hinders decision making.

It might seem unlikely that a Lunenburg matron would be touting such radical ideas; however, Mary's enthusiasm for the rise of socialism is expressed on more than one occasion. Here's one example: "Perhaps the most auspicious event of the past year is the result of the German elections when the Socialists nearly doubled their representation. Representatives took part in a Peace Conference in Copenhagen in 1910, in which it was proposed to Socialists in different countries, that, in case of a declaration of war between two nations, a general strike of all government workers should be declared in order to make war impossible. This would be a more effective measure than that which Ruskin proposed—the adopting of mourning by all women of any country upon the declaration of war."[46]

Socialists were not necessarily pacifist in their thinking, but they regarded war as a capitalist enterprise, so opposed it on that ground. Mary was probably aware of this, but she would have likely welcomed anti-war alliances.

Mary had circulated to all Nova Scotia unions a peace petition initiated by German peace activist Anna B. Eckstein, which was to be presented at the next Hague Conference. Eckstein had sent petitions to the previous two Hague Conferences; the last one contained two million signatures. As would come to pass, the eruption of the First World War precluded all hope of sending Eckstein's "Petition to End all Wars," which had amassed over six million signatures by the time of war's outbreak.

In the year leading up to the war, the WCTU's monthly national newsletter, *White Ribbon Bulletin*, published a number of articles that revealed the divergent voices within the organization concerning military training of young men. Only a month after Mary Chesley had posted information on the international peace petition, the March 1913 issue of *White Ribbon Bulletin* carried an article cautioning against collaboration with the military.

A Word to the Wise

Just a few days after posting my letter, published in the February Bulletin, a notice appeared in the daily papers that the Minister of Militia proposed inviting representatives from the Daughters of the Empire, and the W.C.T.U. to a conference on matters pertaining to the militia, to be held in Ottawa.[47]

That our members may know the extent to which the Canadian Government is infected with the contagion of militarism, I quote from the official organ of the Canadian Defence League: "What the Canadian Defence League has in mind is that the permanent corps of Canada shall be recruited by voluntary enlistment and Canada should have universal military training. The first step is physical and military training for all boys. The second step is after school, a continuation of the training up to the age of 18 in cadet corps. The third step is that all youths, physically fit, beginning at the age of 18, should have four months' continuous recruit training, and during the next three years there will be no question of the efficiency of the Canadian militia for home defence."

According to the Minister of Militia, the combined cost of the militia and navy of Canada in 1912, was $11,404,350. The $35,000,000 already voted for Canada's addition to the British navy, is another matter. The per capita tax for the militia is a growing expense.

We ask ourselves why this waste of money. If ever there was a portion of God's world that had no need of a trained militia, except a sufficient number to act as a police force in case of internal troubles, it is Canada.

But there is more serious "significance" to this matter; that is the effect of military training and camp life on boys.

The effect of all this glorification of war and the warlike spirit, is wholly undesirable. The power rests with School Boards. We have not yet compulsory military drill, though that day may not be distant. It is time that every Provincial Union made a study of the question, and acted.

I cannot but think that if women could use a direct influence upon our parliamentarians, many of them would have their eyes opened and their course altered.

Mary R. Chesley.[48]

The very next issue of the *White Ribbon*, April 1913, contained an article with a pro-military position antithetical to Chesley's, submitted by a leading military officer.

> Canadian Cadet Service
>
> Will the W.C.T.U. Join in Helping the Militia Department make Good Men Out of Our Boys?
>
> There are at present about 350 cadet companies in Canada, consisting of approximately 26,000 cadets, who belong chiefly to the public schools of Canada.
>
> The policy of the Department is to encourage male teachers throughout Canada to take a course during the summer months to qualify to instruct the cadets in physical training, drill, signaling, etc., and to teach them discipline, obedience, hygiene, elementary sanitation, etc., and each instructor, who is qualified, receives a bonus.
>
> The Militia Department furnishes each cadet with a Stetson hat and a brown leather belt, and gives $1.00 a year towards his uniform, which can be purchased for about $2.00 to $2.50, and which is the boy's own property.
>
> Arms and equipment are also given to each cadet. Last summer the cadets were taken to cadet camp for a week and there learned how to pitch tents and take care of themselves under canvas. They were also taught swimming, first aid, signaling, rifle shooting, and camp sanitation, and mounted cadets were taught riding and horsemanship.
>
> At some camps, members of the W.C.T.U. joined the Imperial Order of the Daughters of the Empire, making puttees for the cadets and also looking after refreshments and helping with the messes. They were not only a great help to the officers but they saw the good work done in teaching the boys obedience, discipline, cleanliness and manliness.
>
> Many mothers have appreciated the change for the better in the behavior and obedience of their boys due to the discipline learned in their cadet corps, improving themselves mentally and morally.

The Militia Department wants mothers and sisters of the cadets, and all women to support this good work. The I.O.D.E. have already given most invaluable assistance, and the W.C.T.U. have done so in many cases. We now ask the W.C.T.U. to join as a body and help the Militia Department in this work.

Will the W.C.T.U. join in helping the Militia Department make good men out of our boys?

The following month, the WCTU Dominion Superintendent of Militia, Ida Powell Starr, wrote a column in support of the Department of Defence plans and the importance of supporting the training of the "young manhood of our land": "We think that nowhere in Canada, or in the world, will you find such advocates of Peace, as amongst the force; no one has so great a knowledge of the requirements as the commanding officers of the 'defence.' Our worthy Superintendent of Peace and Arbitration has no stronger supporters than the honored generals."

Mary Chesley did not receive the May issue with Ida Starr's article before writing her response to the April call to support the military. It is obvious that Starr was aware of what Chesley might have been thinking and tried to soft-pedal around her possible objections. If Starr held out hope of Chesley being convinced, she failed to understand Mary. The forcefulness of her article in the June issue of the *White Ribbon* is a testament to her passionate anti-militarism: "I was surprised to read in the April journal (which, by the way, did not reach me in time to make any comments in the May issue), a communication from the 'Military Secretary' under the heading 'Will the W.C.T.U. Join in Helping the Militia Department to Make Good Men Out of Our Boys?'"

Mary related how the Nova Scotia WCTU had, six years previously, passed a resolution against introduction of military drill in the schools. Furthermore, the same resolution was adopted without dissent at the succeeding Dominion WCTU convention. Whether unions adopted Departments of Militia and Defence before the whispers of war were circulating and how widespread a phenomenon it was is unknown. Ida Starr may have initiated the first (and only?) department. Nova Scotia never formed such a department.

The issue over cadet training was not new among WCTU members. As early as 1896, Chesley's predecessor as Superintendent of the Department of Peace and Arbitration, Margaret McKay, wrote in her annual report: "The increasing demand for the introduction of military training in schools is to be deplored. Its tendency is to displace physical discipline of a more comprehensive character. Children should be trained to believe that the interests of the nation are better served by settling difficulties as far as possible by arbitration."[49]

Even gender equity was considered at this early date, for in the same report, McKay wrote of the success of fire drills for both boys and girls as being a much preferred alternative to cadet training. "[In] an exhibition given by a girls' Fire Brigade, in every particular the drill was as well conducted as that of the boys."

Over fifteen years later, Chesley's words regarding cadet training echoed those of Margaret McKay:

> Unless there is an entire change of our sentiments, we can scarcely accept the invitation of the Militia Department to help them "make good men out of our boys."
>
> If war ideals are to be promoted in this Dominion, there is no surer way of doing the work than by perverting the minds of our boys.
>
> Lieutenant-Colonel Winter has made a case in favor of cadet corps and cadet camps, but let us not be too credulous. Equally good results can be attained in other and safer ways, and uniforms and firearms are no necessary part of such culture, nor is there any reason to suppose that the Militia Department is interested in the physical development of our boys apart from their military instruction. We are told that the boys are taught, "obedience, discipline, cleanliness, manliness." Are we at such a straightened [sic] pass that we must hand our young boys to the Militia Department to be taught these virtues, and, if so, on what grounds do we make this particular choice of instructors?
>
> In conclusion, I would ask you to remember that this whole question of militarism is largely one of sordid self-interest—of mere money considerations. I trust many of you have read the

Berlin dispatch and editorial in regard to it in the Montreal Witness of April 22nd, "Militarism Unveiled." Zangwill puts this whole matter in a nutshell in the subjoined lines, which I commend to your thoughtful perusal.

– Mary R. Chesley[50]

The following poem by British writer and political activist Israel Zangwill, quoted by Mary, clearly makes the connection between war and commerce, a topic that Chesley returned to often in her writings on the subject of militarism.

The God of War

"To safeguard peace we must prepare for war"—
I know that maxim; it was forged in hell.
This wealth of ships and guns inflames the vulgar
And makes the very war it guards against.
The god of War is now a man of business,
With vested interests.
So much sunk Capital, such countless callings;
The Army, Navy, Medicine, the Church—
To bless and bury—Music, Engineering,
Red-tape Departments, Commissariats,
Stores, Transports, Ammunition, Coaling stations,
Fortifications, Cannon-foundries, Shipyards,
Arsenals, Ranges, Drill-halls, Floating docks,
War-loan Promoters, Canteens, War Correspondents,
Horse-breeders, Armorers, Torpedo-builders,
Pipeclay and Medal Vendors, Big Drum Makers,
Gold Lace Embroiderers, Opticians, Buglers,
Tent-makers, Banner-weavers, Powder-mixers,
Crutches and Cork Limb Manufacturers,
Balloonists, Mappists, Heliographers,
Inventors, Flying Men, and Diving Demons,
Beelzebub and all his hosts, who, whether

In Water, Earth, or Air, among them pocket
When Trade is brisk a million pounds a week!

Ida Starr wrote again in the August 1913 issue of *White Ribbon*. Sidestepping Mary Chesley's clear-cut analysis and suspicion regarding the aims of the military, Starr wrote:

> In reply to "Peace and Arbitration" article, permit me to say:
>
> If our worthy Superintendent of Peace and Arbitration will tell us how to do better service for Peace, than by helping our Defence, to up-build a character of purity and truth, and love to God and man, your Superintendent of Defence will feel that the object of our organization has accomplished much towards "Peace on earth, good will toward men."
>
> I assure our dear Mrs. Chesley that our departments are striving to accomplish the same good purpose. If the youth of our land received the home training required for the making of pure, true manhood and womanhood, we would not require the many organizations that have for their object the uplifting of humanity.
>
> Therefore, dear comrades, attention! The Department of Militia and Defence of our fair land requires your attention, your prayers, your influence that every man wearing the uniform may become worthy of your trust, worthy as men to protect our homes, our girls from the evils that surround them, worthy to unite their effort with our Superintendent of Peace and Arbitration in the making of peace in all the world.
>
> Yours, in the interests of the youth of our land,
> I. Powell Starr

It is difficult to discern whether Starr's deference to Chesley was genuine or feigned. The two women were poles apart in their thinking on militarism. One cannot read between the lines sufficiently to know whether Starr understood how different the two women's positions really were. Chesley was a long-standing and respected leader in the

WCTU and sixteen years older than Starr. These facts would have had some influence in Starr's decision to play down her differences with the senior member. Nevertheless, she did not hesitate to hold her ground on supporting the military's plan to involve women, Christian women, in their strategic move to make "men out of boys."

During the Victorian and Edwardian periods, the prevailing attitudes regarding manliness emphasized physical prowess and sport over and above intellect for boys.[51] As Chesley perceptively pointed out, Baden-Powell, the founder of the Boy Scouts, was a classic proponent of that ethos, wherein war was compared to a game, and in order to play it well, military or cadet training would be the "ticket." Sadly, the millions of idealistic young men who enlisted once war broke out discovered that war had none of the fun or glory of sport. While camaraderie sometimes persisted among those who went to war, there is much evidence that the war, particularly the Great War, traumatized more than uplifted those who survived. [52]

When Mary filed her peace and arbitration report to the ninth international WCTU convention, held in Brooklyn, New York, in October 1913, she still had hope that war might be averted: "From the Dominion of Canada we have received good reports from Mrs. Chesley, the Superintendent.

"Mrs. Chesley says: 'I do not think there is a warlike spirit in Canada, but our militia department has been unusually active during the past two years and I am afraid is doing a great deal to promote military pomp and display. There is evidence that the churches are awakening to the need of education in regard to the better way of settling international disputes.'"

That the membership of the WCTU was divided on the issue of cadet training is not surprising. In all likelihood, there would have been union members married to military men. However, another strong voice within the WCTU against supporting the military came from Anna E. Gordon, the Dominion Evangelistic Superintendent. Her writing in the November 1913 issue of the *White Ribbon* is as impassioned as Mary Chesley's. While Chesley and Gordon may have been the exception rather than the rule, the following quotation indicates how closely these women were keeping abreast of international and national movements and the ramping up of the military.

Where Do We Stand for War or Peace?

It is frightful to know that nations are expending two-thirds of their net income in maintaining the forces of war, and in maturing preparations for blowing each other to pieces while there are millions who do not know where their next meal is coming from. The air is full of militarism, and our parliament is asked to vote colossal fortunes for defences. All this is wrong in principle, and looks like pouring good money in to the "unplumbed, salt, estranging sea." Has not the time come for every difficulty [to] be solved by international law and reason and arbitral justice? War is an injustice and a curse. Surely we find the keystone of heroism is not in war, but social service.

The burden of militarism is great. The total militia in Canada is 73,000, of whom 56,000 were under canvas in 1913, and costing annually about $2,500,000. This is an advance on last year's total of 19,000 men. Since 1912, 35,000 cadets have been organized in schools, or the Militia Department, of whom 15,000 are over the age of sixteen, and are, in the Minister of Militia's opinion, capable of taking the field in time of war.

Agitation is now being made to introduce militarism into all Canadian schools. It is reported, that to further this end, the Minister of Militia will seek the co-operation of mothers. We, of the W.C.T.U., stand pledged for the principles of peace.

This cadet movement is but the thin edge of the wedge of compulsory service. Do we want this? Again, from a moral standpoint, the soldier factory should be abolished.

The man with a burning revolver in his pocket is too often burning to use it. May we ever remember that the great feature of the millennium is that "the nations shall not learn war any more." Let us all hasten and pray for that happy day.

A.E.G.

Neither Chesley nor Gordon accepted the ideology of heroic manhood or the concept of muscular Christianity, whereas Ida Starr upheld its ideals. No further discussion regarding war and peace occurred in the *White Ribbon* until war was declared in 1914. Chesley's next article, "The European Dance of Death," appeared in the January 1915 issue—its message similar to her annual provincial report.

By the following year's annual WCTU convention in Nova Scotia, Mary had this to say: "Since we last met in Convention, the peace of southern Europe has been disturbed by one of the most bloody and barbarous wars that ever blackened the pages of history. [We] read of men being imprisoned in a mosque and set fire to, of women being outraged and slaughtered, of children being tossed in the air and caught on the point of bayonets. Yet all of this has happened since we last met—and this is WAR."

Ever conscious of economics, Mary saw how politicians and industrialists conspired for monetary gains from the armaments business. She referred to the collusion between Krupps, the German manufacturer of machine guns, and the political powers: "Nor are the conditions better in Great Britain. In London there is a record kept of all the shares held in registered joint stock companies. The list of shareholders in one company found among them thirty-six men bearing titles from earls downwards, and sixty prominent army and navy officers and a chaplain. This was but one company, and not one of the larger ones either. The dividends of the companies average about 10 per cent.

"It is not difficult to discern that at the bottom of many wars lies the almighty dollar."

At this stage, Mary was not aware that the peace petition would never get presented, so she was still receiving reports on the signature-collecting throughout the province. At least six thousand signatures had been collected in Nova Scotia by the time of Mary's report, a not inconsiderable number.

In the report for 1914 she stated: "If there is one truth more clearly demonstrated than another, it is that preparation for war is NOT the best way to preserve peace." Without hindsight or a crystal ball at her disposal, she, like most, imagined an early resolution to the war, and she placed her faith in the United States to take the lead.

Mary read extensively and must have subscribed to a number of newspapers. In her 1915 report, she quoted from political economist

Jean de Bloch, a Pole who wrote *The Future of War*, and Norman Angell, an Englishman whose book *The Great Illusion* also dealt with the economic futility of war. She also quoted from an anti-war pamphlet written by H. G. Wells and George Bernard Shaw, who wrote: "Nations are like bees; they cannot kill except at the cost of their own lives."

She included in this report an account of the Women's International Peace Conference in The Hague. In 1915, women from warring and non-warring nations came together to discuss peace—a radical and unpopular move that was widely discredited by politicians and the press. In fact, at least 180 women in Britain had hoped to attend the conference, but the government required dossiers from applicants and then made a selection limited to twenty-five. At the last minute, when the women were waiting on the docks at Tilbury to embark, the North Sea was declared closed to shipping, so the only two British women present at The Hague were those who had been outside Britain at the time and were able to travel freely.[53] It was as a result of the conference that the Women's International League (later known as the Women's International League for Peace and Freedom—WILPF) was founded.

The following is Mary's 1915 report:

> It is significant that, in the midst of this conflict, an international congress of women met at The Hague last April to discuss ways and means by which war shall become an impossibility. Notwithstanding the slurs cast upon this congress by irresponsible press correspondents, it has been said of the resolutions adopted by it "that they were the most fundamental and most constructive yet formulated by any body of pacifists." It is significant too that one of the measures passed by the congress was to make recommendations for conferences at The Hague and to arrange a peace conference of women to meet at the end of the war. Let us hope that, when this conference meets, the W.C.T.U. will have an honorable place in it.
>
> And let us try to remember that it is not by slaughter of Germans or Austrians war will be ended, but by dethronement of military ideals—whether they be German, Russian, French or British.

The concluding sentence signifies Mary Chesley's understanding of the evils of war. Rather than looking to destroy those determined to be the enemy, she pinpointed the real enemy.

In the following 1916 report, Mary prophetically predicted that eventual settlement of hostilities might only be temporary. "The third time we meet under the shadow of war, and it now seems that Kitchener's prediction of a three years war is to be fulfilled. And what of the outcome? It has been the observation of pacifists that war settles nothing, that rather, by giving rein to all the baser passions, it increases the spirit of enmity and jealousy.

"Is the 'settlement' after the present war to be but the resolving of Europe into two hostile camps—each preparing during a period of armed truce for another and more gigantic conflict?"

Mary feared that if wise counsel did not prevail, "the seeds of future discord might be sown and that the conflict might be succeeded by an economic war which would perpetuate the spirit of enmity and prove fatal to all hopes of permanent peace."

How prescient her thinking was. The "winning" side imposed such awful reparations on the losing side, the seeds of future discord were sown.

The following year, 1917, Mary's report was very brief, alluding to "untoward circumstances" preventing her from putting out a call for reports. Silence falls for the next years. Whether personal circumstances or despair over the continuation of war caused Mary to take a break from her work in this regard is unknown. The Halifax Explosion and its aftermath (of which more will be said later) may have had an impact as well. She only resumed her peace work in 1921.

During the decade of 1910 to 1920, Mary continued her franchise department work. She kept abreast of events on the international front and shared this knowledge with her fellow union members. In 1917, twenty-two years after the defeat of the suffrage bill led by Attorney General Longley, Nova Scotian politicians were finally ready to concede to women the right to vote. The April 12, 1917, issue of the *Morning Chronicle* carried an article with the headline "Women Plead Earnestly for Recognition of the Right to Vote—Case of the

To the Government and Legislature of the Province of Nova Scotia

We whose names are hereto subscribed, being British subjects of the full age of twenty one years and upwards, and having lived in the province of Nova Scotia one year and upwards, hereby pray that you will introduce and pass at the next session of the Legislature an act granting the provincial franchise to women upon the same terms as those upon which it is granted to men, thus placing us upon a level with the women of Ontario, Manitoba, Saskatchewan, Alberta, and British Columbia.

No.	Name	Address	Occupation
1	Mary R. Chesley	Lunenburg	Homemaker
2	Martha O. Oxner	Lunenburg	"
3	Gertie L. Wilcox	"	"
4	Sarah Hubley	"	"
5	Florence Hubley	"	"
6	Bertha Rounsefell	"	"
7	Madge S. Rounsefell	"	"
8	Ettie Hamm	"	"
9	Ada A. Comeau	"	"

1917 Petition for Enfranchisement. [Nova Scotia Archives]

Suffrage Reform was Presented Skillfully and Admirably Before the Law Amendments Committee by Talented Advocates of the Cause of Justice—Not a Dissenting Voice Heard." The following indicates the huge change in attitudes since 1895: "When the advocates had already pleaded their cause Mr. Daniels gave an opportunity to any who had opposing views to present them. No one took advantage of the offer, and only one of two or three inferences can be drawn—either that there was no opposition in the audience or, what is not thinkable of Nova Scotians, that the opponents were afraid to let their views be heard."

There were several speakers that day, one being Mary Chesley. The newspaper's subtitle "The Pioneer Advocate" reveals Mary's central role in suffrage for Nova Scotia, a fact that had been almost completely forgotten. Edith Archibald, who has been more widely acclaimed in the records as a suffrage leader, was the one to introduce Mary:

> Mrs. Archibald then called upon Mrs. Chesley, of the W.C.T.U., "the pioneer worker for woman's suffrage in the Province." Mrs. Chesley esteemed it a privilege to speak. She produced a booklet from Alberta entitled "Why Women Should Not Vote." It was a small booklet, she said, and it would seem that this was because the reasons against woman's suffrage were so few. When Chesley opened the booklet, however, it was nothing but blank paper. (Laughter)
>
> Mrs. Chesley described the disappointments of woman suffragists in Nova Scotia in the past. She said that the W.C.T.U. had always stood for woman's suffrage.

In later years, historians would credit women's support of the war effort as the reason for their winning or earning the vote. Mary would have none of this, not allowing legislators to take refuge in such arguments. The article continues:

> She [Mary Chesley] resented the argument on behalf of suffrage that women, by making bombs and sharpening bayonets, had earned the right to suffrage. All down the ages, by training citizens, women had earned that right. Women would not favor war. The cause of peace would never be promoted unless women had a share in the Government.
>
> We ask this not as a gift not as a favor, but as a debt that is somewhat overdue.

Mary's words also made clear the connection between her work for women's rights and peace advocacy. This is key to understanding her political and social vision for a just and peaceful world. And while it would seem that by 1917 women were, more or less, guaranteed the vote, they were not leaving it to chance. Mary's 1918 Annual Department of Franchise Report chronicles the events that transpired during 1917–18.

> Correspondence with Dr. Eliza Ritchie, President of the Equal Suffrage League, was opened immediately after our last Convention to ascertain how far we could depend upon the

co-operation of the League and the Local Council of Women of Halifax. At a consultation in Halifax, at which the Equal Suffrage League, the Local Council, the Household League and the W.C.T.U. were represented, it was decided to take up the work of petitioning. It was agreed to aim at 40,000 signatures and to secure the help of the Women's Institutes. The forms were to be printed in Halifax, and Mrs. E. M. Murray was appointed to take charge of the work. Some delay occurred in the matter of printing and it was nearly a month later before we secured the forms, which were immediately issued. Suffrage literature was sent at the same time.

Scarcely had this message gone out when the appalling disaster of December 6th occurred.

Nova Scotians will immediately recognize the significance of the date December 6, 1917. It marks the Halifax Explosion, in which two ships collided in Halifax Harbour, one being a munitions ship. Part of the city was completely destroyed, and close to two thousand deaths and a least nine thousand injuries occurred. Until the bombing of Hiroshima, the Halifax Explosion was considered the largest man-made disaster in history.[54]

While the petition work was somewhat curtailed, those who were able to gather names did so, and Mary reported: "The Bill passed with very little opposition. It gives women voting privileges equal to those of men in Provincial and Municipal Elections. By and by we will secure a measure that will do away with property qualification.

"At present the most important work is to arouse women to a sense of their responsibility as citizens and their duty as voters."[55]

Mary then set out the qualifications required for voting and the number of signatures on the petition gathered by each of the unions. Not surprisingly, Lunenburg, with 985 signatures, topped the list. This would have represented a significant majority of the adult population of the town.

With the passage of the bill in 1918, one might assume (incorrectly) that Mary's many years in the trenches of the suffrage struggle were over. At this juncture, not all women could vote, only those who met certain property requirements.[56] As well, Mary knew that women needed encouragement and education to take on their voting responsibilities. The WCTU's Franchise Department became the Department of Christian Citizenship. The last several reports that Mary wrote for the WCTU show the interest she took on the educational side. She searched out and obtained written material for this purpose. As well, she kept an eye on the voters' lists. In her 1919 report, she wrote:

> In Lunenburg it came to light that women's names generally had not been added to the recently revised voters' lists. Committees for each ward were appointed to get the names and hand them to the revisers.
>
> The outcome of this effort was that practically all the women entitled have their names on the voters' lists. Fearing that what had happened in Lunenburg might have happened in other towns, a circular of instructions was sent to every Union and replies asked for.

Mary noted that women had not yet been accorded the right to sit in the legislature. The franchise work was not complete when women still lacked full participation as citizens. She wrote, "Public questions should be discussed in the home. In this way Civic and National ideals would be implanted in the family. Women should use their vote to influence legislation, both national and municipal."[57]

Mary would continue with her work on both the citizenship and peace fronts into the 1920s, up until her death in 1923. This will be addressed in chapter 6. First, we will turn to Polly's life during this second decade of twentieth century.

CHAPTER 5
Polly's International Studies and Adventures

AS MARY CHESLEY WAS ACTIVELY WRITING ON SUFFRAGE AND war and peace issues during this period, her daughter Polly was pursuing her education, both within academia and in the wider world. As mentioned in her Mount Allison senior profile, upon graduation, Polly went directly to the Normal College in Truro for her teaching certificate. According to *The Argosy* of March 1911, Polly had finished her post-graduate work at the Normal College the previous month, and before she reached the age of twenty, she had already been offered the position of vice-principal at the Academy in Digby, Nova Scotia. Mary Albee Chesley received her Class B teaching licence on February 11, 1911, and also received a Physical Training certificate. She was awarded First Rank with the promise that she would be awarded Superior First Rank "upon fulfilling prescribed conditions of successful teaching." Polly subsequently earned Class A, Superior First standing while she was vice-principal of the Bridgewater High School. While teachers in rural settings were typically young during this period, Polly was one of only a handful of university graduates among all teachers in Nova Scotia.

Polly had a yen for adventure and travel. Furthermore, teachers from eastern provinces could earn more elsewhere, so it was not unusual for them to go west to seek better fortunes.[58] The September 18, 1912, issue of the Lunenburg *Progress Enterprise* reported, "Last Wednesday afternoon, 11th inst., Miss Thompson, Miss Holder and Miss Chesley, who was vice-principal of the Bridgewater High School last year, went to Halifax, whence they started next morning for the West. Miss Chesley goes to San Diego, in Southern California, stopping on the way at Fargo, North Dakota, to visit her uncle, Mr. James A. Chesley." (A photo taken in 1925 of Samuel and his brother James in Bridgetown, Nova Scotia—see page 73—indicates that the two kept in touch. This would have been James's last visit to Nova Scotia, for according to Fargo cemetery records, he died in 1926.)

Little is known of Polly's time in California. Two entries in Mount Allison's *The Argosy* help to establish the time frame of her sojourn there. The April 1913 issue reported that Polly was teaching at La Jolla, a suburb of San Diego, and the February 1914 issue provided a San Diego mailing address for her.[59] According to US Naturalization Records, Polly's name was filed on December 27, 1912, in the Superior Court of San Diego County.

Why did Polly choose San Diego? In my Internet browsing I happened upon a digitized edition of the *Lodi News-Sentinel* where I found an obituary for a woman who would have been Polly's first cousin once removed. This person had once lived in San Diego with her family. Her mother, Julia (Chesley) Kinney, was Polly's first cousin, a daughter of Polly's Uncle James.

I traced a granddaughter of Julia's and wrote to her. This woman's mother (Julia's daughter) would have been about four to six years old when Polly lived in San Diego. As Julia's daughter had died at a relatively young age over forty years earlier, my contact knew very little about her mother's family. I found another Chesley descendant through a genealogical website and wrote to him. This spurred some inquiries within the family, and an old photo album was unearthed. I identified a photo of Polly and her friend Lena Bachman of Lunenburg, taken when James Chesley visited Nova Scotia in 1925. The scraps of evidence are minimal but provide a rationale for Polly going to San Diego to teach.

Samuel and brother James Chesley, from Fargo, North Dakota, visiting in 1925, one year before James's death. [AUDREY CHESLEY OLDERSHAW]

Visit in the Annapolis Valley with Chesley cousins. [AUDREY CHESLEY OLDERSHAW]

Polly finished her second year of teaching in La Jolla in 1914. She left for England during the earliest days of the First World War, arriving in London on the ship *Digby* on October 12, 1914. At age twenty-three, Polly, the inveterate student, took on her next academic challenge; she began studies at the London School of Economics (part of the University of London).

In its September 19, 1917 issue, after Polly's return to Canada, the *Progress Enterprise* gave an overview of Polly's time overseas.

> Miss Mary Chesley arrived home on Friday evening August 31st, after an absence of two years and eleven months. During that time she spent two years as an external student of London University and secured the University's degree of Bachelor of Science, with honors in Political Science and spent six months in Oxford reading in the Bodleian Library. After passing the final examinations for the degree she crossed to Paris, where she spent nine months studying French literature and modern history at the Sorbonne and the Alliance Française. At the end of July she received the diploma of the Alliance, certifying her to teach French.

I hope you, dear reader, can appreciate how excited I was when I first stumbled upon one of Polly's letters home, published in the Lunenburg newspaper. It was at a time when I was trolling through microfilm with no clear idea of what, if anything, I hoped to find, coinciding with a period when I was avoiding the writing of my master's thesis. Discovering one letter inspired me to keep looking for others, and eventually I found eleven newspaper entries, letters home written during Polly's years in Britain and France. They convey much detail about Polly's activities and her political and social ideas. One can see that travel and exposure to new experiences and people broadened Polly's thinking. Because of the stature of the Chesley family in Lunenburg, I am guessing that Polly's letters would have interested neighbours and friends in town, which would explain why they were published in the local paper.

In the following entries, I have corrected the spelling of place names where I could, especially those in Welsh, because the errors might simply have been errors in transcription or newspaper typos. The first newspaper entry of September 15, 1915, in the *Progress Enterprise* recounts the studies Polly, "A Lunenburg Lady in London," undertook in England. Included in the list are the names of the professors/examiners in the following fields: economics, British constitution, mathematics, and geography. Of the eleven professors on the list, at least eight of them became renowned in their particular disciplines. The newspaper included the questions for one of the exams.

Polly Chesley and friend Lena Bachman, Meisners Island, Nova Scotia, October 1925. [Tom Gundershaug, Lodi, California]

> University of London
> Intermediate Examination in Science
> (Economics), 1915
> Currency, Banking, Trade and Finance
> Examiners: Prof. C.F. Bastable, M.A., LL.D., R.V. Lennard, Esq., M.A.
>
> Answer EIGHT questions only.
>
> 1."One of the rules for a good monetary system is that the standard coins of the country should be in general circulation and be familiar to people." Do you accept this as rule for modern monetary system? Consider the extent to which it is observed.

2. Explain the way in which money acts as a "store of value" under the conditions of modern credit organisation. How are the other functions of money affected by the changes in economic conditions in recent times?

3. It is said that, "the Bank Charter Act cannot be a scientific settlement of the currency question, since no other country has adopted its principles." Discuss this criticism and explain carefully what the principles of the Charter Act are.

4. Bankers have been described as dealers in "money," and again as dealers in "capital." Explain what is meant by each of these descriptions, and consider the points of connexion between the two forms of dealing.

5. What are the chief causes of the fluctuations in the rate of discount? In the last week of July 1911, the Bank rate was raised by jumps from 3% to 8%; from August 8th, 1914, it has been steady at 5%. Estimate the reasons for this contrast.

6. Point out the different means for "correcting" an adverse exchange. Illustrate your answer by reference to the expedients suggested [by] the variations of the American Exchange with England in the period August 1914 to April 1915.

7. How far, in your opinion, is a country likely to gain or lose by an improvement in the production of a commodity exported by another country with which it has large trading relations?

8. It is a maxim in regard to stock-exchange securities that "the higher the yield the lower the security." Discuss the reasons on which this maxim is based and the limitations to which it is subject.

9. Indicate the characteristics of a commodity which make it specially suitable for being the object of speculative dealings.

Consider the position of (a) wheat, (b) coal, (c) tea, as objects for speculation.

10. Estimate the effects in a time of strain, e.g., a war period, of fixing by state authority (1) minimum price for securities, (2) maximum prices for articles of necessary consumption.

We do not know what questions Polly answered. All we know is that she successfully passed the exam.

What follows are excerpts of letters written by Polly to her family during the next couple of years when she lived and travelled in Britain and France. Already practised in critical thinking, her exposure to people from diverse backgrounds, religions, and ethnicities helped to broaden her perspective. She observed their differentness but was curious and drawn to learning more.

At times Polly was quick to assume that a person might have certain characteristics (she was quite class-conscious and tended to expect the worst from those of the upper classes), and yet she was open to changing her opinion when the persons under her microscope turned out to be different from her expectations. Polly's first letter home appeared in the *Progress Enterprise* on October 6, 1915.

Through England and Wales on a Wheel
Kibworth, July 23, 1915

Dearest Mamma: I will tell you something that I didn't tell you at first for fear you would worry. I am taking a trip through England and Wales [by bicycle]. Miss Overton mapped out a glorious trip for me. I have a beautiful big map (1s.6d.). First I am going to a Students' Convention at Swanwick. I am going to "do" the Lake District and then come back to Chester, and then along the North coast of Wales and down the West coast, under Snowdon, down to the South of Plynlimon to the Wye Valley. I will visit Tintern Abbey and other places around there, then to Gloucester, Oxford, and down the Thames to London.

I am in the Midlands. I have ridden one hundred miles and have hardly been out of sight of a farmhouse, and always there is traffic so it would be hard for anyone to hold me up or run away with me.

The chief drawback has been weather. Wednesday when I started, it was lovely. I went about twenty-five miles. Before I had gone much more than a mile from Endsleigh, whiz! A puncture in my back tire. I felt like turning back, but I found a cyclist and got it mended.

Next morning I started out in rain. I took a muddy path to see the old Roman wall. At a gate where I couldn't get my bike through, I asked some soldiers if they would look after it. I went to see the wall. It is wonderful to think of it (built nearly two thousand years ago). It had started raining, so the soldiers had put my wheel under a tree and one of them tightened the hind wheel. He asked if he could ride with me. I told him I would only I wasn't staying in St. Albans. He was lonesome I guess. By lunchtime I was soaking, but I got a nice hot lunch for 7d. and went on. About 4 I came to a place with a great two story stone wall and immense gateway. It was the Duke of Bedford's estate. Well, a little further on was Woburn, and I was so wet that I went into a shop and asked where I could put up for the night. It was the Bell Inn, and I got a bed for 6d, wonderful. The man insisted this morning on getting me some cocoa and bread before I left. All around were beer and whiskey advertisements and my raincoat was dried in the taproom. Today came through two sharp showers and got pretty wet, but the sun came out so I got dry. I was going to Leicester but it started to rain again, so I inquired at a store and here I am with a maiden lady and her two foster children, supper and bed 2s. 6d. I have come fifty miles today. Not too bad for a novice.

Heart's best love to all,
POLLY

I can imagine Polly waiting until she was on the road before informing her parents of her plans, not wanting to worry them in advance. I view this from two perspectives. I was once an adventurous daughter who did not want to worry my parents, so sometimes I informed them of my activities *after* the fact. Now, from the viewpoint of a parent, I can appreciate that it is better to hear some things once the possibility of danger, real or imagined, is past.

Polly literally counted her pennies, a common practice. Numerous tiny notebooks found in archives and those kept by older relatives in my family attest to this habit of tracking every penny, nickel, and dime.

Coming from a temperance background, this likely was Polly's first time in an inn with a taproom where alcohol was sold. The fact that she found the owners of the inn "awfully nice" must have broadened her outlook.

The next set of letters in the *Progress Enterprise*, published November 24, 1915, provides further insight into the extent of Polly's summer rambles.

> Aug. 2nd, or 3rd, 1915
>
> Dearest Papa:
> I must write home while this wonderful day is fresh in my mind. This morning I had to buy a new tire, 9s. The boy where I was staying last night was very kind and he got this one for me and helped me put it on. When I got a few miles it began to rain hard. At the post office, I got a letter from Madame Cornet. I got something to eat and took it to the shore of the lake and ate and read my letter in the rain; then I went on the road to Ambleside. From the hill there was a lovely view up and down the lake. All around covered with bracken and heather and on the low hills trees and on the gentle slopes near the water typical English fields. I went on through Ambleside to Rydal and was asking a woman where Coleridge lived, to find it was her house that I was standing by, "Nab Cottage" where Coleridge and De Quincey had lived. I asked for a drink and so got in the house. It is just

one hundred yards from Rydal Lake, a little jewel—perfect. In Nab Cottage I saw a front room with a grate, perhaps the one before which Coleridge dreamed Kublai Khan. I went back to see Wordsworth's chair—a big rock by the lake—and the cottage in which he and Dorothy lived—a beautiful place at the end of the lake. Dove Cottage at Grasmere is also quite small, and in front of it now, cutting off the view of the lake, are some larger cottages. Grasmere is larger than Rydal but Grasmere is not perfect, as Rydal is. There is a hotel there, and some rich people have built houses, which mar its perfection. There is a long hill this side of Grasmere, awful to climb, but the view into the valley is glorious, so there I ate and read Wordsworth and then came on past Thirlmere. There are hundreds of little falls down the hills, and I passed an inn Mathew Arnold stayed at and a walk which inspired "Resignation." Then the rain and dark caught me, but it was beautiful all afternoon. I can write no more, so a goodnight kiss to all.

Lovers of nineteenth-century English literature can relate to the thrill Polly must have felt in walking in the footsteps of literary heroes. At present, identification with Wordsworth, Coleridge, and Arnold is, perhaps, rather rare, but for early twentieth-century readers, these writers were touchstones. I recall discovering among the remnants of an older relative's past an envelope that contained a sliver of wood. Written on the envelope were the following words: "A piece of bark from the tree under which Milton sat." This finding helped me to imagine my elderly relative as a once starry-eyed literature major.

Aug. 11th

I am sitting now on the beach at Barmouth. This pretty seaside resort reminds me very much of La Jolla, only it hasn't the caves and shelving rock for beach picnics and the little bungalows. It is full of places where they let rooms. I have found a place for 1s. a night for two nights, so I think, as I can get my dinner at a fish and chip place for 3 1/2d. I cannot do better than stay a day and a half and I can get a real saltwater bath.

Well I have only taken you up to the time when I was at the conference. On the way I passed the Wesleyan Chapel. I found Mark Guy Pearse giving a lecture.[60] I don't know whether I would like him for a steady diet, but after the ordinary run he is refreshing. I am trying to figure out how to make 5-11 last me till tomorrow noon when I get to Dolgelly, where I asked Miss O. to send me £2. I will go bathing and I am afraid that will be 1 bob, also I am going to the pictures but will take a 3 d. seat and get fish and chips for 3 d. so if I don't go in swimming again tomorrow I can make it, or if they only charge me 6d. As I was saying, I tried to discourage Miss E. because I did not think she would want to take the trip I wanted, and I did not think she was the kind of a girl I would enjoy. I hardly knew her at school, though she always seemed friendly, but she is one of the most stylish girls, and always says, "Thanks awfully," with a very British accent, instead of plain "thank you" and I thought that she was not at all the kind for such a trip. However she seemed determined, and there was no shaking her off. (She turned out to be a girl after my own heart).

Went to the top of a hill and got our wheels over a wall and through a field to a little hollow and decided to camp there for the night. In the morning we washed our faces in the dew, ate the rest of our sandwiches and went on. That p.m. we came to Haddon Hall, the home of Dorothy Vernon. We went through it for 6d. It is the most beautiful dwelling that I have ever seen.[61]

We pressed on and climbed up an awful hill about 3 or 4 miles long, with a fine view at the top, then on to Buxton. Then as Miss E. is English and always wants a hot drink, we went and had to pay 4½ d. for a cup of cocoa and a measly little cake. We went out of the town and came to a place near a stone quarry and spent the night there. Miss E had bought some cigarettes she said to cheer us. I did not tell her then I didn't smoke. Well next morning after breakfast Miss E wanted a drink of tea so went to a cottage nearby where it said "Teas." It was so dark the night before that we didn't see how close we were to civilization. The woman was kind of stiff and when we told her we had been sleeping out she froze and said they would lock us up if they found us and charged Miss E 3s.4d. for her teas and when she asked if she might wash her hands said "No, I have no water for you," so when we got outside Miss E. very slowly took a cigarette out and lit it and for once in my life I was glad to see someone smoke, for a woman like that deserved to be shocked. Well we went on and saw a church where Wesley preached and the graveyard where Wesley's sweetheart, Grace Bennet was buried.[62] About noon we got within the influence of Manchester. The city is awful. Back to the station; we asked for the nearest way to the country north, and they told us Greenleaf so we booked there for 12 miles.

It was after 10 when we got there and we had no lights. We rode all the same. We came under a railway bridge where there was a light. Sure enough a cop stepped out and held us up. However he let us off and told us we better not get on again as there were two more cops down the hill. We got on as soon as we got out of his sight. Finally we took a little road and came to a covered haystack that looked inviting so we slept between the haystack and a stone hen coop. We discovered in the morning that the road we had taken led to the munitions factory just below, and about one hundred workers passed us. However the wall was so high that though they passed within six feet only one person saw us. We went on till we reached New Hay, a milling place and more cobblestones. Miss E could stand the cobbles no longer, so we took a train to Rochdale, where she had to take the train to Settle to meet her friend. She wanted me to come on a few miles with her and avoid the cobblestones, but I was too interested in the people. It was totally different from anything I had ever seen. All the women wore shawls and either had them over their heads or woolen caps, and almost every one wore clogs, and the clogs and cobbles between them made the streets resound. Then every one spoke with the quaintest dialect and pronunciation. I liked them; they were rough, but self reliant and sturdy and intelligent, so different from the downtrodden workers of London. It is in Lancashire that men and women cotton weavers are in the same union, and so, as the woman I stayed with that night told me, they were paid the same rates as the men. Both she and her husband tended 4 looms, and often she made more than him. Going out of Rochdale I fell in with a bevy of boys, the oldest did not look more than 12, but they said they were 14 and worked ten hours a day in the mills. They were bright enough and used their Saturday half-holiday to pick berries. I walked through about seven or eight miles more of cobbles and continuous city till I came to the edge of the country. It was getting dark. I saw the Wesleyan Church and asked where the minister lived. When the minister and his wife found out my plight, they were very good, only they were torn up from moving. The minister got me a place with two young cotton weavers. I was so tired that I slept the clock round. I noticed Mrs. Jackson's manner was much cooler than the night before and finally she said, "You will sign the papers?" I didn't know what papers. It seems the policeman had been at the house about five times for me to sign registration papers.

Well I no sooner got them signed when he came again and such a cross-examination as I went through. It was one of the funniest things I ever heard. I had promised to meet Miss E and another of her friends at Chester and we met all right. The next day we passed through some beautiful scenery near Llangollen and saw a lovely Abbey, and Miss E. and I slept that night and the next in the barn of the house where Miss E ['s friend] stayed. The night before we had slept under a tree on the Morris's lawn. At the next place Miss Blake could go no further, and as she wanted Miss E to go with her, they both took the train to Snowdon, much to Miss E's disgust, for she wanted to stay with me. (She is just a lovely girl.) Well I was to meet them that night and could get no sign of them so had to take a room for the night. Next a.m. I looked again but could not find them. However I met two sisters bicycling, and they came with me to Beddgelert—a gorgeous ride, and we spent the night together, and I left them and came to Harlech [which] is very pretty, but not as pretty as here, Barmouth.

Heart's best love to all,
POLLY

Polly, in spite of her aversion to smoking, showed enough of a contrary nature to enjoy the sight of her companion lighting up a cigarette in order to shock the unpleasant woman they'd met. And when Polly and her friend encountered a policeman who told them not to ride any further or they would run into more policemen, like the young folks they were, they figured this was a false warning and consequently ignored it.

Polly's political views are revealed in her observations about the workers in Rochdale. She was impressed by the fact that men and women weavers were in the same unions and that women were making equal pay to men.

The next installment was published on December 8, 1915.

London, N.W. Aug. 22nd, 1915

My dearest Mamma: I have so many things to write. First and foremost I got through my examinations. When I got home I asked for my mail, a lot of letters from you, but none from the university. My heart sank, because they let you know by Aug. 7 if you have succeeded—if not they do not let you know till later. I went over to the other house and went in to see Madame. She said "J'ai observe une lettre depuis un longue temp pour vous de l'université." My heart gave a bound. My name was in the list. It was in alphabetical order, so there is no telling where I came, but now I am going to really study, so that I can add B.Sc. (in Econ. & Political Science) to my name next October. Poor Madame (a Belgium lady, refugee from Brussels) has been ill since I've been away. Madame and her mother were amused with my experience of sleeping between a hen coop and a haystack, not shocked as some of the good English ladies were.

The last I wrote was from Barmouth. I stayed two nights and went to Dogelly, where Miss C. was to send me 2 pounds. I had only 6d. left, and I did not even dare to buy a pair of stockings, so had a great time trying to keep the holes in my stockings from coinciding with the holes in my boots. I got my money and invested in a pair of stockings and felt quite got up. I was away a month from 21st July to 21st Aug. and spent about 6 pounds 5d. and of that 10s. or rather 9d. of it for train fare and 5s.3d, and 9s, on new tires which I hope to get back when I sell my bike, and 4s. for 2 pairs of stockings. So really I have had 31 days and seen about 800 miles of the country for 5 pounds—not bad is it? Mr. P. came to see me just before he left and said he had spent 4 pounds on a nine-day trip and told me I could not possibly do it more economically. I am anxious to see him and let him know.

Well, from Dogelly I went to Aberdovey and got the only dirty place in the whole trip. It spoiled my stay.

Aberystwyth however is different. It is an imposing place, an educational centre for Wales, having amusement places and an old castle and seaside promenade. I stayed long enough for a swim. Spotted a woman with a white ribbon and asked her to watch my wheel and money. I went on to climb up Plynlimon, and it was a climb. I did about four or five miles that night and came to a little village at dusk. The people I was advised to go to were full up. They told me to try next door. I tried, and the woman had no bedroom, but I fared much better than the night before, for she was clean and had a sense of humor, so she fixed up the sofa in the front room. Then she sent the little girl in with the loveliest dish of potatoes and lots of butter and a little meat. It tasted so good, and she only charged me 1s. for the whole. That p.m. I only did 24 miles, but it was lovely, alternate rain and shine, and had about four miles more of climbing till I came to the highest point and the source of the Wye. I followed the Wye Valley to Rhayader and there I put up in a nice temperance hotel. Next day I did over 60 miles to Monmouth, part of it through the Black Mountains. Next morning I went around Monmouth, a quaint town, and then off through the rain for Tintern Abbey.[63]

Then climbed up into the Forest of Dean, which I went through all day, and late in the afternoon descended into Gloucester.

I saw the cathedral and Raikes' first school. Made the 49 miles to Oxford just by dark.

I met a Norwegian girl I had met at Swanwick, so I went out to Lady Margaret's (the biggest woman's college) where she was staying and played tennis with her and a Chinese student, had tea there and swanked generally, and, as he asked us out in his canoe the next p.m. I stayed the 2nd day and went into more of the colleges, and then in the p.m. went punting and canoeing on the river. It was like fairy land, that tiny river through the meadows, with the overhanging trees and the boats and men and girls in white and pretty colors having tea in the boats under trees or on the bank, or punting or paddling along. I don't wonder people love Oxford with those beautiful old colleges with their lovely quadrangles and bordered with flowers and surrounded by the old walls with passages leading into more quadrangles or cloisters and then that beautiful river. I left at six that day and got to a village where I put up at the pub, as a very respectable lady evidently thought I was too suspicious a character to take in, but the lady at the pub was awfully good to me, and it was nice and clean. Yesterday I got back and had a kind welcome at both houses.

Best love to all,
POLLY

Using currency converters to determine 1915 monetary worth of the pound and pence in 2018 values (the latest year available for calculations), Polly spent the equivalent of about twenty-seven dollars per day (current value) over the course of her thirty-one days of travel, which included food, lodging, bicycle repairs, trains, entry fees to castles, and the odd pair of new stockings. Polly was frugal indeed, as will be evident again as her story unfolds.

Robert Raikes (1776–1811) was a publisher, philanthropist, and founder of the Sunday School Movement, initiated in the slums for poor boys working in factories during the rest of the week. Having been involved with those who had been jailed under the Poor Law (that is, imprisoned for debt), he felt that education would serve as a better intervention than punishment. By the early 1830s over a million children (approximately 25 percent of the population) were attending Sunday schools, which predated the first publicly funded state education. Polly's familiarity and her assumption of her parents' familiarity with Raikes and his Sunday schools points to their general knowledge of church- and education-related history even outside of their own branch of faith. Raikes was Church of England; nevertheless, his influence crossed religious lines and oceans. A statue of Robert Raikes stands next to Queen's Park in Toronto.

The white ribbon worn by the woman Polly spotted at the seaside would have indicated the woman's membership within the WCTU; Polly knew this was someone she could trust.

The next *Progress Enterprise* account was published on May 10, 1916.

> Oxford in War Time
> Y.W.C.A., Oxford, Feb. 27th, 1916.
>
> My dearest father:
> Last Sunday I went to the University Church, St. Mary, the Virgin, but was late as they have their service at ten. However, I went this morning and got the whole sermon. It was by a Cambridge man, Dr. Barnes. It was a very scholarly sermon, but I think he was hitting the wrong dog. He condemned, very sensibly, the way in which, while we are fighting for liberty abroad, we are taking it away at home. He spoke of the proceedings the Cabinet had taken under the Defence of the Realms Act, especially the suspension of the Habeas Corpus Act, and he said one of the worst signs was that the people seemed perfectly indifferent to the loss of safeguards to liberty, with the exception of a few eminent lawyers (and, he might have added, a large body of suffragettes and labour people). He spoke too of the tyranny, as in the case of the conscientious objectors whom the majority of the people wish to force to fight. Then too of the false economy which starts

by closing the Museums and turning from 150,000 to 200,000 school children from eleven to thirteen out of school. Now he blamed all these things to the fact that England had a democratic government instead of an aristocratic one. I don't agree with him at all. I think it is because affairs have been—and still are—so much in the hands of the aristocracy who don't think that people need to know more than the three Rs and therefore have not taken the trouble to ensure an educated democracy. We cannot blame the loss of liberties in England to democracy—the only papers that have stood out for liberty have been labour papers.

The minister in the University Church, Dr. Carlyle, is very good. I think he is a Christian and apparently believes in woman suffrage so I like him about the best of any ministers in England. He believes that, according to evolution, we are not born with original sin, but that man is inherently good.

Saturday night we had a nice time at Miss Gloria's (the Indian girl from Hyderabad). There were six girls, three American, one Canadian, one Irish and Miss Gloria, three Indian Hindoo boys and a Dutch boy, who, however has lived in England all his life, does not believe in woman suffrage and is quite an aristocrat. All were students. Sunday we went to Miss Hackings. There is a very nice artist, who worked seventeen years with Burne Jones there, and he took us to his studio.[64] Then we went to a Miss Scott McCrief's who had invited me to come to meet some Canadians, but they weren't there, so she said she would invite me again.[65] There was a very interesting Indian boy there, who told about the desire of educated Indians for independence. They are not allowed to have their patriotic societies in India [but] they have them in the States, especially in San Francisco. They resent the fact that Englishmen with not nearly the education they have are put over India, and they are not allowed commissions in the army, etc.

Well, from there we went to Miss Crocker's. Miss Campbell and I stayed to the last, and had a very interesting conversation with a Polish Dr., who is a graduate here and secretary to the Russian professor of English Constitutional law at the University. He is an Austrian Pole and he was telling how much more democratic the Polish University in Austria is than the English Universities, how it makes no difference there what your father is, and how many of the students are very poor and work their way through as we do in America, only that [they] don't do manual work considered degrading. Still it is an advance to be able to earn money at all without losing caste.

Monday, Miss Campbell and I were in to see Miss Gloria.

Well, Wednesday morning I achieved my wish. A Mr. Durham, a Rhodesman of Christ Church (College) and a very charming Southerner, showed us his rooms and several of the others among them Harmsworth's, nephew of Lord Northcliffe. His room, like most of them, is panelled in oak, and he had about eight paintings by some French artist, worth about fifty pounds each. He himself is a very innocent stupid youth in O.T.C. uniform, about eighteen.

We went afterwards to Hereford College where Mr. Rypons, a Jew from Minnesota, showed us around. We saw the room of an Indian prince, but unfortunately he wasn't in. However, Miss Gloria knows them all, so I am likely to meet some of them. Mr. R. says this one is a nice fellow.

Friday I went for a walk with Miss Gloria. Oh yes, Thursday Miss Campbell left. She sailed for the U.S.A.

Yesterday I was in the Camera all day after 10:45.[66] In the evening I went to hear a lecture on "Women's Work Today and Tomorrow."

Today, I went to two sermons. I went to Miss Hackings to tea. Miss Gloria and Mr. Syrahwada were there, and a Sengalese came in.

Heart's best love to all,
POLLY

It is in this letter that Polly's politics become more obvious. Her labour-leaning, feminist side comes through in her comments on the sermons she heard at the churches in Oxford. She was concerned over the erosion of civil liberties and blamed the lack of democratic process on the ruling class. The Defence of the Realm Act came into effect in the early days of the First World War, giving Parliament powers to restrict personal freedoms and any form of dissent. Habeas corpus is a legal safeguard that ensures anyone arrested must be brought before the court or judge for trial and not be unlawfully detained in prison if there is insufficient cause or evidence. Civil liberties are commonly curtailed in so-called democratic countries in times of war. It would be getting ahead of the story to discuss Polly's eventual move to India; however, this letter gives an indication of her prior exposure to Indian aspirations for independence through the students she was meeting. Because she was intellectually and socially curious, she was mixing with students from all over the globe, which must surely have broadened her outlook in new and stimulating ways.

The next epistle was printed in the *Progress Enterprise* on October 4, 1916. Ever the intrepid traveller, Polly took advantage of her summer break to travel north.

> Miss Chesley in Scotland
> Garty Farm, Delny, Ross Shire, Scotland, July 9th, 1916.
>
> Dearest Aunt Am:
> "The rain it raineth every day." It is simply coming down as though it never would stop, and here we are at Garty Farm, the three of us, Marjorie (Elphinstone), May Campbell, the daughter of the Laird of Jura, who owns the whole island, and myself.
>   Since leaving Oxford, after I had said goodbye to my Hindoo friend, Miss Gloria, I went to Gillett's bank and sent a wire to Marjorie.
>   The first thing I did was get into my tramping rig and get things I needed from my trunk. I got my dinner at the vegetarian restaurant in Holborn. Later I went to Ashley House and saw Miss Overton. I spent the evening with Mr. Tikey (an Egyptian student). He hopes to go to Norway for his holidays. I really was fortunate—I struck a carriage with only three others in the compartment and one of my travelling companions was a severe looking lady, quite well dressed, who drew out her bottle after we

had started, and after taking a draught, and getting a pillow from the conductor, retired in her corner for the night. The other two were a young clergyman and his wife. They preferred leaning on one another to stretching out. So I had all one side to myself. In spite of that I didn't really sleep. I was cold, but the young wife would tuck me in when she saw my rug tumbling off. Then it seemed as though every time I went off a train would pass, so that I doubt if I got half an hour's sleep in all. At 6 I got up and asked her if she wouldn't lie down, I had offered once before, but no, so then we talked.

We got to Edinburgh about 7:30 a.m. I left the station, and walked along Princes Street, said to be one of the finest streets in Europe. I went as far as the Palace, then on my way back went and ate.

I saw two ladies, evidently tourists, going to the castle, so I followed and attached myself to the same guide—6d. They were Australian and quite pleasant. We saw the bedroom of Mary, Queen of Scots, and the banqueting hall, which is very fine—the bedroom is tiny, about the size of mine, but oak paneled. It was too bad that it was drizzling and dull, for the view must be glorious.

After leaving the Castle, I went into St. Giles Cathedral, near which is a heart in stone in the pavement—the heart of Midlothian. In the Cathedral, I saw a Canadian lady whom I had met in London last winter. I was looking disreputable (in tramping rig) and she was fashionably dressed and flitting about with two gentlemen and a lady. They never would have known me, but I just thought I would try an experiment. I wanted to see how she would treat me, for I looked a veritable tramp, so I stopped her and said I thought I had met her. She didn't know me, of course, so I told her where. Well, you would have thought I was a long lost friend. She really was awfully game, she told me if I ever go to St. Andrew's, N.B. where she had a summer home, I must be sure to go and see her.

At 1:45 I took the train. Within half an hour we crossed over the Firth of Forth. After we crossed the Forth I napped till we got to Perth. Then the scenery began to get mountainous and it was picturesque all the way. We climbed 1,450 feet. There were patches of snow. The country is very thinly settled and you wonder what the people there live on, for the land is nearly all rocks. There are many sheep, and in some places cows. In places the hills have woods just scraggy fir and birch, like our woods around home. The rest of the hills were covered with heather, and lower down the broom, in full bloom, and everywhere there were burns (brooks) and every now and then a little loch. Inverness is not a big place. Before we got to Inverness a Cameron Highlander got in. He had had a little too much of "the best," like the sergeant who got in at the same station and who last thing handed the glass, which he had just emptied, back to his wife. The Highlander was very communicative and showed me his notes on a maxim gun, which probably was against orders.

I reached Delny at 11. It was still quite light. I slept till almost 2 p.m. the next day, when I woke up I found that May's brother Colin, a tea grower in India, had come, and they had taken him off to Tain for dinner. After I had eaten I started off to meet them. An old gentleman came along on a tricycle to tell me they were coming back by train. So I came back. Then we all walked to a Mrs. Mac–, where Marjorie had stayed for a while. Mrs. Mac– was very nice and gave us a fine tea. I was quite taken with her. Today Marjorie was telling me that she only gets out once a week and then she comes back with a bottle of "the best" and next day they have to keep her in bed. It seems so funny, for she is quite a superior person, and evidently quite capable—but this is Scotland. We came home, had supper and sat around the grate fire till 12. Unfortunately the talk turned on the war—unfortunately, for Marjorie thinks war a purgative and something that will clear the nation, etc., and May considers the Germans something outside the human species. However we got to bed without quarrelling.

Heart's best love to all,
POLLY

Polly's mention of eating at a vegetarian restaurant indicates her interest in alternative lifestyle choices. It also foreshadows her future time in India. While she may have had no idea at the time that she would be off to India eighteen years later, in small, perhaps unconscious ways she was preparing for that move.

Polly's temperance background shows through in this passage, and it is evident that she was unaccustomed to being around people who imbibed alcohol. While there may be a hint of judgment, it sounds as though she was mostly being observant of these new experiences and sharing them with her family. Polly's pacifist sympathies come through, and although she was not in agreement with her companions regarding war, she avoided an argument. In publishing Polly's letters in the newspaper, her parents revealed a pacifist point of view that would not generally be tolerated, particularly in wartime. It is clear from reading contemporary articles in the paper that the *Progress Enterprise* did not share the Chesleys' perspective.

The next entry occurred in the *Progress Enterprise* of November 15, 1916.

> Highland Manners and a House of Commons Debate
>
> Early in August Miss Chesley returned to London. Of the Highland Scotch, she wrote: "The most wonderful thing about these people is that they combine the simplicity and hospitality of plain country folk with the manner and savoir faire of polished ladies and gentlemen.
>
> "The old ploughman had such a kindly face and the manner of a knight, and today I called at a tiny, white-washed thatched cottage, where the smoke came out through a hole in the roof, but the face and manner of the lady who opened the door would have done credit to a queen."
>
> Aug. 6th. After having parted from her friends, she wrote of the latter part of her motor trip, from Glasgow to London.

Dearest Papa—I did not tell you about Sunday. We went through the pottery district, which, as one might expect, was dirty. I don't see why any one should try to hasten the day when Canada will be a manufacturing country, for it seems to mean millions wretchedly poor with hundreds wickedly rich—and then the dirt and smoke.

That evening we stopped at Daventry, where I found lodging. The next day we got to London. The only remarkable thing we passed was a gorgeous field of green corn aglow with poppies and cornflowers. I never saw such a beautiful color display on such a large scale. That evening I met some of my fellow students, among them the Greek and the Egyptian and Miss Van Merle—and we sat on the little balcony eating Egyptian melons until nearly eleven o'clock.

The next day, I called on Lady Courtney, only to find that she was out of town. So I went to the House of Commons and succeeded in finding Mr. Macdonald [Ramsay Macdonald, MP] who got me a ticket and took me to the lift for the ladies' gallery.

They were still at "questions." Well, I was lucky, for I got in to one of the biggest debates of the session—the one on the Paris Conference, really free trade versus protection.

Polly went into great detail, describing the debate and the debaters, all prominent politicians of the period. Her fascination with political matters is clear. Of most interest to me in this letter was that Polly had tried to see Lady Courtney, whom she presumably knew well enough to drop by her house for a visit. Catherine or Kate (Potter) Courtney was a prominent pacifist, suffragist, and social worker. She and her husband, politician and academic Leonard Courtney, were Quakers and formidable figures in radical circles. Concerned about the costs of war to innocent victims on both sides of conflict, in 1919 Kate Courtney hosted the first meeting of the Fight the Famine Committee, which subsequently became the Save the Children Fund. As will be evident as the story unfolds, Polly would play a prominent role in fundraising in Canada for this cause. The political and social views of Courtney and Chesley were compatible (and they also held common membership in another anti-war organization, the Union of Democratic Control), so it is not surprising that Polly would know Kate Courtney. The same as age as Polly's mother, Kate was cut from the same political cloth. Courtney was an older sister to Beatrice (Potter) Webb. Webb and her husband, Sidney, were founders of the London School of Economics as well as the Fabian Society. Polly's associations with political and social activists were numerous. The interconnectedness and communications among activists across the globe were remarkably strong.[67]

Graduating in 1916 with her degree from the London School of Economics, Polly did not rest on her laurels. She proceeded to Paris to study at the Sorbonne. The following letter in the February 14, 1917, issue of the *Progress Enterprise* was the first of a series from France.

> Miss Chesley in Paris
> Jan. 14th, 1917
>
> My Dearest Mother:
> I am getting quite a list of acquaintances here, partly through the "Students' Hostel," which is run for American and English students. During the war it has been opened to all, and I, together with Miss Lambeth, the English girl from Victoria, B.C., and Miss Jones, Welsh, are the only regular English-speaking people there. The others are a mixture of French, Russian, Poles, Jews, etc., with one Roumanian. Besides the Students' Hostel there is Foyer des Étudiants, a restaurant, where I get my meals every day except Sunday, and when Yuonise and I usually go to a restaurant run for the post office and telegraph girls. The girls at the Guild are very friendly and nice.
>
> I paid 5 sous for 20 of these envelopes. Cauliflowers are 16 sous apiece and most meats range from about 3 francs (57 cents) a kilo [and] up. For a cake of soap I paid 12 cents, and I see now that in most places it has gone up to 16 cents—clothing, especially anything with wool in it, is ridiculously high. For anything like a good boot you have to pay from $6.00 to $8.00, or even more. If it were not for the Foyer des Étudiants, I could

not possibly afford to live here. At the Foyer I can have a good vegetarian meal for from 85 to 130 centimes (17 to 26 cents) never more. Today I paid 180 centimes for my dejeuner, but it is so cold and raw that I was hungry and indulged in a small piece of meat. I don't know how the poor live.

This afternoon I went to see Notre Dame. At mass there were perhaps four hundred people in the central pews, and about two hundred wandering around the outside aisles and the little chapels back of the altar. It is a magnificent Cathedral, but there are only a few of the windows that are worth looking at. I am afraid I am getting a little blasé, it takes a good deal to arouse my enthusiasm in the way of art. There is one comfort; we do not tire of nature—I could never tire of Second Peninsula or Mahone Bay [places near Lunenburg]—and I am looking forward to the Spring, for I am sure the gardens of the Tuileries and Luxemburg and the Bois de Boulogne will be beautiful when the flowers are out and the trees are green.

Paris is more beautiful than London. There are the large spaces and gardens and fountains and grand boulevards, which are entirely lacking in London. In London there is the feeling that everything was built principally for use; if it is possible let it be beautiful also, but useful it must be. In Paris the impression is different—things are to be beautiful first, and then, if possible useful. In London the parks are the only real beauty spots, and they are like eases which one comes upon suddenly, when one is least expecting. I remember when I took Gyrth to Regent's Park, he could not believe that we were almost there, for we were in a regular slum. In Paris it is different; it is evident that everything has been planned so that they may form a complete whole. One could imagine a seething mob of cockneys throwing flour and rotten eggs at the suffragettes or leaders of a non-conscription meeting in Trafalgar Square, but it is impossible to imagine these things even in a Paris market. Every Sunday morning, when I go to meeting (Quakers) I pass through the market at Grenelle, and it is one of the most interesting sights in Paris. It extends under the "metro" with stalls on two sides of this large boulevard. And there are the men and women, bareheaded or with shawls on their heads, and children at the stalls or seated on the cold asphalt, with their wares spread out before them. There is always a crowd buying tout qu'il faut, for there is everything from musical instruments to skinned rabbits. Last Sunday when I went to Madame C's, I met Madame M. at the market near their apartments, where she was buying oranges and a cauliflower, which she put under her jacket, for paper is scarce—and she is a more stylish lady than any in Lunenburg, and when King George visits the front he and his suits stop at the house of her daughter-in-law. She is very sweet and simple in manner all the same, and when she shook hands with some equally stylish ladies with the cauliflower sticking out from under her jacket, she did it with the grace of a princess.

I have not made up my mind about the Parisians yet—as usual city people are harder to get to know than country people. I certainly found the majority of the people I met on my trip (a week in the country) friendly and nice.

POLLY

Polly mentioned going to Quaker meeting in Paris. Although she did not refer to Quakers in her letters from Britain, it seems likely that she did attend meetings there. As well, this is the second reference made to vegetarian restaurants. The fact that she talked about getting a bit of meat when she was feeling especially cold suggests that she generally maintained a vegetarian diet.

The Gyrth Polly took to Regent's Park is Gyrth Russell, her first cousin, a son of Judge Benjamin Russell, Mary's brother. After studying art in Halifax and Boston, Gyrth went in 1911 to attend art school in Paris. When the war broke out he left France for London. He worked as an official war artist for Canada, and he is best known for his depictions of war. Gyrth figures very briefly in this book in a later chapter.

On July 18, 1917, the *Progress Enterprise* published the following:

> [Polly] reached Paris on the 12th of November 1916, and has remained there, with the exception of brief holiday trips and a fortnight at Easter on the Mediterranean coast. As her letters are written in French, the trouble of rewriting them in English has deterred her parents from publishing extracts from them earlier. The following passages are from a letter written the 19th of November.
>
> Have I told you that on Tuesday, Madame (a Belgian lady, wife of a lawyer of Brussels now living as an exile in Paris) took me to see the Place de la Concorde, the Bridge of Alexander, the Grand Palace, the Little Palace, the Louvre and the Tuileries. In the distance I saw the Hotel des Invalides. We saw also the Hotel de Ville, the Chamber of Deputies, and some schools. We went also to the prefect of police to secure my permit to live in Paris.
>
> The streets in Paris are wider than those of London. It seems to me that the majority of the people rich and poor in Paris live in apartments. Many apartment houses are built around a little garden or court. There is always a "concierge" who is an important personage and sees that you wipe your feet on entering.
>
> Paris is totally different from London. I understand why Parisians do not like London. It is much more sombre, the streets narrower, not so many fine buildings or wide boulevards, more smoke, everything looking dark and old. But which place I like best I don't know. London has character, partly because it is so old, so historic. Here historic features are of more recent history. For instance this morning I passed an obelisk commemorating the revolution of July 1830; in London that would seem modern.
>
> All day Saturday I was looking for lodgings. The room I have taken is in a very nice house, on the fifth floor. It is not large, but is well furnished. I am to pay 45 francs ($8.55) a month. [The landlady] has two daughters, still studying, one medicine and the other philosophy.

The location is near the Sorbonne. I can get my lunch at the "Concordia" for 1 franc 30 centimes (25 cts) and my dinner at the "Foyer des Étudiants" for 90 centimes (18 cts.) I have stipulated for hot water in my room every morning to make a cup of chocolate.

This (Sunday) morning I went to a Friends' (Quaker's) meeting—it was very small but good.

Tomorrow I go to the Sorbonne and begin my course of lectures.

A week later Miss Chesley writes from her new quarters:

On Monday I went to the Sorbonne to register.

For lunch Tuesday I went to the "Foyer des Étudiants" for the first time. There I met a young lady who sat at the same table. She seemed agreeable. When I went back for dinner she was there again. She smiled, but I did not recognize her at first, as she wore a different hat. We entered into conversation. After dinner I went with her to her lodgings, where I met her husband. She was married before the war. Her husband was a lawyer, but now he is only a private soldier. As his sight is defective, he is in the reserves, but she told me yesterday that he will probably be sent to the front and possibly be killed, and so they cannot make plans for the future. It is very sad. Before the war his mother had property, but it was at Lille, and now the houses are destroyed. As they have lost everything and the private soldier's pay is only five cents a day, she has to work and is private secretary to a countess. She was ill for months at the commencement of the war, the result of grief. She is better now, but weary of her life—life is so sad for most French people nowadays.

Well, I think a great deal of her, and she thinks a great deal of me. Tomorrow (Sunday) we are going to take a walk and long talk about the war. She is very intellectual and advanced in her ideas. She described to me how a young French girl of good family is brought up. She knows nothing until she is married. Then she looks upon a new world. Before that she could not go anywhere without her maid or her mother. She is obliged to practice devotions till religion is the thing she detests.

The English girl who lived in Canada, a young French girl, and two other English girls are all very nice, but I prefer to be with Mme. A. because she speaks pure French, and I find her more interesting.

This afternoon I took two of the English girls to the "Students' Hostel," and afterwards I spent some time in the library there. Then I went to the "Foyer" for dinner, came home and read Gil Blas. It is now ten o'clock and I must go to bed, because we have to be sparing of electric light.

Living is dear here, dearer, than in England. It was cheaper here than in England before the war, but prices have risen.

I embrace you all with all my heart.

your affectionate

POLLY

What strikes me as remarkable is not that Polly's letters were written in French but that her parents translated them into English.

The following week, on July 25, 1917, the *Progress Enterprise* printed the next installment:

> Dec. 3rd, 1916:
> Yesterday I worked all morning. I take three courses at the Sorbonne, one on contemporaneous history, one on three classical French books, and for the third, the history of the 20th century. At Mr. Signebois' lecture on Wednesday I understood nearly every word, but at last I got so tired, and the air was so bad, that I could only understand about half.
>
> On the afternoon I took a walk with Yvonne and we went to the Gallerie La Fayette, a stylish shop. We met four Canadian nurses, two of them from Antigonish. They invited us to go to the hospital to see them. Today I went for the third time to the Quaker meeting, and this afternoon Yvonne and I went to the Luxembourg [garden].

Christmas evening she writes:

> It is Christmas night. This morning I went to two masses. After leaving church I went to Yvonne's and we went to a woman's restaurant. In the afternoon we went to the Gounod festival, where they sang and played Gounod's works. Concerts are dearer here than in London. At the opera the best seats cost $2.00. But I must go sometimes, must I not? Because I do not know when I shall be in Paris again. After the concert I went to a reception for the Students' Christian Association. There were perhaps thirty students. They sang and recited, and then we had refreshments and conversation. I met there, three Russians, a Pole and a French girl whom I had met at the Students' Hostel, so I passed an hour very agreeably. Such was my Christmas.

A day or two later she writes:

> I found Yvonne, and we took a walk. Thursday, when I went to see my Madame, as she was not at home I took a walk in the Bois de Boulogne and could hear the cannons as if they were on the other side of the hills. It was terrible. If one can hear it so plainly at 40 kilometres (26 miles) or more, it must be terrible near at hand.
>
> Yesterday I went to see my Madame. She was not at home, but I spent the afternoon with her mother.
>
> I had a good time yesterday with three Russians, two Poles (one named Meisner) and a French girl named Bachman. Have I told you that the Alsatian girl who is studying medicine is named Deihl?[68] We ate lots of cakes and I am paying today. Afterwards we went up to the library and found the Christmas tree and presents, all sorts of things, handkerchiefs, stockings, little jackets, even umbrellas. I chose bedroom slippers. Afterwards we sang Christmas carols. We left after seven and I went with a Scotch Irish girl to Yvonne's.
>
> This morning I gave my pupil an English lesson, and later dining for the first time at the "Concordia."[69] G. is with her

step-father today. He is 46 years old, but has been at the front and is on leave for a few days.

During the past week I have taken tea two or three times at the "Students' Hostel"—a rich American lady pays all the expenses of the institution.

On the 29th of December she commenced a letter mailed later.

I did not tell you I planned to a take a trip in the country because I wished to spare you an uneasy week.

This morning I started out from Paris on my bicycle. Fortunately Paris is not London, but it is extensive enough. I followed the Seine. At one kilometre from Paris, I lunched at a little restaurant. They always ask what wines you wish and are surprised when you say you do not wish any. I lunched for 27 cents.

The road for 23 kilometres was bad, full of little stones, but when I reached the forest it was asphalt. The town where I am now is 32 kilometres from Paris. I was rather tired when I arrived and I decided to remain. I found a restaurant readily enough and, as it is not warm, I sat in the kitchen with the family.

December 30. A perfect day, the sun, the country, fine.

Dec. 31. La Chapelle de la Reine. I commenced to write last evening but, as the people with whom I stayed were great talkers, I conversed with them till half past eight, when I went to bed and slept till half past six. I left early, but came to grief for want of a little piece of rubber. I walked a little over two miles, but as I can't get the tube I need, I am going to take the freight train to the next town, 8 miles. The station agent has tried to secure me a tube. Now he is going to put me on this train, which does not ordinarily carry passengers. I am going to travel as freight, by weight.

Yesterday I had a perfect day. I went 8 miles through open country to Melun. Eleven miles from there was the battle of the Marne. From there I followed the Seine several miles. It was beautiful. Then I crossed the Seine and entered the forest of Fontainebleau.

> I remembered that it had a celebrated chateau. After I had seen the gardens, I started again on the road, when I saw another great building. I asked a man what it was, and he told me it was the same chateau, and that one could see the apartments. I went to see them, and it was worth the trouble. They were magnificent. There were two apartments, including the great ballroom of Napoleon Bonaparte, the great entrance corridor of Francis I, his chapel, the throne room, the apartments of the favorite of Louis XIV.
>
> I am now at Malesherbes, I came by freight in a baggage car but I paid nothing, only a "thank you, Sir" to my friend the stationmaster. But nobody has a tube for my bicycle. I have had lunch, and have taken a little walk, and am now waiting for my train.
>
> January 5 – Paris – As you see I have arrived safely at Paris. Yesterday forenoon I passed very agreeably at Tours, where I climbed to the top of the tower built by Charlemagne over the tomb of his wife. The view from there is magnificent.
>
> POLLY

Another week later, on August 1, 1917, a further installment of Polly's letters appeared in the paper. If all the letters were in French, her parents had much work to do to translate them.

On the first of January Miss Chesley writes:

> Monday morning I studied. In the afternoon I went to see Madame. She is almost perfect, always the same, under all circumstances and with all sorts of people. In the evening I studied.
>
> Tuesday I had two lectures in the forenoon, and in the afternoon I attended the lecture of M. Strowski on Lamartine and his epoch. I was early, and there was not a seat left. Fortunately, a lady in the front row made room for me. The lectures are very interesting.
>
> Thursday I studied and then I found the girls from Ulster— and we went to the reception which takes place the first and third Thursday of each month. On those days some of the professors' wives entertain the students. We three were the only students. It

is a pity when those ladies give their time, that students do not generally attend.

Friday at dinner a young lady gave me two tickets for the Odeon. I went with one of the girls to see "The Two Orphans." We got good seats, and I understood the play very well.

Saturday morning I gave my only English lesson for the week. This morning I went with Miss Lambeth to a Protestant Church at Passy. We went from Grenelle on foot, and returning I walked along the Seine from Passy to rue de Bac. I passed the Eiffel Tower, which is a wonderful structure.

They are going to close the pastry shops Mondays and Wednesdays in Paris and they are going to shut off the electric lights in the house at ten o'clock every night. After ten we will have to use candles.

On the 29th of January she writes:

This week has been very cold. One day the thermometer went down to 8d below zero, and that night, the water froze on the river. For several days there was no coal to be had, everybody nearly frozen. Consequently I have a cold and stayed in bed this morning.

I have a second pupil. The lady wished me to give two lessons a week to her daughter, and when she asked the fee, and I said 3 francs an hour, she agreed so readily that I was sorry I had not asked for more.

Wednesday I went again to the Students' Hostel and met the Scotch Irish girls and a French girl, who told us that "The Blue Bird" was being played under the direction of Mme Maeterlinck, and that this was the last week. We paid 44 cents, which was 25 cents too much, it seems to me. But the play was fine.

February 6th, she writes:

Friday I was at the Students' Hostel after the lecture on French history and general history between 1830 and 1870. Miss Morgan gave me a ticket for a rehearsal. M. Henri Robert spoke, and they played and sang compositions by Rameau. I went with a French girl, Miss Breton. The same afternoon I met Miss Diehl, the girl who is studying medicine. She asked me if I would like to skate next day with her sister. She lent me her skates, and Saturday morning I skated for the first time in years.

Yesterday I went to the concert at the Sorbonne with Yvonne. It was very good. Saint Saëns accompanied the orchestra in a composition of Mozart's and the orchestra played some of his compositions. The batonnier of the Paris Bar spoke, and they sang and recited war poems and La Fontaine's fables.

This morning I attended the lecture on Voltaire, because they told me it was very good.

I see everything black today. I am afraid to look at a newspaper. If America enters the war it will seem to me that civilization is lost. Certainly I have seen too much of the goodness of the human heart for that. But just now, it is very difficult to keep from growing pessimistic.

The same mail by which I received a letter from Sylvia (Pankhurst) brought me also a very nice letter from Mrs. Bridges. She had asked me to let her know the result of my examinations at the London University, and this letter was in reply to mine.

It was snowing again today, and again there is no coal. Paris has not experienced a winter like this for years. At times I wish to be where there is no lack of coal or of love. But Lunenburg also is in the war and I would feel badly about that. Enough of this. I shall probably feel differently next week.

I embrace you with all my heart.

Polly

An article in the Halifax *Morning Chronicle*, dated February 1, 1917, corroborated Polly's account of the cold. With the headline "France in Grip of Jack Frost," the article stated that the country was experiencing the most severe winter since 1893.

Polly's spirits were unusually low in this letter, in part due to the dark, cold winter in Paris with no coal for warmth and also her sense of pessimism because of the war. Her homesickness for warmth and love in Lunenburg is counterbalanced by the knowledge that her hometown was also "in the war." Polly's belief in humanity's basic goodness even in the face of war keeps her motivated and defines her life path and her commitment to peace and social justice.

The fact that she was receiving mail from Sylvia Pankhurst and Mrs. Bridges attests to Polly's associations with the radical and intellectual Britons of the period. Sylvia Pankhurst was a socialist and suffragist whose parents, Dr. Richard Pankhurst and Emmeline Pankhurst, were early members of the Independent Labour Party. Along with her mother and her sister Christabel, Sylvia was instrumental in forming the Women's Social and Political Union, which quickly became the radical edge of the suffrage movement (the suffragettes whom Polly's mother, Mary, defended in a newspaper article).[70] While it is uncertain how they might have met, Polly and Sylvia could have been connected through various political/social channels. Later, in the 1930s, both were members of the Friends of India Society.

The Mrs. Bridges Polly refers to is Monica Waterhouse Bridges, who wrote and collaborated on projects with her husband, Robert Bridges, at one time the British Poet Laureate. Monica was well connected to various prominent intellectual, artistic, and business people of the period.

This was the last letter published from Polly's time in France. As was reported in the Lunenburg newspaper in September 1917, she arrived home at the end of August after almost three years abroad. The following letter, which was submitted to the newspaper by Polly's mother (M.R.C.) and appeared on Christmas Day, 1918, is from an unnamed location in Canada. It is evident that there had been other letters in the paper, both before and likely after this. As mentioned previously, a complete run of the *Progress Enterprise* is not extant.

> Trying Experiences of Mary A. Chesley in Hospital
>
> Dear Editor of Progress-Enterprise:

Perhaps these letters of Mary A. Chesley who last month offered as night nurse in an improvised "Flu" hospital may be of interest to your readers as giving a glimpse of the sad occurrences in influenza hospitals all over this Dominion and the United States during the past two or three months.

– M.R.C.

I will tell you some of my experiences as night nurse. The first night I was one of two helpers, on a women's ward with seventeen patients. Matters were not bad at that time. The other helper was a Methodist minister's daughter and she knew no more about nursing than I did. I had not met her before but we saw a good deal of each other during the first four nights, for, though we were never in the same ward again, we took our lunch and breakfast together, and I missed her greatly when she came down with the Flu. I performed some very unpleasant tasks that night and was feeling quite sick when a nurse took me into the woman's worst ward to help her give a cold sponge to a woman who seemed to be dying. Imagine my feelings when she said she wanted me to be able to do that the next night alone. However, I guess I was broken in that night for the close air, smell of new drugs, etc., never made me so sick again.

The next night the awful shortness of help began. One nurse who had only had two wards and three helpers the night before now had four wards with the same number of helpers. She did not discover till morning that one woman had a temperature of 105 and then she had no time to do anything. Is it any wonder people died?

That night I was alone, on a ward that had twenty men patients—two of them delirious. One of them was continually sitting up in bed and I would have to make him lie down. The poor fellow died a few nights later. The other man would strip off his shirt whenever I left the room and the patient in the next bed would call, "Nurse, that man's got his shirt off again" and I would have to go and put it on him. The following night I had the same ward but they had taken away my two delirious patients, and I found time to do what needed to be done, that was to put paper shade over the lamps and to tie the doors so that [they] would not bang and wake every one up. Some of the trained nurses would come in during the night banging the door and switching on the lights needlessly, so, I saw that these things were done in the wards on my floor.

The next night I was put on the worst men's ward. It was not a hard night as far as the work was concerned, for there were only twelve beds, and there was another helper and we had two orderlies. Besides that, the nurses came in off and on. But there were things happening that took your heart-strength. One man was dying a slow death—just gasping—for five hours, while his wife—the sweetest woman—who was brought in from another ward, lay beside him. She was so brave; though she was quite sick, she wanted nothing for herself, but would ask us to relieve his suffering. They had been married but three years and had been in the city only two months. Then there was one poor boy of seventeen, in the next bed, who was quite sane and, with proper care, I think might have recovered but there he was right beside the poor man gasping for breath for hours while another fine looking young fellow was talking nonsense all night long and another screaming and fighting with the orderlies. Poor fellow, he would say "nurse it scares me," and it seemed to comfort him to have me hold his hand. Well—[that] night poor Milford died, and five others out of the twelve the hours I was on duty. It was an awful night. The next night, the fifth one, I felt obliged to take a rest but the sixth night I went on duty again in one of the women's pneumonia wards. There were only seven patients, so I had a fairly easy night. The only troublesome patient was a poor girl, who was so wild and strong that they had to tie her down to the bed.

The seventh night I was again alone with three pneumonia patients, one of them my dear little Mrs. Aitkens, whom I mentioned in my last letter, and another an old lady who was dying.

She and the third one, also a young married woman, both died the next day. The next night I went early, so that I might be on the ward where Mrs. Aitkens was, and I felt repaid when, on recognizing my voice (I had my gown and mask on) she said "Oh here's my dear night nurse." They had moved five other pneumonia cases in that night. But it was the next night—the ninth—that took all there was of me, that night they moved in four new patients, two women and two little children, about seven and nine years; altogether there were nine. Both women were delirious, one wanting continually to know when she was going home, and the other, poor thing was always asking for the doctor. I got him for her once, and he ordered a prescription. When, after some time, the medicine hadn't come, and she was asking for the doctor, I went to see about the prescription, only to find that the nurse had been too rushed to see about getting it made up. The poor woman had a baby girl at home and she'd say "Will I live, nurse?" I tried to comfort her. I had learned the next day that she had died. I was almost distracted that night. I would just start to rub one woman's chest with olive oil when another would call me. I could not begin to do what needed to be done. I felt my ignorance, and there was no one to help. The next night I was on the same ward, but it was somewhat easier, as there were only seven patients, but two of them were pretty sick. Mrs. Aitkens said to me that night, Oh, nurse, I dread the day—I wish you were twins so that one of you could be with me during the day! Poor little woman—I learned later that she died within the week. I had the satisfaction of seeing one woman pass the crisis—or so it seemed to me. She was terribly sick all the first few hours. I supplied plasters, put an ice bag to her head, fanned her, etc., and she seemed decidedly better when I went off duty late in the morning. Before I had finished my breakfast I felt that I was coming down with the "flu," and my temperature was taken by one of the nurses. The next day I was taken to another hospital—the one for nurses in training. Of my experiences there, I will write you another time.

This concludes the most extensive collection of Polly's personal writings. Most knowledge about Polly otherwise comes from newspaper or organizational sources and the accounts of individuals who knew her. Polly's peripatetic path is sometimes difficult to follow, and there are holes in the timeline; however, it is still possible to capture glimpses of her passions and activities.

There is no mention of where Polly carried out her volunteer work during the great flu epidemic in 1918, but based on my research, I assume that it was in Vancouver. The first clue that Vancouver was on Polly's map came from her 1936 obituary, written in *The Friend*, Britain's Quaker journal. Among her teaching posts, it mentioned that Polly had taught at King Edward High School in Vancouver. Subsequently, I found references in the *Progress Enterprise* (July 7, 1920, and September 1, 1920) to Polly's arrival in Lunenburg from Vancouver to spend summer vacation with her parents and her later departure to return to British Columbia. What I did not know is when Polly might have first gone to Vancouver. Further research in the Mount Allison *Argosy* revealed that by April 1918, Polly was teaching in Vancouver. In the November 1918 issue of the journal, there appeared a further note to say that Polly was teaching English and French in the high school. The Vancouver City Archives proved valuable in establishing Polly's tenure with the Vancouver School Board. While the records are scanty, one account book notes that Polly was appointed in September 1918.[71] (The fact that she was already teaching in April may mean that an earlier account book is missing or that she may have been teaching without a full-time contract.) Her yearly salary plus bonuses are recorded for the years 1918–1921. There is a note that she resigned June 30, 1921. Other than this documentation, nothing is known of Polly's three years of teaching in Vancouver.

The *Progress Enterprise* account of her volunteering during the flu epidemic in the fall of 1918 at first seems to contradict the evidence that she was teaching at that time, but schools and other public institutions were closed at the height of the epidemic. The improvised or makeshift hospital that Mary Chesley referred to in introducing Polly's letter may or may not have been in the high school itself, but it seems reasonable to assume that Vancouver was the city where Polly carried out this work. According to one report, almost one-third of Vancouver's 100,000 citizens came down with the flu, with 900 dying from the virus. Based on information from a contemporary *Vancouver Sun* article, during October and November, schools, churches, and theatres were shut down for weeks along with pool halls, swimming pools, and gyms.

Having now experienced the COVID-19 pandemic, one can vividly imagine the horrors of the flu of 1918.[72] One hundred years ago, modern medicine and technology were non-existent. Volunteering on the front line of the epidemic put Polly at serious risk of sickness and possible death. Fortunately, she lived to see another day. That she should succumb to a flu-like infection with pneumonia and fever less than ten years later is a sad irony.

CHAPTER 6
Mary Chesley's Final Days and Polly's Emergence as an Activist

ON JULY 21, 1920, *THE WESLEYAN* PUBLISHED THE FOLLOWING news item:

> Lunenburg. July 14 – A serious accident took place today. Judge S. A. Chesley went up to the second story of the Lunenburg outfitting company to get some rope. He tripped and fell down the hatchway, his collarbone is broken, and his skull fractured. He was taken home where he is still unconscious, and in very serious condition. Mrs. Chesley and her daughter were at their summer home and a car was sent for them.
>
> The many friends of Judge Chesley will devoutly pray for his recovery. It is difficult to fully appreciate the service which this devoted man has rendered to the church during the past more than 40 years.
>
> Since the above was written a note from Rev. A. R. Reynolds says Judge S. A. Chesley though still in a very critical condition seems to be improving slowly, and hopes are entertained for his recovery.

Polly would have been still teaching in Vancouver but was home for summer holidays when the accident occurred. It is unknown how long Samuel's recovery took, but he would outlive his wife Mary and have another ten years of good health and active travel.

Mary was still active in the WCTU. The 1920 annual report of the Citizenship Department included union news. Windsor members had tried to elect one of their own to town council. Mary wrote: "They did not succeed but we trust that they will remember that 'If at first you don't succeed' the motto is 'Try, try again.'" A provincial election brought out women for the vote, one union reporting, "those who had cars kept them going for the women voters all day long." For those women who fought for the right to vote, it would be impossible to understand the indifference and voter apathy of today.

Mary's last Report for the Department of Christian Citizenship appeared in the annual WCTU convention records for the year 1922. She instructed women on becoming better informed, both as to their responsibilities as voting citizens and also regarding their rights. Through an arrangement with the Extension department at Dalhousie University, a series of lectures was planned on "the Laws of Nova Scotia Relating to Women." In her last few years, with women's franchise finally won, Mary must have reaped some satisfaction, and yet, she did not rest. In fact, there is a sense that she had renewed energy. She believed that women could influence the world of politics and lead in peace work.

It is only in the 1921 annual WCTU conference report that it is apparent that the Department of Peace and Arbitration had ceased to function for the duration of the war. In one of the executive meetings of the 1921 conference, we find the following: "It was moved and seconded that we resume the Department of Peace and Arbitration that had been discontinued during the war, also that Mrs. M. R. Chesley be again appointed Superintendent."

At the WCTU's first public meeting during the conference, Polly was the chief speaker. "Her mother's mantle has assuredly fallen on Miss Chesley who held the rapt attention of her audience as she made a strong appeal to the women of Canada to work for World Peace." Polly's growing peace activism reflected her mother's influence, but Polly would expand upon Mary's work, becoming a vocal peace advocate on the international stage.

When Polly resigned her teaching job in June 1921, she did not return to Vancouver. The next news clippings that record her activities occur in the fall of that year. It may be that for the next couple of years, Polly did not teach but spent the time lecturing and fundraising.

On October 7, 1921, the *Evening Mail* published the following article:

> An Interesting Personality
>
> Miss Mary Chesley, who arrives in this city tonight, is an interesting personality. A graduate of the University of London from which she received her degree of B.Sc. she has traveled far afield, knows France well, has bicycled thru Scotland and knows every part of the United Kingdom. She is interested keenly in life out of doors and takes to "hiking."
>
> With the zest of a finely vigorous woman, having lately walked from Lunenburg to New Glasgow [240 km] to visit a friend, what would our Halifax women who think it a hardship to walk from Inglis Street to Mahon's Ltd. [1 to 2 km] think of this? She is described as being very fond of sailing, and as interested in aquatic sports. She is to address a mass meeting in the Women's Council House next week and the meeting has been thrown wide open to all. She is to speak on "Peace and Disarmament."

One week later, the *Evening Mail* of October 12 reported:

> Miss Chesley's Lecture a Striking One
> Vigorous pleas for "Peace and Disarmament and Strong Arraignment of War"
>
> Last evening a large audience assembled in the Women's Council House and keenly enjoyed the striking address by Miss Mary Chesley, daughter of Judge Chesley of Lunenburg, and a graduate in Political Economy of London University. Miss Chesley, taking as her subject "Peace and Disarmament."
>
> Every pulpit and every newspaper, said Miss Chesley, should counsel universal demand for a peace founded on justice, not on revenge; on love, and not on hate.

Maynard Vane, one of England's strongest writers has written against the "secret diplomacy" of the four great leaders in whom unlimited confidence had been placed. Millions have died and millions more are starving because of the Great War, and, the mistakes of diplomats since the war. All the warring nations are burdened with debts, yet the countries are spending five times as much in military preparation as was spent ten years ago.

One big gun, once fired, costs as much as a boy's education. Morally and physically a standing army is a menace, and the speaker alleged that one of the causes of unrest today in India is the order of Lord Roberts regarding prostitution.

Waste in war is inevitable and impacts business life. Moreover, indemnities do not make up for the loss. The speaker analyzed caustically why this is so.

At the Hague Conference in 1915, a Women's International League was suggested by the suffrag[ists] (non-militant). It is now organized in 33 countries. Why, asked Miss Chesley, do not Nova Scotian women join this organization and also work for reform in education.

In reply to questions by Miss Hume, Miss Chesley stated that troubles in Mexico were largely caused by oil interests. In India, a common saying is "drunk as a Christian."

At the conclusion, Mrs. George Black moved and Dr. Jane Heartz Bell seconded a hearty vote of thanks. Rev. E. E. Graham, who enjoyed Miss Chesley's acquaintance at college, said that so long as we have hell on earth, we will have the concomitant evils. Loss of life, said he, is not the worst thing about war. It is the spirit of hate which it engenders.

The newspaper's reference to Maynard Vane, I believe, is an error. I think that Polly was referring to Maynard Keynes—John Maynard Keynes—renowned British economist and philosopher. He resigned his post with the British Treasury because of his disgust over the collusion of the principal players at the Versailles Peace Conference.

Polly's radical politics are apparent in her address. Her allusion to the troubles in India refers to the regulatory control of prostitutes through the Contagious Diseases Act. Originally enacted in the late nineteenth century, it targeted prostitutes or any woman presumed to be a prostitute. Women under suspicion could be arrested, physically examined, and incarcerated. Feminists were outraged by these regulations and protested the double standard that penalized women while allowing men who consorted with prostitutes to remain free. Polly's critique of the use of the Act in India is also a critique of the British military presence in India. Her analysis of Mexico's troubles being due to oil interests also indicates her questioning of the motivations of big business.

A couple of days after this meeting, Polly made a presentation in New Brunswick. On October 14, 1921, the *Saint John Standard* carried the following report:

> Address on Peace and Disarmament
>
> The necessity for peace disarmament was brought before members of the St. John Local Council of Women in a lecture given by Miss Mary Chesley, of Lunenburg, N.S.
>
> Miss Chesley described conditions among women in the countries recently fought over and pointed out many of the results of war. Miss Chesley named big financial concerns whose interests are served by the conquest of some country and war being held before children as noble and virtuous. She pointed out that almost all boys' books are war books and urged women to improve education schedules and eradicate the war spirit.
>
> In Alberta, she stated, a committee had been appointed to revise schoolbooks and to eliminate everything savoring of militarism.
>
> Miss Chesley then spoke of international peace organizations, particularly the Women's International League for Peace and Freedom of which she herself is a charter member. Miss Chesley named prominent British women who are members of this League which is now organized in twenty-one countries and has a branch in Canada. Another organization was one of ex-soldiers, of whom two million had pledged themselves never to take up arms again. Still another society is called "The Union of Democratic Control."[73]

> Women should organize to kill the war spirit. Miss Chesley said we must get away from narrow patriotism.
>
> Mrs. W. Frank Hathaway spoke in appreciation. Mrs. E. A. Young referred to the sacrifice of Canadian soldiers in France and Flanders saying that they died for a just and righteous cause. Mrs. Raymond spoke of Miss Chesley's enlightening talk and thanked her for coming to speak.

Mrs. Young's defence of a just and righteous war hints at the difficulty many would have had in accepting the pacifist position that Polly espoused. Meaningless sacrifice of so many young lives would have been too horrible to contemplate. No doubt, Polly had difficulty convincing some of her audience of her peace and reconciliation message. However, those who personally fought in the war, especially a significant number of writers and artists (notably Siegfried Sassoon, Robert Graves, Wilfred Owens, and Otto Dix), shared Polly's view of "meaningless sacrifice." Their writing and painting portrayed the bleakness and horror that was in contrast to the nationalist rhetoric being promulgated in the "official" story of honour and heroism.

As mentioned in the Saint John article, Polly was a charter member of the Women's International League, founded in 1915 after the Peace Conference at The Hague. Whether the Canadian chapter that Polly referenced was the Lunenburg branch or a group in Vancouver is unknown. It is possible that the Lunenburg group had been established by 1921, although the first written account of it appears in the 1922 annual report for the WCTU. In addition to discussing the circulation of petitions urging universal disarmament to be sent to Sir Robert Borden, Canada's representative at the Washington Disarmament Conference, Mary's 1922 report mentions the unions' work of collecting funds for the famine victims of Russia and states that in Lunenburg this fundraising was under the care of the Women's International League "which is organized there." The Women's International League for Peace and Freedom still exists. Polly would have been instrumental, along with her mother, in instigating the Lunenburg chapter, which was one of the first Canadian chapters, if not the earliest.

That a chapter of the Women's International League existed in Lunenburg at this early date is significant. Without WCTU records and a reference or two in the Lunenburg newspaper, this fact would be unknown. Regrettably, no record of the Lunenburg chapter exists in the WILPF archives either in Britain or in the United States. Records from this period were only sporadically preserved. Vancouver possibly had the first Canadian chapter, established in 1921, according to the Vancouver WILPF chapter's website. Swarthmore College holds American WILPF papers, and the records they hold from Vancouver are dated from 1922 onward. The Vancouver and Lunenburg chapters began about the same time and before other chapters were formed in Canada. Laura Hughes and other feminists in Ontario were involved in the organization from the earliest days but may not have formed a chapter. It would appear that once Mary Chesley died and Polly moved to Britain, the chapter in Lunenburg ceased to continue.

It is probable that the Lunenburg branch affiliated through Britain rather than the United States. When the Women's International League first organized in 1915, Polly lived in Britain, and she is listed as a charter member in the organization's records. Housed in the London School of Economics (LSE) archives, the early league records are scant but, nevertheless, Polly's name is listed among the first members.[74] I would like to imagine that she might have been one of the women who had tried to attend the Women's Peace Conference at The Hague but was turned back at the port of departure; however, there is no record to reveal whether this is true or not.[75] That she became a charter member indicates that she was aware of the conference and the subsequent decision to form an organization that continues even today. The WILPF marked its one-hundredth anniversary in 2015.

It is uncertain whether Polly was in paid employment during the next year or two. Based on news clippings, she spent considerable time giving public lectures and presentations. Related to her peace and reconciliation message were her fundraising lectures in support of Save the Children, the organization Kate Courtney helped to establish. The following article appeared in the *Sydney Record* (Nova Scotia) on May 1, 1922:

> Appeal for Relief for Starving Russia
>
> Miss Chesley Heard in Fine Address at the Palace
>
> Before some 800 people who crowded the Palace Theater, Frank Grierson, of the Department of Finance, Ottawa, and Miss Mary Chesley, representing the "Save the Children" committee, spoke with effect on the movement to raise funds to save the starving children in Russia.
>
> Miss Chesley made an eloquent plea for donations to the fund. In opening her remarks she said that she had given $1,500, which she saved against old age. She said it was well worth the sacrifice, as it would probably be the means of saving some 300 children. She also referred to criticisms made that a lawyer in London was getting big profits out of the subscribed funds. She explained that there was a lawyer hired by the committee, but that he was acting as a publicity agent and was being paid on a commission basis of one and one half per cent.
>
> She declared that in the famine area, out of a population of 35,000,000 no babies under six months were alive. She said that according to relief workers that six to seven million must die between now and harvest time.
>
> The lecture concluded with slides, depicting the horrible conditions under which the people are living and also showed how the money now being collected by the Save the Children Committee is used to relieve these conditions.

A reference to Polly appeared in the May 1922 issue of *The Argosy*, the Mount Allison journal: "Miss Chesley, a Mt. A. graduate, was here in the interests of the Russian Famine Relief. A collection and generous response was given."

The next reference to Polly appeared in the *Progress Enterprise*, February 21, 1923:

> Interesting Meeting
>
> An open meeting of the Women's International League was held in the Women's Institute room on Friday evening. Miss Mary

Chesley had the chair. She spoke on the Ruhr occupation and what a mistake the French people were making. She also spoke about the German reparations. Rev. F. C. Ward-Whate, who was invited to address the meeting spoke on the Ruhr occupation. He did not speak as a German or Englishman, but took the stand of a Frenchman, and said that the French people had been so cruelly treated by the Germans, that the treatment they were receiving now from the French was very mild in comparison.

The WILPF considered the Treaty of Versailles, signed in 1919, to be unduly harsh in its reparation demands on Germany. Pacifist women felt that such demands would effectively set up the preconditions for another world war. In January 1923, the French government, fed up with Germany for defaulting on payments, sent in its troops to occupy the Ruhr—the industrial heartland of Germany. It is obvious that Polly and Rev. Ward-Whate were of different minds. Again, Polly's peace and reconciliation position was not universally accepted; in fact, it would have been a minority opinion. However, later historical analysis would suggest that the harsh reparations did indeed contribute to the rise of Hitler.

Reverend Ward-Whate was, at the time, the Anglican priest of St. John's Church in Lunenburg. A noted Orangeman and closely tied to the military, he served as a recruiter and army padre during the First World War. According to his obituary (*Toronto Star*, August 27, 1935), a "distinguished gathering of Clergy, Orangemen and Canadian Legionnaires" attended the funeral. Writer Susan Lewthwaite, in an essay on Ethelbert Lionel Cross, Toronto's first Black lawyer, discussed Cross's challenge to Ward-Whate for a public debate after the minister spoke from the pulpit declaring that if he were the attorney general, he would imprison and deport rationalists and "disinfect" the office of the *Christian Inquirer*. Cross, a vocal advocate of civil liberty and justice, found Ward-Whate's rant abhorrent, and as legal council to the Rationalist Society and their newspaper the *Christian Inquirer*, he threatened to sue Ward-Whate for slander. [76]

Polly probably could not have had a more vigorous opponent than Ward-Whate to her pacifist point of view. The fact that the WILPF organized the event indicates that women chose to air both pro-war and anti-war perspectives.

Polly continued her speaking engagements throughout 1923 and 1924. One of the Halifax papers, the *Evening Echo*, had the following announcement in the June 12, 1923, issue:

> Miss Mary Chesley, daughter of Judge Chesley, of Lunenburg, will give an address on the League of Nations from the woman's viewpoint, in the First Baptist Church on Queen Street, on the evening of June 13, at 8:15 p.m. Miss Chesley is an Honor Graduate in Political Science of London University and was associated with English women in their efforts to obtain the franchise, speaking at Hyde Park. She is very well informed on the subject of European politics and is an effective, forceful speaker. The public is invited."

A week later, on June 20, the *Berwick Register* carried the following:

> Kings County was favored last week by a visit from Miss Chesley, daughter of Judge S. A. Chesley of Lunenburg. On Sunday afternoon she took the service at Cambridge, and in the evening she spoke on Peace and Disarmament in the Baptist Church at Berwick. Monday evening she gave her lecture on The League of Nations in the schoolroom of the Baptist Church at Waterville, which was filled to capacity. Interesting discussion followed.
>
> During her years in post-graduate work at London University, Miss Chesley came in intimate touch with leading pacifists in England. She was a charter member of The Woman's International League and one of the earliest members of the Union of Democratic Control. She belonged to the U.D.C. in those early days when its meetings were broken up by organized mobs, and its paper was not allowed out of the country. Miss Chesley is one of the best authorities in Eastern Canada on questions relating to Peace.

According to the custom of the time, Polly is referred to as Samuel's daughter only, with no mention of her mother, the major influence in Polly's political development.

The next word about Polly comes in the form of a small note in the *Progress Enterprise* on November 21, 1923, under the heading "Lunenburg Lady Heard on the Radio":

> On Armistice Day, Sunday 11th, Miss Mary Chesley, of Lunenburg, previously announced over the continent by radio as a graduate of London University who had spoken in Hyde Park (London) demonstrations, was one of three speakers whose addresses were broadcasted from Philadelphia by radio.
> The other two were Bishop Paul Jones, an Episcopal Bishop, and Frederick Sibly [probably meant to be Libby], a prominent Quaker, President of a Peace Society in Philadelphia.

Through a notice in the December 26, 1923, issue of the *Progress Enterprise* I discovered that Polly was in Philadelphia doing volunteer work with a Quaker relief organization. It is not certain when she arrived in Philadelphia; it would appear to be early autumn. How long she planned to stay there is also unknown, for her time there was cut short by the death of her mother. Two sources of information on Polly in Philadelphia helped me to fill in the picture.

From September 2004 to June 2005, I was living outside of Philadelphia at Pendle Hill, a Quaker Center for Study and Contemplation (established in 1930). I had been awarded a scholarship so I could work on my dissertation. Several of my dissertation subjects had spent time or lectured at Pendle Hill in the 1930s, and one had lived there briefly in the 1970s. Remembrance (or Armistice) Day in Philadelphia on November 11, 2004, was a cold, wet day, but I took the train into the city to the public library to search through microfilm to possibly establish Polly's presence in the city, and to follow up on the Lunenburg newspaper notice of Polly's presence among those giving radio broadcasts. Sure enough, the *Philadelphia Record* of November 11, 1923, published an article, "Armistice Day Marked by Appeals for Peace," giving news of many ceremonies and services carried out by veterans, churches, and peace and patriotic groups. I discovered researchers' gold.

Under the heading "Plead for Peace on Streets," was written, "In many sections of the city, open-air meetings were held under the auspices of the Women's International League for Peace and Freedom. The article described the gatherings of Quakers and other peace organizations and individuals, quoting extensively from the speech of Bishop Paul Jones.

Polly was among illustrious company that day, including the following:

- Paul Jones, Episcopal Bishop of Utah and a prominent advocate of pacifism. He was forced to resign his post when the House of Bishops pronounced him guilty of "promulgating unpatriotic doctrines." He would become a founding member of the Fellowship of Reconciliation (FOR) as well as the Episcopal Peace Fellowship and during the Second World War helped to resettle Jews and others who fled Nazi Germany.

- Dr. Jesse Holmes, a Quaker philosophy professor and an active participant in the relief work of the American Friends' Service Committee (AFSC) following the First World War.

- Edward Evans, a Quaker pacifist and lawyer who was instrumental in the founding of FOR, taught international law at the University of Pennsylvania and was active in educational and peace programs.

- Janet Payne Whitney, a British Quaker who married an American Quaker and wrote biographies of early Quaker women.

- Dr. William I. Hull, another Quaker pacifist, who taught history at Swarthmore College.

- Walter Longstreth, also from a Quaker family; a prominent lawyer and pacifist who defended conscientious objectors in the Second World War.

- Frederick Libby, a pacifist and Congregational pastor who eventually became a Quaker; in the period following the Great War, he carried out relief work with the AFSC in Europe.

- Walter Abell, an art historian and professor who spent fifteen years teaching in Nova Scotia at Acadia University. Abell joined the Society of Friends while attending Swarthmore College and also served in reconstruction work in France with AFSC in the postwar period. During 1922–23, he was in Philadelphia and serving as publicity manager with AFSC.

- Allen Olmsted, another lawyer and judge, who became disillusioned after serving as a sergeant major in the First World War and became active in civil liberties and pacifist causes. Married to Mildred Scott Olmsted, a prominent figure in WILPF, he gave pro bono legal services for several organizations.

- Bernard Walton, another Quaker pacifist and social worker, who served as chair of FOR and secretary of the Committee on Social-Industrial Relations; there is a memorial lecture series named in his honour. [77]

- Gladys Boone, originally from Britain, who went to Columbia University for her PhD and remained in the United States. She was an economist and labour specialist, best known for her book on women's trade unionism in Britain and the United States.

- Harold Evans. Although I have not been able to confirm this, Evans may have been a brother of Edward Evans, mentioned above. Both were Quakers, born in Germantown in the 1880s, and both went into law.

- Henry E. Close, a socialist who ran as a Pennsylvania representative in several US House elections and also for Lieutenant-Governor of Pennsylvania in 1926.

The only members of this group of speakers for whom I could not find any information were the two single women, Rachel T. Jones and Christine Doyle. It is possible that they married, took their husbands' names, and, therefore, are difficult to trace.

Today there is no official recognition of Polly's place within the peace movement and Quaker circles, and I had imagined her as a lone and relatively unknown figure. The fact she was invited to give public lectures and participate in something as large as the Philadelphia radio broadcast and was among such impressive company in Philadelphia indicates that her profile at the time was significant and that she was more connected to Quaker and peace activists than the historical record would indicate.

As to Polly's personal life, another proof of her sojourn in Philadelphia came from the surviving correspondence, now housed at the Nova Scotia Archives, of Elizabeth (Bessie) Hall (1890–1969). Bessie was from Bridgewater, another town in Lunenburg County. She and Polly were friends; perhaps they attended the Lunenburg Academy at the same time. Also a bright young woman, Bessie was, at the time, working on her doctorate in social work at Bryn Mawr, a women's college near Philadelphia. The following excerpts from Bessie's letters to her parents during the autumn of 1923 reveal something of Polly's personality and interests.[78]

On October 10, 1923, Bessie wrote, "Now I will tell you all about my trip. Soon after we left B'water I noticed Judge Russell on board the train (Polly's uncle), so I spoke to him and had a nice talk, in which he scolded me for that boat trip of Polly's and mine. He is a cute old thing. He got off at Liverpool. I must get in touch with Polly." It is unknown with whom Bessie was travelling on this particular occasion, but she and Polly had had adventures together, and the two were travelling companions the following year. Bessie's last remark in the following letter of October 25, 1923, suggests that Polly was already in the Philadelphia area:

> I must tell you—Polly has been out here twice already! The girls are getting quite habituated to her appearance. She is my scout in town to buy cheap opera tickets, or tickets for good plays. She can scent a bargain as quickly as anyone I ever knew and I see where under her judicious supervision I shall be able to indulge in a whole galaxy of things for the price of just one or two of the prodigal "Hall" purchases.

> P.S. Sunday evening
> Polly came out yesterday afternoon and played tennis, and then we made a "campfire" and had tea outdoors. Polly has got cheap seats to "Faust" for next week, and I am going. Isn't that grand!

Bessie's letter of November 4 confirms Polly's talent for living "on the cheap." She wrote, "Last Monday evening I saw 'Faust'! It was perfectly lovely. Our seats were 55 cents! Polly got them for us but didn't go herself as she had seen it." On November 12, Bessie wrote: "Polly was out on Sunday. She comes for our plentiful hot water as the hot water where she boards is apt to be a minus quantity. Today she is giving some street addresses in Philadelphia on the world peace movement. Good old Pol!"

"Sunday…Polly meanwhile has been making herself at home in my room and the family bathtub."

On November 26, Bessie wrote, "This is Sunday. I was to the 'Friends' [Quaker] meeting this morning, a mile or so from here. They have a quaint sweet service. Everybody just sits quiet till the 'spirit' moves them and then one of them gets up and speaks a little. Then quiet again, and so on. It is quite impressive." On December 8 she wrote of Polly being among "some girls" Bessie was having "in to tea."

Then, on January 2, 1924, Bessie mentioned in a letter that she had "a message to do for Polly," which I think refers to the writing of a condolence note. Polly's mother, Mary, died on Christmas Day 1923, and so Polly cut short her stay in Philadelphia and returned to Lunenburg.

It is unclear what group Polly volunteered with while in Philadelphia. I was unable to find any references to her at the Swarthmore archives or in Philadelphia at the AFSC archives. Nevertheless, the newspapers and Bessie's letters confirm Polly's involvement in the peace movement.

That fall of 1923, Mary Oxner gave the WCTU report for Christian Citizenship. After thirty years of carrying the torch for enfranchisement and then citizenship, Mary finally had someone to replace her. Not surprisingly, Mary Oxner was a member of the Lunenburg union. In 1922, according to the annual WCTU records, the Lunenburg union was the largest group in the province with 100 paid members. Halifax had only 60 members, and there were 937 in the entire province. Lunenburg also took the lead in the number of active departments. Mary Chesley's leadership must have been a factor. Another indicator of the strength of this union can be found in W. A. Letson's *Lunenburg by the Sea* (c. 1896).[79] Primarily a tourist promotion vehicle, the photographic guide included salient facts about the town. Throughout the entire text, the only hint that women actually had an existence in Lunenburg is found in the following statement: "The fraternal organizations are well represented by such societies as the Masons, Oddfellows, Foresters, Orange, Sons of Temperance, W.C.T.U. and minor organizations." The fact that the WCTU was the sole female organization mentioned indicates its strong and forceful presence in the community.

Mary Chesley made her last Peace and Arbitration report at the same WCTU convention in 1923, only a couple of months before her death. Again she referred to the work in Lunenburg:

> The barrels of clothing reported [for Russian relief] were sent by the International League for Peace and Freedom, but as the leader and most of the members of this are W.C.T.U. women, and as the collecting and packing were done by two of them and also as there is only the Lunenburg branch of the League in Nova Scotia, I have given this item in my report.
>
> The posters mentioned in the reports were suggested by my daughter. They contain figures of the cost of war and show what good measures might have been accomplished at far less cost. It surely devolves upon us, the mothers and grandmothers of the rising generations, to do what we can to impress upon children, the horror and futility of war.

On Christmas Day 1923, Mary Russell Chesley died at the age of seventy-five. Her obituary appeared in several newspapers, both in Halifax (in the *Morning Chronicle* and the *Acadian Recorder*) and on the South Shore (in the *Lunenburg Progress Enterprise*, *Lunenburg Argus*, and *Bridgewater Bulletin*).

> LUNENBURG, Dec. 25 – Mrs. Mary R. Chesley, wife of Judge Chesley of Lunenburg, and sister of Hon. Justice Russell of Halifax, died at her residence, Tuesday evening. She had been ill for several days, having been stricken with paralysis on Friday the 14th. Mrs. Chesley is survived by her husband and daughter, Polly, now in Philadelphia doing volunteer relief work as a member of a Quaker Relief organization.
>
> The deceased ranked high among the distinguished women of the Province, having been prominent in the work for Temperance and Woman's Suffrage, and other branches of social reform. In the cause of woman's rights she was a pioneer, having been among the first and most ardent advocates. Her correspondence, which frequently appeared in The Morning Chronicle, was always trenchant and convincing and her views were presented and enforced with great ability and distinction. She will be greatly missed in the ranks of social reform where she has been one of the most outstanding figures.

The memorialist concluded with this final paragraph: "The deceased was one of several sisters of Hon. Justice Russell of Halifax. The eldest sister, Alma, now over eighty years of age survives and lives with the Chesley family. Mrs. Chesley was predeceased by a son and daughter, whose death by drowning in Lunenburg harbor over twenty-five years ago is still remembered as one of the tragic events in the town."

Mary was also memorialized in *The Wesleyan* and in the national WCTU publication *The Canadian White Ribbon Tidings*.

In the February 20, 1924, issue of *The Wesleyan*, A. R. Reynolds, formerly a minister in Lunenburg, wrote the following:

> In Memoriam
>
> MARY R. CHESLEY
>
> An Appreciation
>
> As former pastor of the church where Mrs. Chesley worshipped, I would like to bear this tribute to her memory. The newspaper

references spoke of her as one of Nova Scotia's most distinguished women, and she was. Her achievements in temperance and social service, and in advancing the cause of women's rights, were unequalled by any contemporary Nova Scotian woman. She was endowed with many intellectual gifts, and she did not use her endowments selfishly. She freely consecrated them to promoting the welfare of others. But with all her endowments and achievements, Mrs. Chesley possessed the true Christian grace of humility. She was a woman of genuine character, with a high ethical standard, not as a measure for the character of others, but to live up to herself.

In the home, she was a devoted wife and mother, and a gracious hostess.

During my pastorate I found in Judge Chesley a true friend, and wise counselor, and I learned to depend upon his unfailing judgement and advice. When through an accident, in the summer of 1920, his life hung in the balance, my concern for him was as great as for a father. I was in his home many times over two weeks. It was then that I learned to appreciate Mrs. Chesley in a way that I never had before. I saw there her devotion and gentleness, and yet, at the same time, her strength and courage. With all her anxiety, she never for a moment forgot the needs of others. It is in these times of crisis that true character is revealed. My high estimate of Mrs. Chesley's character was enhanced by my contact with her. Her character was as admirable as any that I have ever known. Her calm courage and poise of soul were a real inspiration.

Mrs. Chesley will be greatly missed in the church and community where, while health permitted, she was in labors abundant.

– A.R.R.

The February 1924 issue of *The Canadian White Ribbon Tidings* contained a couple of tributes to Mary. Sara Rowell Wright, the national WCTU president, in her monthly letter wrote:

> With a heavy sense of loss we record the "passing" of one of our most honored and valued Superintendents, Mrs. Mary Chesley. Dear Mrs. Chesley never once wavered in her allegiance to the White Ribbon cause which she served with distinguished ability as one of the first Presidents of the Nova Scotia Provincial Union, and later as a National Superintendent. At a time when allegiance to the cause of Women's Enfranchisement involved courage, both Mrs. Chesley and her husband, Judge Chesley, fearlessly championed the cause. Mrs. Chesley, as Superintendent of our Department of Peace and Arbitration set herself to promoting "peace on earth, good will to men." Her only daughter, Miss Mary Chesley, is in full accord with the fine ideals instituted by her mother on behalf of world peace, and as Associate Superintendent will take up the work her mother so efficiently performed.

Ada L. Powers, another leading figure from the Lunenburg union, wrote in her Nova Scotia report:

> In the death of Mrs. Mary Russell Chesley on Christmas Day, not only Lunenburg W.C.T.U. but the Canadian Union as well has suffered a distinct loss. The late Mrs. Chesley was one of the pioneers for Woman Suffrage, which she advocated for so ably. She held the offices of President and Corresponding Secretary in the Provincial Union and was for years the President of her home Union. For years she held the offices of Superintendent of Citizenship and of Peace and Arbitration, both in the Provincial and Canadian W.C.T.U.
> We will miss her—not only in her public capacity but as a kind friend and good neighbor.

Later that year, after the provincial WCTU convention had been held in Windsor, Ada Powers reported in the November issue of *Tidings* on the memorial service that was held for the twenty-one members across the province who had died since the last convention.

Only two members were mentioned by name. "The most widely known was Mrs. M. R. Chesley, who as a pioneer for the enfranchisement of women when that subject was most unpopular, had a continent-wide reputation. She [also] gave her sympathy and support to the cause of Peace and Arbitration, a work which she passed on to her brilliant daughter."

Although Mary Russell Chesley always maintained her personalized signature rather than going by Mrs. Samuel Chesley, which was remarkable for the time, in a report of the WCTU's annual conference in 1924 listing those among their membership who had died in the previous year, Mary is listed only as Mrs. Chesley. Of the twenty women named, only one (a widow) was not listed by her husband's name. Among dozens of named women in the rest of the conference report, the only other ones that were accorded their own first names were single women.[80]

With Mary Chesley's last report comes the silencing of an intelligent and passionate voice for peace and equality. In her lifetime she gained recognition for her writings and advocacy, particularly as a suffragist, as witnessed in her inclusion in *Women's Who's Who in America* and *Canadian Men and Women of the Time*. Nonetheless, Mary Chesley has all but disappeared from the story of women's contributions both regionally and nationally. Memories of her outstanding leadership on suffrage and peace issues faded with time, perhaps because she didn't have family members to carry on the memory of her work after her daughter died and because she lived outside the capital city of Halifax.

Mary Chesley lived a full life of activism. She probably held high hopes that voting women would contribute to a more peaceful world. One would hope that she died feeling that her life's work had not been in vain. Her "brilliant" daughter Polly was carrying on in the family tradition.

~~~

When Polly returned to Lunenburg, she served temporarily as the superintendent of Peace and Arbitration with the WCTU, a position made vacant by her mother's death. Neither Polly nor her mother made temperance their chief cause; however, the following article from the *Progress Enterprise*, published on January 23, 1924, less than a month after Mary Chesley's death, does focus on temperance.

> The meeting of the W.C.T.U. on Tuesday was marked by an interesting discussion, started by Miss Chesley who told the members that she had promised her mother to move the following resolution but had neglected doing so until then. "Resolved that the W.C.T.U. as the temperance organization of the town ask all ministers to preach temperance sermons on the evening of Jan. 27. Making special reference to the rum running which is such a disgrace to our town, Miss Chesley said that her feelings on this subject were even deeper than when she had promised to move the resolution for since then she had lived in the city of Philadelphia. She said that in the largest daily in Philadelphia there had been an article on the rum running which had made special mention of the Lunenburg vessels, formerly fishing vessels, but the men of Lunenburg had found there was more money in rum than fish. And so Lunenburg is becoming known in all the cities, being regarded as one of the worst plague spots. About four weeks ago there were 300 arrests for drunkenness in one night and doubtless hundreds of drunken men and boys got home without being arrested. Do the men and women of Lunenburg as they buy a new car or a fur coat with the profits from their rum shares, think of the mothers and wives made sad by the money that bought that coat and the little children, who went this Christmas cold and toyless because their fathers were enriching the men and women of Lunenburg?
>
> The speaker said her heart was sick as she heard of those whom she had respected and believed true Christians who had sold their soul for rum money.
>
> When the motion was seconded a large number of members spoke to it. One member spoke of what she termed "A conspiracy of silence" among all those whose voices should be heard.
>
> At the suggestion of one of the members who felt deeply because, like many of the women there, her own husband was

making money out of the business and refused to sell his shares it was moved and seconded by two other members and passed unanimously that the secretary send a copy of this discussion to the Lunenburg papers: "That the men may know how we feel."

Although Canada had fairly strict restrictions on the sale of alcohol, the United States' prohibition against the liquor trade, from 1920 to 1933, was even more constraining. Lunenburg was considered the prime centre of the illegal rum-running. For cash-strapped fishermen, the rum trade was more lucrative and, perhaps, more exciting too. While living in Lunenburg in the 1980s, I talked with my elderly neighbour whose deceased husband had been a captain of a fishing schooner that made trips to the West Indies, taking lumber and salt cod south and returning north with sugar and rum. During the era (which coincided with the Depression), rum-running provided good income. My neighbour showed me a photograph album with pictures taken from the stern of her husband's boat, capturing images of the US Coast Guard in pursuit, revealing the daring adventure that rum-running must have offered.

A gap existed between the men and women of the town on this issue. It must have been difficult to be a member of the WCTU and also know that your own family income was based on the rum trade.

Polly's talk to the WCTU on the temperance issue was to honour her mother's request that a resolution be put forward. All other talks Polly gave had to do with peace, disarmament, reconciliation, and relief of poverty in war-torn countries. In the next few months, Polly would campaign and fundraise for Relief of the Children in Germany, a cause that found both supporters and detractors. Her earlier campaigning for Russian aid had not aroused the same reactions. Because of the war, Germans were still seen as the enemy. For several issues of the Berwick and Truro papers, a debate ensued on the question of Germany's need for aid.

The coverage of Polly's fundraising lectures in the Berwick *Register* was likely due to the friendship and support of Eunice Buchanan and her husband, John. Eunice was an active member of the WCTU and also a pacifist. Eunice's family, originally from England, settled in

Nova Scotia in 1894. John, a Scotsman, came to Canada in 1900. The Buchanans were apple farmers in the Annapolis Valley, and Eunice also contributed articles to the *Canadian Horticulturist*. In 1921, when Polly was lecturing and fundraising for Russian famine relief, Eunice and John also campaigned, gathering funds that were then directed to the Friends' (Quaker) Committee for Russian Relief in London, England. In 1924, Eunice again campaigned to help children in Germany.

The first notice of the appeal for relief in Germany appeared in the February 20, 1924 issue of *The Register*. It outlined the serious conditions in Germany and listed well-known men and women of Britain who supported the fundraising. Organizations involved in the co-operative effort included the Society of Friends, Save the Children Fund, the Universities Relief Committee, Fellowship of Reconciliation, German Distress Relief Fund, and the British Council of the World Alliance for Promoting Friendship through the Churches. The Nova Scotia Committee for Relief of German Children had been formed with Justice Russell, Polly's uncle, as chair. Polly served as secretary and also travelled throughout Nova Scotia and New Brunswick presenting lantern-slide talks in churches and theatres. After nine months of fundraising, the campaign wrapped up in October. Throughout 1924, the *Register* carried regular reports by Eunice Buchanan as well as ongoing conflicting letters to newspapers regarding the issue of helping Germans.

On April 23, 1924, the *Register* published the following response from Polly to an earlier letter questioning Germany's need:

> Sir,
> Re: a letter in your issue of April 9, headed "Those 'Poor' Germans." The writer quotes from the London National Review that the tax on wealth in Britain, is $1,985,000,000, and in Germany $62,500,000. He argues from this that the German rich are being let off.
>
> I wish to point out that [the figures] may mean something totally different from what he infers. Jim Jones who lives in the little house down the street is not taxed nearly as much as John Davis who lives in the big house next door, and yet his taxes

weigh on him as heavily. The reason why the wealth of Germany is not taxed as much as the wealth of Britain may be simply that there is not as much wealth to tax. Also in England, with free trade, practically all taxes are direct, while in Germany, as in Canada, a great part of the taxes never appear on the tax collector's book but are paid in the form of customs duties that raise the price of all imported commodities.

Whether these explanations account for the difference in the figures or not, the fact remains that the "British Appeal for Relief in Germany," signed by Mr. Ramsay Macdonald, Mr. Asquith, Mr. Lloyd George and 55 other leaders in English life, states "Unemployment has been prevalent throughout the year in the Ruhr and Rhineland, and now to add to this sum of human misery has come a general industrial collapse. It has resulted in the closing down of factories with consequent unemployment all over Germany, and the workers as well as the middle classes are now faced with hopeless poverty. Strenuous efforts for relief have been made. Soup kitchens have been opened in all the towns. Private institutions and individuals are helping generously. But the need is too vast to be covered by a bankrupt government and the present help is inadequate.

The British organizations working in Germany have first-hand evidence of wholesale suffering and privation so intense that they feel bound to make the facts known.

For English political leaders to appeal for a people richer and more lightly taxed in proportion to their wealth than the people of Britain, as your correspondent suggests, would be to court a crushing defeat at the next election. No! They must be convinced of the need and of the inability of the German people to meet that need or they would never dare appeal to the people of Britain.

MARY CHESLEY
Sec. N.S. Branch of the Canadian Committee for Relief of the Children in Germany.

Eunice Buchanan, as treasurer of the fundraising campaign, regularly published a list of donors and their donations and contributed further facts and figures on the crisis. In the April 30, 1924 issue of *The Register*, she wrote:

> In Aachen, Germany, one-fourth of the school children are either already infected or threatened with tuberculosis. One-sixth of all the children in the Dresden elementary schools are reported ill as a result of hunger. Lady Bonham-Carter, daughter of the ex-Premier Asquith, confirms reports of starvation from personal knowledge recently acquired while travelling in Germany.
>
> The British appeal says that "The greatest help English people could have today would be the restoration of normal conditions in Europe, and normal conditions cannot be restored if the population of Germany sinks deeper in misery and despair." The Economist says, "Characteristic of conditions 30,257 horses, and 6,430 dogs were slaughtered for food during the third quarter of 1923."
>
> As for it being unpatriotic to plead for German children, Major-General Henry T. Allen is head of the American Committee for the Relief of German Children. When writing to General Allen the Archbishop of Philadelphia said, "You are doing a humane thing to raise funds in this country for the relief of children in Germany. It is praiseworthy that a soldier like you is leading in this charitable enterprise."
>
> EUNICE BUCHANAN, Treasurer.

A series of articles and letters also appeared in the *Truro Daily News*. It was apparent that the newspaper itself had little sympathy for the cause as witnessed in the following article from May 19, 1924:

> Speaking in Truro Church for Germany's "Starving" People
>
> Miss Mary Chesley, spoke in Pleasant Street Methodist Church in the morning and in the First Baptist Church in the evening on Sunday.

> She is spending some time and effort in Truro for funds in aid of "Starving Germans."
>
> Miss Chesley is a graduate of Mt. Allison University and Edinburgh University [sic], and for some time was associated with the Women Suffragists in England.
>
> The speaker on Sunday quoted the Prime Minister of England, Lloyd George, Mr. Asquith and a variety of prominent English politicians favorable to the scheme.
>
> She told stories of German children and babies suffering from hunger.
>
> On the other hand returned travelers in Germany tell of luxurious and extravagant living and signs of wealth on every side. Bankers and Financial men tell of Industry loosening and of Germany capturing markets in all parts of the world.
>
> The stories of suffering children in Germany told by Miss Chesley were along the line of revelations published by Montreal newspapers not long ago concerning "Starving Children" in that city.
>
> There is a great diversity of opinion as to whether or not Germany is in poverty or financial affluence. Reports differ.
>
> The good book says "Love your neighbours" and "Do good to them that hate you" etc. There is also a trite addage [sic] "Charity begins at home."
>
> Each one will have to use his or her judgment. There are doubtless many cases of need; but look around even in Canada for needy ones first, and make sane comparisons before being carried away with magnanimous sentiment.

Apparently the paper was in error about the Baptist Church address, for the following note appeared a couple of days later. The tone leaves no question as to the writer's feelings of antagonism toward the very idea of speaking on behalf of the cause: "In your issue it states Miss Chesley spoke for 'German Children' in First Baptist Church last night. I beg to state such was not the case; she did not speak at all and we don't desire her to do so; or to permit such an address."

Several other short articles and letters from someone who only signed off as "Citizen" were in the same vein. One J. D. MacKay wrote two letters in response to the letters from "Citizen" with information from various British and American sources that supported the idea that German poverty and starvation were real issues. Polly wrote the following letter in response to the original article published in the *Truro Daily News*:

> Editor The Register:
>
> May I be permitted a brief reply to an article in your issue of May 28, copied from the Truro News. This article suggests that Germany is a wealthy country, with enormous foreign investments, feigning poverty.
>
> The Experts' Reports should have proved the falsehood of such reports. No one would deny that there are very wealthy Germans, some of them selfish and unmindful of the sufferings of their countrymen. That Germany is a poor country is proved conclusively by the Dawes Report. This report reduces the yearly payment of $4,600,000,000 demanded in 1921 to $2,500,000,000. The Report states, moreover, that it will be four years before Germany will be able to make even these greatly reduced payments.
>
> We are reminded of the suffering among the children at home. We would not seek to blind anyone to its existence, but we are thankful that it does not exist on the scale prevailing in Germany. In none of our schools would every fourth child be found to have spinal curvature as was found in one of the Dresden schools. In none of our provinces is every sixth child tubercular, or threatened with tuberculosis, from undernourishment as in Saxony. In no province have 4,600 children fainted in schools, from hunger in one month as was the case in Silesia.
>
> Let us not neglect the children who are suffering at home, but let us not make these children an excuse for hardening our hearts to the sufferings of those across the sea.
>
> MARY CHESLEY

While we do not know all of Polly's activities from the fall of 1924 until November of 1925 when she set sail with her father for England, it would appear that she was busy giving lectures on the issue of peace and raising aid for children in Europe. Polly found time, though, for recreation and renewing friendship. On September 15, 1924, the following article appeared in the *Halifax Herald* under the heading, "Ladies on Hiking Tour of Province": "Miss Mary Chesley of Lunenburg and Miss Bessie Hall of Bridgewater paid a visit to Chester on Sunday, while on a walking tour; they intend to visit several counties and a number of towns. Miss Chesley and Miss Hall arrived in Chester from Lunenburg making the first lap of their journey by boat and left by the Post Road for Kentville via Chester Basin and New Ross. Both hikers are experienced, having toured several different countries in this way."

In conversations with two older women whose mothers had been friends with Polly, I gained further glimpses of Polly from about this period. Elizabeth Hebb's mother, Marion (Holder) Hebb, had been a schoolmate of Polly's. Like the Chesleys, the Hebb family had a cottage at Princes Inlet. It was not uncommon for families in Lunenburg to move to their cottages for the summer, and according to Elizabeth, her mother, Marion, and her sister spent holiday time with Polly. Elizabeth had a childhood memory of Polly standing on the steps of the cottage with a faraway look in her "vivid blue eyes" and saying something deep, something that made Elizabeth ponder. Polly wore a middy blouse. This "uniform" is evident in a number of photographs of Polly. Always economically minded, Polly could never be accused of extravagant spending or fashion consciousness! Elizabeth Hebb also remembered that Dickens had made a strong impression on Polly and had a part in inspiring her social ideas. [81]

The other person who had particularly vivid memories of Polly was Natalie Corkum (1915–2017), the daughter of Lena Bachman, Polly's closest friend in Lunenburg. As previously mentioned, the Bachmans and Chesleys shared a cottage at Princes Inlet. Natalie's memories included the senior Chesleys. Two of her recollections stood out for me: the image of Samuel walking from downtown Lunenburg to the summer cottage after work, holding a velvet bag that held his swimming trunks; and that the Chesleys dubbed the outhouse "The Parliament Building," an indication of their sense of humour and their preoccupation with the body politic. As Corkum said, "That way you [could] give the Government the devil!" [82]

Natalie remembered when she was having difficulty with math and Polly tutored her. They would take the rowboat and go to Bachmans Island to study. Natalie also talked of walks she and Polly would take to Blue Rocks, a community seven kilometres from Lunenburg. Apparently Polly was knowledgeable about the flora along the way. On night walks, Polly would point out the constellations. One interesting memory Natalie held was of Polly sitting under a tree studying Esperanto. This became particularly relevant when I discovered references to Esperanto in the Women's International League for Peace and Freedom (WILPF) records. Not surprisingly, for those promoting peace and international understanding, the idea of having a universal

Alma Russell (Aunt Am), Samuel, Mary, and Polly Chesley at camp, Princes Inlet, 1922. [PHOTO TAKEN BY FRIEND EUNICE BUCHANAN, COURTESY AUDREY CHESLEY OLDERSHAW]

language that ignored country boundaries, a language of "hope," appealed greatly. Polly, as apparent by her studies in France, was someone who valued the learning of other languages, as is further corroborated by this anecdote.

Polly Chesley, c.1920s.
[NATALIE CORKUM, LUNENBURG]

Another of Natalie Corkum's memories of Polly involved a time when Polly and Natalie's mother, Lena, walked back from downtown Lunenburg. Polly had a nail sticking up through her shoe, and her friend was scandalized by Polly's removal of her shoes and her walking barefoot the rest of the way home, something a "lady" would never do. Ever the practical one, Polly could not abide suffering for the sake of propriety. Polly had little concern for convention, not necessarily out of a need to rebel so much as it was an extension of her sensible nature. In the same way, her practicality and lack of concern for fashion suggests that Polly was not trying to impress anyone but was merely maintaining comfort and limiting expenses to necessities such as keeping the body clothed.

In what would be the last year that she lived in Canada, Polly stepped into her mother's role as interim Dominion Superintendent of Peace and Arbitration of the WCTU. Her admiration for her mother is reflected in her words and deeds. The mother and daughter held common concerns, and Polly did her best to honour and carry out the work initiated by Mary. In 1925, she gave the following report to the national body:

I am glad to report that the number of provincial unions in which the Peace Department is regularly organized, with a Superintendent, has increased from two to four, the old ones being Saskatchewan and Nova Scotia, the new ones British Columbia and Montreal Northern District. Quebec has also a Peace and Arbitration Department under its sub-executive. I have also just received a sympathetic letter from the president of the New Brunswick and P.E.I. Union, and I hope that this year will see the formation of the department in all the remaining provinces. Let us redouble our efforts, for the forces of militarism were never stronger. After thousands of our boys have made the sacrifice to crush militarism it not only still survives but flourishes in our own fair land as never before. At the time of the St. John Convention in 1909 when the Dominion W.C.T.U. passed its first resolution against military training in our schools there were about 10,000 cadets. Today there are well over 100,000. I hope we will not only reaffirm our opposition to this system but that during the coming two years one of our main efforts will be directed against this growing effort to instill the military spirit into our boys.

Although there has been no Peace Department in New Brunswick, the President of the Fredericton Union and several of the members helped me by standing at the doors of their theatres and taking an offering for the suffering children in Germany. This public work for the children of a former enemy showed that the women in Fredericton have that spirit of love, which is the surest promise of peace. One mother, who gave her little boy to help with the collecting, had had her other three sons killed in the war. She felt that they had given their lives to end war, and that the spirit of hate breeds war.

Over a year ago my mother received a letter telling her that the unions [in B.C.] had joined with the Parent Teachers' Association, University Women's Club, and others in protesting against war pictures presented to the schools by the Imperial Daughters of the Empire calculated to glorify war in the minds of the children and nourish the spirit of hate. My mother was asked by the W.C.T.U. of British Columbia to write to the National Regent and did so. Owing to my absence from home and my mother's poor health at that time, I do not know what action was taken.

The most interesting report is that of the New Glasgow Union where a committee conferred with the principal of the schools and had his promise that the teachers be asked to instruct the pupils on the cost of war with copies of this poster. I hope that many more unions will follow this plan. At a Peace lecture which I delivered in Halifax, I showed this poster, and the wife of the provincial leader of our Conservative party was so impressed by it that she offered to place one in every schoolroom of the city.

In closing, may I pay a word of tribute to my mother. She realized, as so few of us seem to that the next war, for which we are still heading will be "a concentration of bombs and poison upon the great centers of population." Let us in memory of her, in memory too of those many millions who died "to end war," awaken from our slumber and make this "next war," of which our militarists speak so glibly, impossible.

Prior to Polly's 1925 report and following Mary senior's death, Lulu DeBlois Porter, a WCTU member from Kentville in the Annapolis Valley, stepped in to become the Provincial Superintendent of Peace and Arbitration. Her 1924 annual report shows what individual unions in the province were doing to promote peace. The report submitted to her by the Roberts union (in Halifax) made reference to Polly's work: "Last September Miss Chesley of Lunenburg was in the city and the Superintendent made arrangements for her to speak in three schools on the cost of War and how we might better use our money." And from the report of the Lunenburg union: "The Superintendent co-operated with Miss Chesley in her work as Acting Superintendent for the Dominion W.C.T.U. Letters were written, literature distributed and financial aid rendered for the relief of starving German children."

The following year, Porter's report included further references to Polly's work:

At the request of Miss Chesley, acting Superintendent of the Department in the Canadian National W.C.T.U., I sent out letters asking that a resolution be adopted and sent to Government members asking that Cadet training in our schools and Officers' Training Corps be abolished. A similar resolution was to be sent to the Superintendent of Education.

Lunenburg endorsed copies of the resolution re military drill in schools and colleges. Prof. Mercer gave two lectures under the auspice of this department. Miss Chesley addressed a meeting.

United Victory. Resolutions re Cadet training endorsed after lively discussion. Miss Chesley at a special meeting answered questions concerning these resolutions. An amendment recommended the Department of Education eliminate from our school readers war stories, and substitute stories of inventors, explorers, reformers, nurses and others who have given their lives for the service of mankind.

Professor Charles H. Mercer taught in the Modern Languages Department of Dalhousie University, and his papers, housed in the Dalhousie Archives, indicate that he was involved with a number of progressive organizations. In the mid-1930s, he was the local liaison for the League of Nations Society in Canada. In response to communication with the National Secretary, dated October 20, 1934, he shared a similar concern to the Chesleys with regard to glorification of war. He wrote, "I agree, between

Polly Chesley, c.1920s.
[NATALIE CORKUM, LUNENBURG]

ourselves, about the I.O.D.E.: we tackled them last year on some of their war pictures and nearly caught a Tartar, but here I think there is a good deal of variation of opinion and some I.O.D.E. groups can be induced to abandon, to some degree, the more extreme forms of imperialism with which they are associated."[83]

In October of 1924, less than a year after her mother's death, Polly's beloved Aunt Am died. According to the obituary in the Halifax paper, Alma Russell, older sister to Mary, had been in failing health for about nine months.

Now, with both his wife and sister-in-law gone and a daughter who had a tendency to move around, Samuel was potentially facing a solitary life in Lunenburg. He chose to join his daughter on her next journey. Leaving Halifax on the SS *Orbita*, Samuel and Polly arrived in England on November 10, 1925. In the weeks previous, the *Progress Enterprise* carried a couple of notes regarding the imminent departure. Samuel's IOOF Lodge presented him "with a well-worded address expressing their appreciation of his services to the organization" and a gift of a ten-dollar gold coin. The group expressed "their regrets at his removal from our home town, and their best wishes for his happiness in the mother country." Further to that, the following: "S. A. Chesley, K.C. and Miss Mary Chesley sailed from Halifax on Monday for England where they will make their home."

What little is known of Polly during the next year comes from the annual WCTU Peace and Arbitration report written by Polly's friend, Eunice Buchanan. In 1926, Eunice took on the role of superintendent for this department, on the national, provincial, county, and local union levels. Of note is the following: "Perhaps it will interest many of you to know that my predecessor in the Canadian National W.C.T.U., Miss Chesley, is devoting much of her time to peace work in England, speaking before audiences in Hyde Park, or on other London platforms once a week. When she wrote last she and Judge Chesley were attending the Sixth International Democratic Peace Conference a few miles outside of Paris. Mr. Chesley is writing an article on this Peace Conference for *The New Outlook*."

In 1925, when Methodists, Congregationalists, and some Presbyterians came together to form the United Church of Canada, the older Methodist newspaper, *The Wesleyan*, ceased to exist. *The New Outlook* took its place, and Samuel's article on the peace conference appeared in the September 29, 1926 issue of the journal. The conference, the sixth organized by Marc Sangnier, a liberal French Catholic pacifist thinker and politician, brought together many youth, mostly from European countries, with a smattering of students from across the world. Samuel's enthusiasm is apparent. Held on a beautiful estate, with inexpensive food and accommodations, a swimming pool, and plenty of concerts, folk dancing, and theatre performances on peace subjects, the idyllic setting and positivism undoubtedly inspired hope in a future without war.

When I imagine Polly at Speakers' Corner in Hyde Park, I see her as part of a continuum of passionate campaigners for innumerable causes. The Wikipedia entry for Speakers' Corner lists some of the well-known people who spoke there over the years, but no woman makes their list, even though the well-known Christian pacifist Muriel Lester, the famous Pankhurst suffragettes, and numerous other politically active women have played their part in the history

Polly Chesley, taken in Berwick, Nova Scotia, in 1928 on a visit with her good friend Eunice Buchanan. [AUDREY CHESLEY OLDERSHAW]

of free speech at this illustrious location in London. While it seems likely that Polly would have met Muriel Lester at some point through their various joint interests, I have no evidence of this. They both had involvement with the Friends of India Society, and both were friends with Gandhi. And Polly received a letter from Sylvia Pankhurst when she was living in Paris (Pankhurst, too, was connected to the Friends of India). While Polly would never be a famous figure (except briefly at the time of her death), she shared much with and travelled alongside the leading radicals in Britain.

The next clue as to Polly's activities comes from a Change of Address notice in *The Friend*, the British Quaker journal, on December 24, 1926: "At the end of January Olive Warner and Miss Chesley hope to be established in their new schoolhouse, St. Margaret's, Quaker Lane, and the pupils of the school now known as St. Michael's will be housed there as soon as circumstances permit." The school was in a small town just north of London called Potters Bar.

Based on scant records, Polly and Olive, about whom more will be said later, began their school in January of 1927. On July 30, 1927, Polly travelled back to Nova Scotia with her father for a visit, then returned to Britain in September to begin another school year. Samuel did not go with her this time.

Where Samuel spent the following year and a half is only partially known. He maintained contact with the extended Chesley family in Annapolis County. An October 12, 1927 notice in the Bridgetown *Weekly Monitor* reported: "Judge Chesley, of Lunenburg, who just returned from England, accompanied by Miss Lucy Chesley, of Upper Granville, were visitors on Thursday at the home of Mr. and Mrs. B. F. Chesley." And in the *Bridgetown Spectator* of October 27, 1927, is the following item: "Upper Granville: Judge S.A. Chesley, of Lunenburg who since his return with his daughter Mary from England in July has been renewing old friendships in his loved Nova Scotia, recently spent a few days here visiting his cousins the Misses Chesley and Mrs. John McCormick."[84]

Samuel is found on the passenger list of the *Canadian Fisher*, a boat that travelled from Bermuda, arriving in Halifax on March 14, 1928. Presumably, he spent the winter in Bermuda. The address given on the passenger list was that of a friend, Mr. D. Smith, of Lunenburg. The following year, on March 7, 1929, Samuel arrived back in Britain on the *Scandia*, and his address was again with Polly in Potters Bar.

In the meantime, along with her teaching in Britain, Polly continued to engage in political campaigning and the promotion of peace and disarmament. An article appeared in the *Norwood News* on July 27, 1928, regarding Polly giving a talk: "Women and War: the Only Way to Ensure Peace" for the No More War Movement.[85] In October 1928, Polly attended the National Labour Party conference in Birmingham as the representative from St. Albans district. When she was studying in England over a decade earlier, she had become a member of a number of political groups, including the Independent Labour Party, the pacifist wing of the Labour Party.

Numerous newspapers reported on Polly's proposal for total disarmament, some more sympathetic than others. The reporter for an October 6, 1928, article from *The Times* painted Polly as a nuisance to the conference and to Ramsay MacDonald, the MP who would lead the Labour Party to victory in 1929. In reporting that "The Labour Party Conference was concluded in the Town Hall, Birmingham today," the writer said, "The last subject of the conference was disarmament. Miss Mary Chesley (St. Albans) [said that] nothing but total disarmament would give safety, and she asked that a Labour Government should call a conference of the nations to consider plans for achieving that end."

Debate ensued and "Mr. MacDonald was subjected to considerable interruption, particularly by the St. Albans woman delegate, and at last he appealed to her and others to follow the argument. Disarmament by example he regarded as impossible. It would do no good and would only increase difficulties. If they started a policy of disarmament by themselves, it would take years to carry out, and on account of the policy of disarmament they might have a change of government and corresponding reaction.

"Miss Chesley's motion was negatived by a majority."

Polly's speech was recorded in the report of the Labour Party on its 28th annual conference: "Miss Mary Chesley (St. Albans D.L.P.) said she rose to support the last woman speaker; in other words, she wanted to tell the Conference that she stood for the united organized motherhood of the Labour Movement; because the women at the Conference at Portsmouth asked that the Labour Party should pledge itself to complete Disarmament."

After hearing from various delegates, the chair of the conference made some remarks, which were followed by Polly's response:

> All that we are asking is that we shall have a definite pledge and we believe we are entitled to a definite pledge—that the labour government within a year of coming into power will call a conference of Governments through the League of Nations, or otherwise, to prepare plans for Complete Universal disarmament to be accomplished, let us say, in a term of four years, so that it can be accomplished in the life of one Labour Government and not be upset when a Conservative Government may again come into office. I am asking this on behalf of the 300,000 organised women of the Labour Party, who by 640 votes out of 650 delegates at Portsmouth, voted in favour of the Party giving this pledge. The mothers ask this because they are sick of limitations. They realize that limitation is bound to fail, because it depends upon measuring armament against armament, and the last word is always with the military expert. And because the decision rests with military and naval experts, it is bound to fail. Even if it could succeed, even if the Labour Party were successful in getting the armaments reduced by one half, what good would it do? We are told that less than 30 aeroplanes could wipe out the eight million people of London. If armaments were reduced by one-half, France and ourselves would each have over 400 aeroplanes, enough to wipe out all the great cities. Nothing but Total Disarmament will give us safety. Under Capitalism war is inevitable. The only way in which we can defend ourselves under the capitalist system is by removing from the capitalist the means of making war. I want to quote the words of our Chairman [George Lansbury], written only a few weeks ago. He said: "Shout from the housetop, 'No more war.' Mobilise public opinion so that when Labour comes to office and power all this

awful business of preparing for peace by building up more and more armaments shall stop. Do not be misled about partial disarmament." If our Party on going out of office leaves one-eighth of the armed forces that there are in the world it will have signed the death warrant of our civilization. If any feeble heart thinks that this pledge will lose us the Election, let me say what more glorious appeal can be put to the millions of young mothers who will vote at this Election than that we are out to rid the world of war and save the children.

As the *Birmingham Mail* wrote on October 5: "Much earnestness was imparted to the discussion on disarmament. Miss Chester [sic], St Albans, in appealing a declaration that Labour, within a year of being in power would call for an international conference to encompass total disarmament in four years, made the most emotional speech of the whole conference."

There is no question of Polly's earnestness and passion regarding the subject of war and peace. Ever the idealist, she looked for the best in people and fervently hoped that "her" party would make the courageous move to lead the world powers in the direction of total disarmament. Even though Ramsay MacDonald was a pacifist during the First World War (and either vilified or admired because of that position), he was not entirely ready to take the initiative on this proposal and was, perhaps, more realistic than Polly in recognizing that there would be too much opposition to total disarmament, particularly from the military and the armament industries. So too, the mere threat of job losses would scare many civilian workers (and their families) from supporting such a position.[86] What is patently clear is that Polly viewed capitalism as a largely destructive force.

Although her impassioned plea for the Labour Party to commit to a policy of total disarmament failed to gain traction in 1928, Mary Albee Chesley was at the Labour Party conference the following year, reiterating the same points. By this time, the party was in power. Here is part of her speech: "Let our Government appeal, over the heads of the military experts, to the workers of other countries, to the fathers and mothers. We believe that if they make that appeal to save the children of the world—we believe that the fathers and mothers will force their Governments to join us. The resolution asks our Government to urge a policy of complete disarmament. We have the support of two of the biggest Trade Unions in our country and also of several other Trade Unions, so that their vote alone would carry the resolution."[87]

Polly was not a lone voice in the wilderness—there were many others within the Labour Party who supported disarmament. However, there were the idealists on one hand and the pragmatists on the other. Arthur Henderson, appointed by Prime Minister MacDonald as Foreign Secretary in the Labour government, would eventually be awarded the Nobel Peace Prize in 1934 for his efforts at peacemaking, but in 1929, his response to Polly was one of pragmatism:

> I think that no exception can be taken to either the questions or the discussion that has ensued, and I am much in agreement with most of it. The last speaker [Polly] made a very earnest appeal. She used the phrase, as other speakers have, "complete disarmament"—total disarmament within the lifetime of the present Parliament. Well, we are deceiving ourselves by expounding such ideas. I am sure that there is no member of this Conference who would ever seek to persuade the public that it was within the power of his or her Government to carry such a policy into operation. Now we are tackling this problem seriously. We have tried in a few short months to give you an earnest [idea] of our determination. We will not attempt that which is practically impossible. I only wish that she and other speakers would tell the Conference what they mean by total disarmament. What we really must try to get down to is a reasonable standard of policing forces. The world will have to be more advanced and human nature more perfect before you will be able to do without policing forces. That you must have progressive disarmament down to a reasonable standard of policing is most important. It is a policy that we will do our best to put into operation during the coming year, and I hope we shall have something to say to you next year.[88]

From a principled perspective, the absolutism of total disarmament resonates with pacifists: wars beget wars, and if every nation would put down their arms, it would be a different world. But, as Henderson pointed out, humans have not achieved perfection, so it would seem that some form of law and order is necessary.

Polly Chesley's investment in the causes she espoused is clear. With her impassioned speeches made on behalf of famine victims in Russia and Germany, at Speakers' Corner in Hyde Park, and at Labour conferences on peace and disarmament, Polly chose to be a spokesperson for the protection of future generations. As a teacher and an activist, Polly kept the welfare of children at the forefront. Childless herself, she nevertheless cared passionately for children's rights to proper food, shelter, safety, and well-being.

For the last year of the 1920s, Samuel lived again with Polly in Britain. At the turn of the 1930s, father and daughter would make their final trip together.

CHAPTER 7
A Canadian Activist in England

ON JULY 19, 1930, POLLY AND SAMUEL CHESLEY SAILED FROM Southampton, England, to Nova Scotia. Unexpectedly, Samuel died on board ship. His obituary, written by his long-time friend and brother-in-law, appeared in the *Progress Enterprise* on July 30.

> Judge Chesley, Former Lunenburg Citizen Dies Suddenly At Sea
>
> By Hon. B. Russell
>
> It will have come as a shock and regret to all his friends to learn that Samuel Chesley died on board ship when crossing from England to Canada with his daughter on the Pennland. He had his eightieth birthday shortly before sending his last letter, dated June 21, in which he expressed hope that he would see all his friends towards the end of July. After being on board a few days, and seemingly enjoying perfect health, he had a pleasant conversation with the purser of the ship and went to his cabin where he fell asleep, never to wake.
>
> He had been living with Miss Chesley, where, with her partners, she conducts a successful school. He enjoyed life perfectly until the end.
>
> Judge Chesley was the son of a Methodist minister and he was an effective member of that communion. He was one of four

at Mount Allison University. Of the four members, Mr. Justice Wheelock Burbidge of the Exchequer Court of Canada was the first to pass away. The late Dr. Weldon, Dean of the Faculty of Law at Dalhousie, was the second; Judge Chesley is the third, leaving this writer the only survivor.

Chesley was an excellent student. After teaching at St. John's, Newfoundland, he returned to Nova Scotia to study law in the office of the late Judge Savary. He entered the office of the late Mr. Justice James. After his admission to the Bar he became a member of the firm of Russell, Chesley and Geldert, better known as reporters and journalists than legal practitioners. They were for years, the joint editors of the Halifax Citizen, established and owned in the first instance, by McDonald and Garvie.

Mr. Chesley's articles were always well written. His work displayed wide knowledge and great literary ability. Mr. Chesley then went to Lunenburg, where he had hardly acquired a law practice before he was appointed Judge of Probate.

Judge Chesley became a life member of the Methodist conference and the conference of the United Church of Canada. His wife a sister of the writer was a well-known advocate of "Women's Rights" and he became a convert to her views so that where one of the leaders of the Conference opposed the appointment of deaconesses in the church and sneered at it as merely one of the ambitions of the "New Woman" movement, Judge Chesley calmly replied that whatever the "new woman" might have in the movement it had certainly encountered a violent enemy in one of the "Old Women" of the Conference.

Samuel was buried at sea. A conversation with Natalie Corkum revealed that her mother, Lena Bachman, Polly's closest friend in Lunenburg, was upset by Polly's decision not to bring Samuel's remains to Lunenburg for burial with his wife and children. Natalie believed that Polly's decision was based on practical considerations, which would have been true to character. Polly would not have seen any point in spending money unnecessarily. The cost to bring home her father's body for burial undoubtedly seemed like a poor use of funds that could better be used for the living. Traditionally, ordinary seamen were buried at sea, and I had assumed that would be the case for anyone who died at sea, but I have yet to discover much information on the protocols around sea burials, particularly for civilians. Preserving a body at sea would have been costly. Ice might have been at a premium. According to one account, in order to return Lord Nelson for burial on land, the Admiral had been preserved in a barrel of brandy. Such a solution certainly would not have suited a temperance family like the Chesleys!

Shortly after Samuel's death, the *Evening Mail* of August 14, 1930, reported that Samuel had planned to move back to Nova Scotia on a permanent basis. It is, perhaps, fortunate for him that his death came peacefully in the midst of seeming robust health (a reference in the *Bridgetown Monitor* of September 5, 1928, when he was visiting cousins, described Samuel as being in "splendid health"). He likely enjoyed being with his daughter in England, but his friendships, extended family, church, and community involvements were all in Canada. He was spared not only the hardships of diminishing health, but also being torn between being near Polly or among his other family and lifelong friends in Nova Scotia.

While the Chesleys may not have been wealthy, they were financially comfortable. Samuel was generous in his support of the church, and Polly's academic life and travels must have been supported by family money. According to the records of probate, Samuel left a relatively small estate of less than $1,000, so he must have given over most of his estate to Polly while he was still alive. Undoubtedly, Samuel helped Polly in the purchase of the house/school in Potters Bar. As will be evident from Polly's activities and concerns for the duration of her lifetime, money meant little to her personally and was something she felt compelled to share.

By September, Polly had wrapped up her affairs in Nova Scotia and sailed back to England, likely to resume her teaching. Her teaching partner, Olive Warner, left for South Africa that same year (of which, more later) and sometime after that, Martha (Pat) Blyth joined Polly in the running of the school.

Having spent some of her formative educational years at the London School of Economics and Oxford, Polly likely thrived in the rigorous intellectual milieu of the city. London was exciting in its diversity, and the political and social contacts she made there would have been more invigorating than any she could have experienced in Nova Scotia or even elsewhere in Canada at this time. Her friendships with international students, both in Britain and France, helped to broaden her outlook. For the next few years, Polly engaged in political, social, and economic involvements that had an impact on her future life choices.

What little is known of Polly's years living and working in Britain comes from her obituary and also a chance discovery of a newspaper article written by her in 1932. After years of attending Quaker meetings, she formally became a member of the Welwyn Garden City Preparative Meeting in 1931. Very few records from this meeting exist. The Hertfordshire Archives holds a small notebook containing minutes of the overseers of the meeting. In the minutes of February 1, 1932, the following brief mention is made: "Overseers are asked to bear in mind Mary Chesley of Potters Bar and to invite her to a meal on Sunday sometimes, when she is able to come over to Meeting."[89] The distance from Potters Bar to Welwyn Garden City is approximately ten miles, and Polly likely would have taken a train to get there, so perhaps she did not attend on a regular basis.

Polly's impassioned speeches in various arenas did not go unnoticed. Her interest in India came under the scrutiny of the India Office Records (IOR). An intelligence arm of the Public and Judicial Department, concerned with what the British Government considered subversive elements, the IOR kept track of individuals and organizations supporting Indian independence. The Friends of India was one such organization, founded by Reginald Reynolds in August 1930 after he had spent time in India. Reynolds, a British Quaker, became a staunch supporter of Gandhi's movement. According to a couple of IOR intelligence reports, Polly was a member of the Friends of India. An "Extract from New Scotland Yard Report dated 4 March 1931" contained the following: "A meeting was held at the Bull Ring Birmingham on Sunday, 22nd February under the auspices of the

'Freedom of India.' Each speaker spoke from a caravan—the Meeting was opened by the Reverend Will Hayes, who acted as Chairman. Others who spoke were Miss Chesley and B. P. Sinaha [sic]. Their remarks were of stereotyped character. About 250 persons were present."

And another entry, dated November 11, 1931: "The Indian Caravan came into being to distribute the literature of the Friends of India Society and to prosecute a more vigorous and direct propaganda throughout the country. It used 11 High St., Hampstead, the address of Miss Payne [Richenda Payne, Quaker and fiancée of Reginald Reynolds] and Miss [Bertha] Bracey as a base. A tour of some four weeks' duration was completed in February and March, 1931, some 34 meetings being held in 18 towns. The speakers included Atma Kamlani, Miss Mary Chesley and the Rev. Will Hayes."[90]

This entry in the IOR provides concrete evidence of Polly's interest in India's struggle in the years prior to her moving there. Polly was travelling in illustrious company. Laurence Housman, Bertrand Russell, and Sylvia Pankhurst were but a few of the more famous Britons who supported the Friends of India. Between her involvement in the Labour Party, The Neighbours, the Oxford Group, Quakers, and Friends of India, Polly was deeply immersed in radical social, political, and religious organizations and undoubtedly knew many of the leading leftists of the era. Among them there were common causes. For example, Bertha Bracey, one of the Friends of India executive members, started out as a teacher but in 1921 went to Vienna where she served in Quaker relief and reconstruction work. Throughout the 1920s she worked in several German cities with needy families and established clubs for young people. During some of this time, Polly was busy fundraising for German relief throughout the Maritimes. Bracey would later be instrumental in getting Jewish children safely out of Germany, but in the early 1930s, Polly's path and her own must have crossed through sympathy with the plight of India in its struggle against imperialism. According to a website for a Unitarian church where Reverend Will Hayes served, he was "a visionary who promoted inter-faith co-operation [and] became the leader of the Free Religious Movement which sought to create 'a Brotherhood of Nations through the Sisterhood of Religions.'

Rev. Will Hayes also founded the Order of the Great Companions, to encourage the emergence of an eclectic and universal world religion."[91] Through all my research on this period, I found a remarkable number of interconnections between human rights activists across continents, cross-pollinating ideas and strategies.

Based on the account in Polly's obituary, it seems that she gave over the running of the school to Pat Blyth sometime prior to setting off for India in 1934. Perhaps she did not resume teaching when she returned to Britain from her last trip to Canada or only resumed teaching briefly. It is likely that when she was travelling with the Friends of India caravan she was not teaching. The caravan was not her only enterprise at this time. According to the obituary, "She gave up the school work two or three years ago to spread the practice of Christian economics, nationally and internationally. She was a member of Professor Bellerby's group, The Neighbours, who restrict their personal spending to £150 a year—the average wage of the country."

John (Jack) Rotherford Bellerby, an economics professor, wrote a number of books on economic matters, but I would have known little of his group The Neighbours were it not for stumbling across *The Memoirs of Earl of Listowel* on the Internet (I am no longer able to access it online; however, the memoir has now been published).[92] During his student days, William Francis Hare, Earl of Listowel (1906–1997), was a member of the group. His vivid description of Bellerby and his aims and Hare's own experience help to flesh out a picture. Hare, coming from aristocracy but with a left-leaning idealism that shocked and dismayed his family, had this to say:

> What might have made matters even worse than my escapades at Balliol, was that I fell into the clutches of someone even more dangerous than the Master, a Christian socialist who was the nearest approach to a socialist saint that I ever met. His name was Jack Bellerby, a Fellow of Caius College. He was engaged in organizing what he called a "contributive society" in place of the acquisitive society in which we live—a new kind of Friendly Society called "The Neighbours." This Society was registered

under The Industrial and Provident Societies Act, and the first Articles of the Rules read:"The Society should be called Neighbours Limited, and its object should be to collect, provide and administer funds for the promotion of art, science, social welfare, and fellowship."

Every member was obliged to hold at least one share of one penny, but for each share he must donate £100 to the Society. The donation of members would be invested, and the income used for the above purposes. There was one benefit, and one benefit only, which the members themselves would derive; being a safety net for those who gave away all of their property. If their income were less than the national average wage earned at that time, it would be made up to 3 pounds a week for a single person and 4 pounds per week for a married couple, with 10 shillings extra for every child. Though the aim of every member of the Society was to live on no more than the average wage, the only qualification was a commitment to reduce personal consumption in order to release surplus income and capital for the purposes of the Society. There was no obligation not to exceed the average wage, and I am afraid this feat of self-denial was always beyond me. But I hovered for a time close to the edge, and this was enough to cause intense worry to my parents.

The founding of this Society and my connection with it did not escape the attention of the press. I was interviewed by the Daily Sketch, and the result was an article headed "Peer's Son to Give Up Fortune" and beginning with the following sentence: "An Extraordinary Friendly Society has been formed to enable wealthy men and women to give away their money for social purposes and live on a mere pittance allowed by the Society."

My fortune consisted of an allowance from my father to cover food, clothing and tuition fees, and a capital sum of £2,000 given me by my grandfather when I was 21. I had told Jack Bellerby that I might be willing to hand over my capital, but before accepting he thought he should discuss it with my mother. He told me, after having a cup of tea with her at our London home, that it would evidently cause distress to her and my grandfather if I parted with my money, and advised me to keep it for the time being. As my father had now banished me from the family home, I had nowhere to go during the university vacations. So my mother had come to my rescue by taking a bedsitter for me until accommodation with my father made it possible for me to return home. The basis of this accommodation was that I reverted from Mr. W. Hare to Viscount Ennismore.

But to go back to my friend Jack Bellerby and the Neighbours Limited. I do not believe that it ever attracted many supporters, and those who joined it were worthy rather than wealthy. I am sure that Jack Bellerby did not expect it to transform society, but rather to offer a unique opportunity for those who believe that the accumulation and inheritance of private property and the manner of its acquisition are obstacles to the good life. This belief has inspired secular socialists and many devout people throughout history. But, whereas the utopian socialists and monastic orders organized their new societies outside the community, The Neighbours was a new society within the existing community. You could therefore be a "Neighbour" and remain a husband, a professional man, a good citizen standing as an active participant in local or national politics, but you became a better person by using income or capital for the common good. This was the essential originality and ingenuity of Jack Bellerby's conception. He certainly deserves a niche in the history of British socialism in the 20th century.

While I have not been able to discover a paper trail on the Friendly Society that Bellerby initiated, his book outlining his socio-economic theories, *A Contributive Society*, first published in 1931 by Education Services, was considered worthy of reprinting in 1988 with additional essays and appendices, which argued that Bellerby's ideas were remarkably original, accessible, and still have relevance. One of the contributors, a colleague of Bellerby's, described him as "a very nice, rather saintly person." It is uncertain when The Neighbours ceased to function, although according to J. O. Jones, one of the contributors to the 1988 edition of Bellerby's book, "At least two threads of continuity can be traced. Much of the accumulated surplus income of The Neighbours was invested in a charitable trust and association known as Education Services. Jack Bellerby was a most active member of the Association until his death in 1977, and continuity has been maintained by a succession of new members. Over the years Education Services has been able to assist and collaborate with a wide number of students, authors, and projects. Often help has been provided at highly critical stages in careers and project development"[93]

In his introductory essay to Bellerby's book, Jones quotes from a pamphlet that Bellerby's wife, Frances, wrote about the society. M. E. Frances (Parker) Bellerby was a poet and part of the group; she and Bellerby married in 1929, and although their marriage did not survive a number of later tragedies, one can read enthusiasm, joy, and humour in her description of The Neighbours' aims:

> The Neighbours, consists of a small group desirous of expressing concretely a variety of emotional drives ("religions" if you like) and agreed that as good a way of doing this as any other is to be as contributive as possible and that you cannot contribute what you have spent on yourself. Another advantage of being one of a group (is) the unfailing comfort that if you are on a wild-goose chase you are in good company. If it turns out to be something more valuable, there will be others with you to share the excitement. The group belief of The Neighbours is in the creative power of Beauty, Truth and Love; which belief leads to desire for expression in works.[94]

An appendix of the reprint provides a list of publications and charitable groups that had been assisted through the years 1974 to 1988. It speaks to the generosity of the members of The Neighbours, whose contributions provided for so many good works well into the future. It also speaks to the good stewardship of the fund that was amassed in the 1920s and 1930s. Perhaps donations continued to Education Services, even after The Neighbours no longer existed.[95]

The *Times* obituary for Bellerby, published April 5, 1977, mentioned that he was, at one time, a Quaker but that he then became involved with the Oxford Group. This group would, perhaps, not be relevant to this story if it were not for the fact that Polly, too, became engaged with this group to the extent that when she rewrote her will before leaving for India in 1934, she specified that part of her estate was to go to the Oxford Group (Polly changed her will a number of times over the years).[96] This part of Polly's story is obscured by lack of information on her last years in Britain. It is apparent, though, from the writings of others on the subject of the Oxford Group and its founder, American Frank Buchman, that that this charismatic leader managed to draw in many Christians, among whom were distinguished clergy and scholars of the time.

I did not begin to tease out Polly's story and consider the significance of the trajectory of her life until I received her death notice from the Friends Library and Archives in London with the mention of her association with Gandhi. Readers will remember that my initial aim in hunting down information on Polly was to find out more about her mother. The discovery that Polly died in India precipitated a whole new avenue of inquiry (or I should say new avenues, for my dissertation encompassed a larger group of women I found along the way).

When I was at the very beginning of this project, the Internet was new and yielded almost nothing useful for my research. As newspapers and other documents become digitized and various archives post search aids online, new information occasionally turns up. Such was the case with the discovery of an article published on July 20, 1932, in a paper in northern Britain (more or less between York and Newcastle-upon-Tyne), the *Teesdale Mercury*. Subsequently I found that the same article appeared in the the *Motherwell Times* (Lanarkshire, Scotland) on July 15, 1932, and in the *Edinburgh Evening News*, on July 20, 1932, under the title "This Mad World: Thousands Starving in the Midst of Plenty" (discovered through the British Newspaper Archives: britishnewspaperarchive.co.uk). And at least three Australian newspapers—*Westralian Worker* (Perth, WA), September 30, 1932, *Bunyip* (Gawler, South Australia), November 4, 1932, and *West Coast Sentinel* (Streaky Bay, SA), December 23, 1932—carried the article.[97]

The article, originally titled "Why are all so poor," was Polly's take on the economics of the time and her proposal for improving the situation. She argued that overproduction without a commensurate rise in wages meant that people could not afford to buy the goods produced, and as a result people were thrown out of work and were far worse off than they should have been.

In considering all of Polly's writings, one gains a clearer idea of her background knowledge and concern for economics. Even though she majored in economics at LSE, it is only in covering all of her rather limited legacy of letters (and the letters of her friend Bessie Hall) that it is possible to see that economics was not merely an intellectual pursuit, but a personal, social, and political preoccupation that shaped the way she lived her life. From her thrill at travelling on a very limited budget, to her joining The Neighbours and giving away "surplus" income, to leaving, in each of her wills, legacies to organizations and people that she felt could use her money, Polly was conscious of her financial privilege and was eager and willing to share her good fortune. Polly was not wealthy, but she was comfortable. A penchant for economizing and a generous nature were part of the equation.

How did she come to be published in newspapers so far from where she lived in London? Had she been travelling around Britain on a mission, as indicated in her obituary? It would seem that this article was likely published through a syndicate and may have been even more widely distributed.

In addition to Polly's economics article, two articles relating to Polly's disarmament speech at the 1928 Labour Conference are available through the British Newspaper Archive. At least four Parisian newspapers reported on Mary Chesley's disarmament speech.[98] The numbers of newspapers that still remain to be digitized are countless. Researchers in the future will have wider access.

CHAPTER 8
Voluntary Poverty in India

THE *TEESDALE MERCURY* ARTICLE IS THE LAST RECORD WE HAVE of Polly's time in Britain. In the autumn of 1934, she sailed to India. What we know of Polly from then on comes from her time in that country. The following letter is the first and only surviving personal account from Polly after her arrival in India.[99]

> c/o Nur Jehan, Ph.D.
> Inspectress of Schools
> Shahjehanpur, United Provinces, India
> Dec. 24th, 1934
>
> Dear Friends:
> Here I am with my Indian sisters! When they left England four years ago they begged me to go with them and ever since have been writing. When they returned, their uncle wanted them to live with him. However, my friends, especially Bibi were indignant with their uncle, because he had cheated some cousins, also it would have meant going back into purdah. Bibi soon got this job, as an Inspectress of girls' schools in the United Provinces. They live in a big bungalow with a glorious verandah. Only one of the three living-rooms is in real Indian style, having no chairs but a "tugt" or low platform and big bolster to lean against. It is very comfortable. The real Indian way of furnishing is both

beautiful and comfortable. A Hindu diningroom is spotlessly clean. You sit on one board slightly raised, possibly with another sloping board for your back, and your big metal tray with metal dishes on it, is put on another board in front of you. All must wash hands and mouth before and after eating. I would not be allowed to enter this room in an orthodox home, as I am "untouchable." In one home, when, in their hospitable way, seeing me out sight-seeing, they invited me in to eat, after showering dishes on me—on the big verandah—none of them would touch the leaf-plate from which I had eaten, but I was asked to pick it up and led to a refuse-bin.

To Hindus we are unclean because we eat meat, and to both Hindus and Moslems we are unclean because we drink liquor. The Hindu religion insists on daily bathing before devotions, and the Moslem on washing every exposed part and the mouth each time before prayer, that is five times a day.

Bibi and Bagi, my Indian sisters, are good Moslems. Bibi is very religious. When she is not working or eating she is at her devotions. This is the month of Ramzan, when they eat nothing between 3 a.m. and sunset. She says that this fasting not only helps her to have more sympathy with the poor and hungry but also to feel God's presence. Yesterday I found a man with his rug spread out among bushes saying his afternoon prayer.

I must tell you what I have been doing since I reached Bombay on Oct. 24, two weeks of which I have spent on tour. Bibi had to go over her district. We went two hundred miles going through Lucknow, and stayed ten days at a Public Parks Inspector's house. These houses are scattered all over the place for officers on tour. Then we went to the guesthouse of the Rajah of Barampur, a grand place, where we stayed five days. From these places Bibi went out inspecting schools. Only the biggest villages have girls' schools. Thousands of the villages have no school. Now that education is more in the hands of Indians the number is growing, but lack of funds cripples growth. Unfortunately as Indians get the offices Englishmen have filled, they demand to live in the same style, so that all live in a style altogether out of proportion to the country's resources and you compare it with the five to ten rupees a month (rupee = about .37) got by the majority of the people in this country. Bibi's salary is 320 rupees a month ($118.40 about). Gandhi wanted to limit salaries to, I think, 30 rupees ($11.10), which I feel is reasonable. Money goes about twice as far here as home. Bibi keeps five servants.

Now for my most interesting news. After staying nine days at Bombay during Congress, which I attended (I never saw such a huge crowd as the 60,000 at the meetings, where loud-speakers enabled all to hear) and two days at the Christa Seva Sangha Ashram ("Christ the Savior Missions") at Poona started by Jack Winslow (he has written the best book I have read on the Oxford Group Movement), and I think I sent Edith Russell a copy which I hope she will lend you all.[100] If I didn't send her one, you could get one from Eunice Buchanan, Waterville, Kings Co. or Lena. I went to the Quaker Mission at Itarsi on my way here.

At Poona I had a talk with the Indian R.C. Priest, who together with a young English priest has now taken Jack Winslow's place. He is a deeply spiritual man. He prays that Gandhi may become a Christian, because he feels that with his deep spirituality he will be able to interpret Christ's teachings as no one else has done, and bring Christianity closer to the original message. I had little idea that within a month I would have spent sixteen days with Mahatma, had many long talks with him, and be adopted as one of his family, that in less than a month I should have a letter from him in which he says:

"Do write as often as you feel the impulse. Treat this as your home whenever you feel like coming &c.
Love
Bapu"

[Gandhi was known to many as Bapu, meaning "father," and he referred to his closest Western women friends as daughters.]

When I was at Itarsi I was told of a Wesleyan missionary, Mary Barr, who after eleven years had left the mission to live in a nearby village. I decided I would go see her. With no time to wait, I went without writing. She welcomed me warmly, and soon asked me to stay four or five days. I found she had become a follower of Gandhi, doing her work more or less under him, and that she was intending to go in a few days to the Ashram at Wardha. She wanted me to go and the chance seemed too good to miss.

While we were there one of two English communists who were imprisoned four years ago at Meerut, had talks with him, at which we were present. He tried to turn Bapu's soul inside out, and Bapu helped him, all the time trying to win him from his belief in violence. One question he asked was: "Do you not delight in punishing yourself for youthful misdeeds, perhaps in fear of the brute within you?" Bapu said that such an idea was contrary to his whole belief, that when he had truly repented of his sins, and had the realization of God as his Father, he knew that they had been wiped out, and there was no more need of punishment. He told Mary Barr and me how, when he has exhausted thought, and is still unable to know what step to take, then God shows him the next step. We can never have this guidance unless we are humble before God and lead a disciplined life. And by being absolutely honest Bapu means that one keeps for himself no more than all could have, which, in India, is not a great deal. He believes that all people must live in simplicity unless they are going to exploit others. I have thought a lot about this, and I believe that the English standard has been kept up largely by exploitation and because they paid too little to the producers of the raw materials, and asked too much in proportion for their services in manufacturing them. By "honesty" Bapu also means absolute honesty of thought, ridding one's mind of prejudices, making no efforts at self-excuse. In fact Bapu is the best grouper I know, living and teaching the four absolutes.

I'm hoping the "Montreal Witness" will take some articles. I have written offering some.

As I've written a long letter, could you send this on to Lena Bachman. And Lena, will you send it to Miss Hewitt and Miss Hewitt, will you send it to Bessie [Hall].[101] It will have to be my New Year letter and it bears my good wishes.

> A few more words about Bapu. Though he is no longer the official leader of Congress, he is still the real leader. The last night the leaders all came to Wardha to talk things over with him before the meeting at Patra. He rises at four, when all meet for prayers. At 5:30, just before sunrise, he starts on his two-mile walk, and at 5 p.m. he takes another two-mile walk. I always went with him on the latter. There are always six to twelve people, but often we would walk, he with one arm over my shoulder, and the other over that of the person on the other side and we would have our long talks. At seven we had evening prayers again on the roof. An atmosphere of beautiful peace seemed always to surround him. One would think he lived a carefree life, yet his hours are carefully planned. It is the peace of those who have absolute trust in God, and he told us that only once had it deserted him.
>
> Love to all

Polly's first letter to friends and relatives from India is packed with information. While we cannot know all the triggers that played a part in drawing Polly to India, she gives us a clear identification of one influence: her Indian friends, Bibi and Bagi, had been urging her to come. We know from her letters home while attending university in England that Polly had made friends with Indian students as early as 1916 and had been learning about Indian politics from them. In a talk given in Halifax in 1921, she referred to the British implementation of the Contagious Diseases Act in India.

In Polly's letter, without criticizing her friend Bibi, Polly made it fairly clear that she found the idea of the new Indian elite making so much more money than the average worker distasteful. With her egalitarian principles and radical stance on economics, she would have to find her own way of living ethically in India. While it was not a given that she would so quickly become personally acquainted with Gandhi, it is not surprising. Even before the thought that such an event would come to pass, Polly was immersing herself in Indian politics by attending the Indian Congress meetings that were held not long after her arrival in India. As well, her visit to the Christa Seva Sangha, the Indo-Christian ashram, points to her awareness of religious activity in India, which sought to bring Christians, Hindus, and Muslims together for contemplation and religious unity. The founder, Jack Winslow, was an Anglican priest who greatly admired C. F. (Charlie) Andrews, another ordained minister and great friend of Gandhi and Rabindranath Tagore, the world-renowned poet. Winslow returned to Britain in 1934 and, like so many clergy of the period, engaged with the Oxford Group Movement. Polly's earlier reference to Gandhi being "the best grouper I know" stems from her enthusiasm for the Oxford Movement. What she likely did not know is that Gandhi had serious reservations concerning the Oxford Group's leader, Frank Buchman.

Polly mentioned writing to the *Montreal Witness* to offer articles concerning Gandhi. Having searched through the *Witness and Canadian Homestead* (the newspaper's complete name at the time) for the years 1934 to 1936 and finding no mention of Gandhi, I believe that the editors declined her offer. From late 1932 through 1936, the weekly devoted a significant section of the paper to news about the Oxford Group. However, in early 1932, the paper carried a very negative article about Gandhi. On February 24, 1932, a "lady doctor" wrote in response to the Editor of the *Witness*:

> Sir, I am sorry to inform you that I do not intend continuing the Witness. Some little time ago an editorial appeared which dealt uncharitably with Mahatma Gandhi, the Indian Nationalist Leader. Such articles do not promote international understanding and goodwill, which you say is your aim. He is a great personality and deserves respect from everyone whether they agree with his methods or not.
>
> As for the churches, every time they have been put to a test as followers of the Prince of Peace they have invariably failed. They have not, in any country, shown themselves fit for spiritual leadership.
>
> DOCTOR

The editor felt compelled to write a response: "The above writer thinks it is right to tell truth about the churches of Christ but not about Mr. Gandhi. His present attitude of demanding democratic government for ignorant millions of antagonistic religions, mutually repellent castes, wholly diverse languages communicating with each other only in English, is preposterous."

It is true that the situation in India was riddled with complex difficulties because of religious and caste differences. The position of the newspaper was firmly in favour of continued British colonial rule. A letter from "Another Missionary in India" on April 27, 1932, also questioned the earlier negative editorial. Based on the heading "Another Missionary" and the fact that most female doctors of the period served as missionaries abroad, it is reasonable to assume that the "lady doctor" was a missionary in India (the early female graduates of medicine were often refused positions to practice in Canada, and thus, most went to India, China, and elsewhere under the auspices of missionary societies).

What follows is a portion of the letter to the editor. The very lengthy editorial rebuttal provided further evidence of the *Witness*'s antipathy to Gandhi. It is interesting to note that while the missionary was critical of the paper's attack on Gandhi and the independence movement, he still supported the British Raj. It appears that he had written before.

> Sir,
>
> You strongly criticize and condemn policies and methods of the Canadian governments, but refuse the same liberty to the Indians and advocate even sterner methods for their repression. I have studied and followed Indian problems and politics. Any man who lacks national aspirations for his mother country is not worthy of any place in any country, yet we are refusing that right to Indians.
>
> You label anyone disloyal "who sees things from the point of view of the nationalist movement." You feel that "the movement has an impossible and disastrous goal." Is that any reason why we should blind our eyes to the possibility that the past and present ordinances may be ensuring and hastening that evil day?
>
> You as a loyal Canadian have raised your voice against many acts of our government, but at the same time you refuse the friends in India the same liberty of speech. You ignore the large

> body of missionaries in India who do not approve of the terrible ordinances as they see many of their honored Indian friends among victims of these ordinances.
>
> We who wish to keep India within the British Empire believe that the surest and swiftest methods are an action to sever forever that desired relationship.
>
> I have the best interest at heart for the British Raj in India, for the mission cause and for the great people of India.
>
> ALEX NUGENT

Thus, with the editor's lengthy argument in response, concluded the newspaper's coverage of anything to do with Gandhi, at least over the course of the years I studied the paper's content: 1932, 1934, 1935, and 1936.

Another account of Polly's early days in India comes from *Bapu: Conversations and Correspondence with Mahatma Gandhi* by F. Mary Barr. Because of Barr's recording of events involving Polly, I quote liberally from her book. Here are her recollections of their first meeting:

> Not long after my return to Khedi, a Canadian Quaker, Mary Chesley caused great excitement in the village, as it was rare to see any white person. She had come to India to visit friends and with the idea of doing village work. After concentrated conversation it seemed a likely plan that she should take on the Khedi work if I went on to the Gond hamlet.[102] She saw something of Khedi and we walked to the Gond village one day. She arrived just at the right moment for, although no definite scheme of work had yet materialized in Khedi, I was loath to break the contacts there, and yet wanted to accept the Gonds' offer. So it was decided that we should put the plan before Gandhi and we went to Wardha. His first brief talk with her brought out two points:
> 1. That she should not promise anything precipitately, and before visiting her Mussalman [Muslim] friends in the north.
> 2. That if she was to stay and work in India, she would be wise to concentrate on learning Hindi.

> The following day, Mary C., as she soon came to be called, and I were fortunate in hearing two interesting conversations, one between Bapu and Dr. Stanley Jones, the noted American missionary and writer, the other between Gandhi and an English communist.[103]

In her letter home to Canada, Polly recounted her impressions of this talk with the communist. Mary Barr transcribed the whole conversation, and according to her account, Polly interjected with a question that was a truly Polly-type inquiry: she asked how exploiters could be persuaded to give up their wealth. "Through love," Bapu replied.[104]

Polly had landed where she felt at home among people who held common values and goals. Choosing a life of voluntary poverty and becoming useful in the most basic of ways spoke to her economic principles. Having a friendship with Gandhi meant that she could engage in serious conversations that encompassed politics, philosophy, and social issues. Mary Barr, with whom she was developing a friendship, also had intellectual and spiritual inclinations that would have meshed with Polly's. She was ready to embrace her newfound mission in India.

Some background information on Gandhi is useful at this particular juncture so Polly's life and activities in India can be put in context. Following is a brief overview from the time of his return to India up until the time of Polly's arrival.

Gandhi's return to India in 1915 after years of living in South Africa marked a new chapter. At the time, he was forty-five and had not stepped on his native soil in twelve years. To familiarize himself with the country and its people, Gandhi took the advice of his mentor, one of India's leading nationalists, Gopal Krishna Gokhale, who urged him to take a year for observation before getting involved in any active political work. During his years in South Africa, Gandhi had honed his leadership skills and through experimentation had developed political and social ideas as well as strategies that he would further refine in India. He had worked out the philosophical and spiritual foundation for non-violent resistance in South Africa, calling its practical application *satyagraha* (truth-force or soul-force). The underpinnings for non-violent resistance required that those engaged, *satyagrahis*, adopt the principles of *ahimsa* (non-violence, love) and *tapasya* (willingness for self-sacrifice). Using *satyagraha*, Gandhi's basic objectives were *swaraj* (self-governance or independence) and *sarvodaya* (social uplift for all).

Within his first year back in India, Gandhi established Satyagraha Ashram in order to train satyagrahis for the country's struggle for independence. Relocated alongside the Sabarmati River near Ahmedabad in Gandhi's home province of Gujarat, it was renamed Sabarmati Ashram.

The events of Gandhi's first years back in the country are not addressed here. What will be said is that in the years leading up to the famous Salt March, Gandhi had stepped back from active protest, and his focus had been on developing constructive work and on fighting prejudice against so-called "untouchables." Nevertheless, by 1930, Gandhi gauged that the time had come for direct action once again.

The British charged Indians a tax on salt that was harvested from the country's shores. Poor Indians, therefore, could not to afford this essential. Gandhi understood that the salt tax symbolized the injustice of British imperial policy in India. On March 12, 1930, Gandhi and his fellow *satyagrahis* began their two hundred–mile march from Sabarmati to Dandi, on the seashore. With the world press watching, Gandhi, the brilliant strategist, gathered up salt from the shore and inspired hundreds of thousands of Indians to do the same. Over the following year, the crackdown by the British was severe; police violence perpetrated on the peaceful *satyagrahis* and the imprisonment of Gandhi and approximately ninety thousand other Indians only helped to galvanize the public. From this time onward, Gandhi gained increasing sympathy internationally, but more importantly, he built support among Indian women who entered into the spirit of *swadeshi* (meaning made in or belonging to one's country), depending on the resources and manufactures of India rather than on foreign imports. By organizing pickets against the sale of liquor and foreign cloth, women participated in public life, the majority of them for the first time.

In January 1931, after eight months in jail, Gandhi was released. Later that year, he and his entourage sailed to England to attend the Second Round Table Conference, a meeting to which the British authorities invited representatives of numerous Indian factions. The discussions to work out resolutions involving India's political fate failed abysmally.

Almost immediately upon return to India in early 1932, Gandhi and many members of the National Indian Congress were rearrested. Over the next years, Gandhi would spend time in and out of prison. He disbanded Sabarmati Ashram so the government could not confiscate the land and or more of its contents than had already been seized, and moved the ashram community to Wardha in Central India.

Gandhi's involvement with the Indian National Congress had been constant since his return to India in 1915. He had his detractors among Congress members who did not approve of his civil disobedience tactics; nevertheless, he gained the support and following of a growing number of new Indian nationalists. Gandhi reorganized the party, transforming it from an elitist urban-based group to one that represented Indians from all across the country. He ensured that leadership within the Congress became more dependent on a member's social service work than on their wealth and social standing or caste. Although he remained a powerful influence in the Congress, in late 1934 Gandhi stepped down from direct leadership to focus more of his energy on constructive work and set up the All India Village Industries Association (AIVIA). This was just at the time of Polly's entry to India. Mary Barr had already been engaged in village work, and Polly would now join her.

Some biographical information on Mary Barr is also pertinent. It is through Barr's book that we gain crucial information on Polly's activities. They had much in common in terms of their social and political outlook.

By the time Polly and Mary met, Mary had been in India for fourteen years, having arrived in 1920 for a teaching position in a Methodist mission school. In 1931, she was on furlough in England during the time that the Second Round Table Conference was convened. She recounted in her book: "I began to take an interest in [Gandhi's] writings and speeches and to read books about him."[105] Her increasing concern regarding international peace and conflict issues had taken her to the Rhineland with War Resisters' International where she observed the rising nationalist tensions. She had contemplated joining a group of peacemakers who would serve as buffers in conflict zones. However, she decided that her calling was to return to India, although it was clear that teaching in the mission school might not be the way to work for peace and change in India. By chance or fate, Mary returned to India on the SS *Pilsna*, the same ship that Gandhi was sailing on. They met and thus began a friendship that endured until Gandhi's death in 1948. Because of Gandhi's arrest upon arrival in India, Mary's early contact with him was mainly through letters. She was particularly interested in his spiritual philosophy and his ideas on social reconstruction. She had been contemplating moving to a remote village to do service work. Meeting Gandhi at this particular juncture in her life was timely, and after giving the school time to find a replacement, she resigned and moved first to the Sabarmati Ashram and later to Gandhi's new headquarters in Wardha.

At the time of Polly's arrival, Mary Barr had been working in the village of Khedi, near Betul in central India. Mary had been invited to move farther into the hinterlands to work with the previously mentioned Gonds; however, due to a number of factors she continued at Khedi for some years, with the periodic help of others, like Polly.

The term *khadder*, also spelled *khaddar* or *khadi*, refers to the homemade cotton cloth that became one of the cornerstones of Gandhi's self-reliance program. Gandhi was interested in decentralization, and the All-India Village Industries Association paid particular attention to developing spinning and weaving within the villages. Among projects initiated by Mary Barr and her colleagues who worked in Khedi over the years, spinning and weaving took a primary place.

Although Gandhi made himself available to many people, it seems that he and Polly developed a special friendship, and a couple of conversations between Gandhi and Polly were considered worthy of recording in *The Collected Works of Mahatma Gandhi* (CWMG), the multivolume collection of Gandhi's letters, speeches, and other writings, which has been published over the course of many years and is downloadable in the Collective Commons.[106] Those who knew Polly had noted her intellectual brilliance. Additionally, she had an inquiring mind on matters of faith as well as a good sense of humour. All of these qualities, plus her passionate empathy for the poor and disenfranchised, would have appealed to Gandhi. The following transcription of a conversation that Polly and Gandhi had on the subject of religion can be found in Barr's book and was subsequently published in *CWMG*. Barr introduced the dialogue:

> In 1934, Gandhi was busy inaugurating the All-India Village Industries' Association, a successor to the All-India Spinners' Association and the Harijan Sevak Sangh (the Servants of Harijans Society). Several of us who were interested were allowed to attend the sessions. At the close of one of them, Gandhi, knowing that Mary C. wanted to have a talk with him said, "Come along this afternoon and we can have some quiet talk." A small group of us listened to the following conversation:
>
> **Mary C.** – Do you believe your guidance comes from sub-conscious reasoning or from God?
>
> **Gandhi** – From God—but sub-conscious reasoning may be the voice of God. Often, after seeing the way to go, I consciously reason out why that is the best way.
>
> **Mary C.** – Then does following conscience lead to mystical experience?
>
> **Gandhi** – It may or it may not. But one thing is sure that humility before God is necessary for mystical experiences, such as those of Saint Francis and Saint Augustine. On the other hand, a Bradlaugh or a Marcus Aurelius, though following conscience, felt themselves not dependent on God, and so they could get no mystical experiences or joy. To me, following conscience is following a living force, not an ethical code.
>
> **Mary C.** – How do you understand what is God's guidance for you when it is a question of choosing between two good things?

Gandhi – I use my intellect and if I don't get any strong feeling as to which of the two I should choose, I just leave the matter, and before long I wake up one morning with the assurance that it should be A rather than B. Of course, it is necessary to be utterly humble and go wherever the decision should take you, even though it should be to difficulties and suffering.

Mary C. – Is it not necessary to lead a disciplined life in order to receive these assurances as to what to do and not do?

Gandhi – Yes, of course, one's mind must be attuned to the five necessary rules of love, truth, purity, non-possession and fearlessness.

Mary C. – Do you include bodily discipline such as fasting?

Gandhi – If you follow the five rules already mentioned, you will find that bodily discipline follows automatically. You should read Rajayoga by Swami Vivekananda on this point.

Gandhi – If rich people could see us poorer ones really content instead of hankering after wealth, it would become the fashion to dispense with wealth. Unfortunately the higher castes have failed to identify with their humble fellows. This is the darkest hour of Hinduism. I have no excuse to offer.

Mary C. – What is your remedy?

Gandhi – Village Industries, Khadder, Harijan work, etc.

Mary C. – From what sources do you get your conception of God?

Gandhi – From my childhood, remembering my mother's visits to the temple. Also my nurse used to tell me I must repeat the name of God if I felt afraid.

Mary C. – Are not your own experiences sources of your conception too?

Gandhi – Yes, but they did not begin until later, in South Africa. Before that I had a period of doubt and it was during that time that I began to study Islam and Christianity.

Mary C. – How far have these two religions coloured your conception of God?

Gandhi – I began with a prejudice against Christianity because it had meant to me drink, eating meat, and Western clothes. I had no such prejudice against Islam. Later when I met some fine Christian people my prejudice went, and for a year I studied Christian books, attended the Keswick Convention, met famous divines and absorbed Christianity, seeking to know if I should do as some of my friends were begging me to do—become a Christian. But in the end I felt I could not do so. I believe in the historic Jesus, for the gospels bear the stamp of the real experience of devotees.

Mary C. – Is the conception of God as Father only to be found in Christianity?

Gandhi – No, it is also to be found in Hinduism. Read the second chapter of the Gita in which the conception, not only as father, but also as mother is to be found. This is not the case with Islam, for among all its ninety-nine names for God, "Father" is not one. Mahomet, like Christ, had the note of God-consciousness. If you judge a religion by the changed lives of its adherents, Islam seems to me to have as much to show as Christianity. Anyway, two thousand years is a very brief time in which to judge the merits of a religion.

Mary C. – I know some people who are praying that you become a Christian.

Gandhi – (laughing) If they wish me to say that Christianity is the only true religion, I cannot do so. I can say, however, that Christianity is a true religion.

Mary C. – What do you think is the special contribution of Christianity, Islam and Hinduism to the world?

Gandhi – I think Christianity's particular contribution is that of active love. No other religion says so firmly that God is love, and the New Testament is full of the word. Christians as a whole have denied this principle with their wars. The Ahimsa of Hinduism is a more passive thing than the active Christian love. The great contribution of Hinduism is its recognition of the unity of all life. Like Christianity, Hinduism has not lived up to its teaching.

If either had done so, there would have been no need for Islam. Islam's contribution has been the brotherhood of all men. Later this idea was limited to the Islamic brotherhood, so Muslims too have failed to live up to the teaching of their religion. Khan Sahib, with his teaching of the service of all humanity, is bringing them back to the original idea.

Mary C. – You once said that the idea of Jesus as the Son of God was a mystical conception. Would you enlarge upon that, please?

Gandhi – I believe that Jesus was a man born in the natural way, and that people, seeing the wonderful things he did, ascribed divinity to him, and then described it mystically by saying that he was the Son of God.

Mary C. – Do you think such writers were imposters?

Gandhi – No. They were just expressing their conception mystically. The whole book of Revelation is a description of mystical experiences. For example, it does not mean literally that streets were to be paved with gold. Many mystical expressions would be gross if they meant literally what they said.

Mary C. – Have you had any mystical experiences?

Gandhi – If, by mystical experiences, you mean visions, no. But I am very sure of the voice which guides me. Of course, some unbalanced people have claimed to hear voices too—but I do not think anyone has suggested that I am unbalanced.

(This remark was said in such a droll way that we all burst into laughter.)

Mary C. – You have spoken of your sense of uneasiness which preceded your twenty-one days' fast last year, and also said that generally, when obeying your inner voice, you find a reason for your action afterwards. Did you find a reason for the twenty-one days' fast?

Gandhi – It is true that a sense of uneasiness drove me to that fast. Usually, even under strain I can remain quite buoyant, but when I lost that buoyancy and could not even sleep, I decided to fast and immediately found peace.

Mary C. – You have said sometimes that consciousness of sin brings a feeling of separation from God. Did you feel any such separation before your fast?

Gandhi – No. I felt only great uneasiness and restlessness. I could not even joke in my usual way.[107]

Polly delved deeply into questions of Gandhi's approach to religion and spirituality. It speaks to her inquiring mind and also reveals her willingness to approach Gandhi not only as a mentor, but also as an equal in conversation. Public speaking and academic training gave her the confidence to engage easily with him.

Gandhi's list of "five necessary rules of love, truth, purity, non-possession, and fearlessness" are similar to the attributes to which Quakers aspired. That many of Gandhi's closest Western friends were of Quaker faith is not surprising, what with their mutual adherence to non-violence and simplicity.

Gandhi coined the term "Harijans," meaning "Children of God," for the so-called untouchables. As he kept refining his overall vision for reform in India, eliminating the inequality of the caste system became a strong mission. The weekly journal that he published changed its title from *Young India to Harijan* in 1933. Untouchables themselves did not identify with the term Harijan, and the term "untouchable" was declared illegal under the Indian constitution in 1949.

Over the next year and a half, Polly enthusiastically entered into Indian village life, combining physical and social work with the challenge of learning Hindi, and visiting Gandhi in Wardha and Delhi. The record we have comes from the letters Gandhi wrote to the "two Marys" and accounts in the *Harijan* and Mary Barr's book. Polly acquired an Indian name, Tara (meaning "star"). Using the honorific given to unmarried women, she became Tarabehn (variously spelled Taraben or Tara Behn), *behn* meaning "sister," used for a single woman. Mary Barr was known as Marybehn.

In late 1934 and early 1935, Gandhi was camped at Delhi, "five miles out of the city on the grounds that became a Harijan Training Colony," according to Mary Barr. She wrote:

Mary C., who had left Wardha to visit friends, suddenly arrived one day at the camp at Delhi. He greeted her with a good deal of light-hearted banter.

Mary C. had, like myself, recently read "My Experiments with Truth" and was puzzled by Gandhi's attitude to sex, placing a Bramachari (celibate) on a higher plane spiritually than a married person. When she asked about it, he cleared up the matter as follows: "I agree with you that a Bramachari is not necessarily on a higher plane. A bachelor may be a blackguard and a married man deeply spiritual, but the point I want to make is that anybody wishing to serve humanity in any special way, will be able to do so more fully as a Brahmachari, for, having no self-possessions and having no special service to render to one group (his family), he is free to serve all."[108]

Gandhi's attitudes toward sex were complex, based on his own personal history and his adoption of *brahmacharya*, a Hindu spiritual practice in which celibacy is merely the beginning, a form of self-discipline in which total non-desire is the goal in order that sexual energy (vital force) can be transformed into pure spiritual energy (or godliness). Gandhi first adopted the practice in South Africa in 1906. Western writers, in particular, have been obsessed with Gandhi's relationship with women and have been prone to believe that sexual tension or repressed desire was inevitable in these relationships. In actual fact, Gandhi had a remarkable capacity for intense friendships with both men and women, and there is no evidence to suggest that his relationships with Western women were carnal. There was a period late in his life when Gandhi wished to prove to himself that he was beyond desire, and he slept naked with a couple of the younger Indian women in his circle. These experiments aroused intense discomfort among many of his friends and fellow workers. And while Gandhi's motives were in keeping with his overall search for truth, and the women said that they had not felt threatened sexually, his use of the women in his experiment raised questions. In my study of the various Western women friends of Gandhi, I found that a number of them commented at one time or another on their disagreement with

Gandhi on his attitude regarding celibacy, an ironic twist considering all were single and presumably celibate.

Back to Polly's story as related by Mary Barr.

> Mary C. asked to join me in Khedi and I was glad. We told Gandhi our plans and asked him if he would send a Hindu woman who would help and teach us. We wanted someone free from caste distinctions. There was no one like that in our village, so Gandhi promised to try to find someone. After some weeks, I could then leave the two together and go back to the Gond hamlet.
>
> Mary C. was ill during the last days of our stay in Delhi. As we sped south in the train she seemed to be in a comatose condition, but just before we reached Betul where she and I were to get out, she woke up sufficiently to ask Gandhi, "What ought we to do about snakes, kill them?"
>
> "The first thing to do," Bapu replied, "is to kill our own evil passions which are like snakes. I suppose that until we have succeeded in doing that, we must kill snakes if they are in a position to do us harm. Out in the jungle it should not be necessary. We must remember that many are not poisonous, and that even the poisonous ones do not wish to harm us unless we willingly or unwittingly, harm them." [109]

Gandhi's first *Harijan* account concerning Polly, published March 8, 1935, follows:

> WELL BEGUN
>
> A sister who has just begun work in a village in Central Province writes an interesting and earnest letter from which I extract the following :
>
> "I have had 11 days of village life. So far I am enjoying it. I like the physical exercise in the cool of morning and evening. I have carried over 100 basketsful of mud on my head from the pit about 11 yards away where I dig it, to the back of our house where I am making a verandah. Two days I carried 40 each day. This verandah is a bit of selfishness, but there is a beautiful view from the back

of the house—open country and distant wooded hills—and it seemed foolish to only be able to enjoy it from two little windows, so the verandah 14 x 9 is to be our chief living and sleeping room.

Mary Barr and I had our first and only real disagreement about this as she wrote to you. She felt that I was likely to do a lot of unnecessary work and that we should have a coolie. I thought that I enjoyed the work, that one should not have help for things one could do oneself and that in a village, where most people did their own building, one should be able to get enough free information not to go wrong.

After the verandah I am going to garden. I think the earth is quite good and they are going to fence it to keep out the cattle. I am going to build up a mud trough with a wooden floor in which we will stand for our baths and which will have a hole near the bottom, as I had planned (with a tank, so that our bath water will do for watering the garden, for the great snag in village gardening is water). Also the man who has the nearest good well says I may plant some fruit trees near and use his water."

There is much that is valuable in this letter. If these two sisters are blessed by God with health and can stick to their work, they will certainly make of their village a model—not merely because they have begun with physical labour, but also because of the propriety of their scheme of work and the selfless love of the villagers, which fires them.

Gandhi's personal response to Polly's letter is included in the *Collected Works of Mahatma Gandhi* and is dated March 1, 1935:

> My dear Mary C.
> I have your wonderful letter. You must shed this fear complex of your inability to earn your bread by the sweat of your brow. You must continue to give me a vivid description of your labours and I will tell you whenever I think you are wrong. Both of you must keep well.
> Love,
> Bapu

Gandhi's concern for the health of his workers was not unfounded. India presented many challenges, both for the native population and for Westerners unaccustomed to the climate and at high risk of diseases for which they had no immunity. Recurring bouts of malaria were endemic. A host of other dangers lurked in the water, the food, and the general lack of sanitation. One of Gandhi's biggest missions was to educate villagers on the importance of sanitation. In addition, he had an interest in diets and cures. He developed his own theories, sometimes rather eccentric and off the mark. He also had a strong nursing side and personally took care of many of his associates over the years. It was evident from a letter Gandhi wrote to Mary Barr on February 1, 1935, that Polly was already experiencing some adjustments to diet. Also evident is that Gandhi was utterly open about bodily functions: "I am glad Mary Junior had an enema. It must have given her considerable relief. Mary must become strong and fit."

It is not surprising that the two Marys had different approaches to this question of manual labour. Mary Barr had lived in India for close to fifteen years, and she would have been accustomed to having helpers or servants for physical chores. In countries where imperialism existed, it was a given that white people and higher caste Indians would have servants. Polly, on the other hand, was someone who would resist having things done for her that she could do herself. Both her cultural background and her desire to live as simply and as equality-minded as possible would have influenced her approach.

From Mary Barr's book: "Gandhi is of a naturally generous disposition, yet he is nothing if not economical. His next letters to the two of us were both on one small sheet of paper and came along with Sumitraben, whom he had chosen to be our fellow-worker and mentor. She was a member of the Wardha Ashram.

> Chi. Mary,
> Sumitra is a good, hard-working woman. But you will test for yourself. If she is not the type you contemplated, you will send her back."[110]

Mary Barr's reference to the economical Gandhi does not begin to describe his frugality in many areas. Unfortunately many of the letters people wrote to Gandhi are no longer extant, because Gandhi tended to reuse the paper of incoming letters for drafts of speeches and outgoing correspondence. He could be very generous with strangers but tyrannical when it came to what he viewed as excesses or wastage by his family and closest friends.

Mary Barr's account from this time further illuminates the unfolding life of the two Marys as they settled into village life together: "We found Sumitra a delightful companion and helper. She stayed nearly six months in the village. During part of the time, she and Mary C. did not get on very well together, but later events cemented their friendship."

From Gandhi, the following: "Mary C.'s method of doing everything herself even at the risk of losing time is not to be lightly disposed of. Local circumstances should determine the choice of a particular way where more than one is open to us."[111]

At some point after Sumitra's arrival, Mary Barr felt she could leave Polly and Sumitra in charge of the work at Khedi. She returned to the Gond hamlet. Barr mentioned that the two women came to help her clean and whitewash the place she was living in. Within a few days of arrival, Barr had a malaria attack and ended up in hospital. Over her convalescence, Gandhi kept in touch. In a letter dated June 28, 1935, Gandhi wrote: "Mary Chesley expects to come here on or about July 7 and bring Miss Ingham with her." According to Barr, Mary Ingham had journeyed from England in answer to Polly's suggestion that she should come to India to do village work. I do not know how Polly knew her, whether this was a friend through Quakers, her political work, or otherwise. For Ingham to pick up and go to India at the urging of a friend indicates that the two women must have had a close enough relationship and an interest in common causes.

Mary Barr's book offers more details of life in Khedi during the time she was recuperating in a nearby village hospital:

> A letter from Bapu to Mary C. while I was in Miraj concerned a trained spinning and weaving master who had been sent to look after the Khedi work, but who soon showed himself to be unsatisfactory. Bapu was apparently feeling that Mary C. and Mary I. (Tarabehn and Shantabehn) needed more training than Sumitrabehn had been able to give.[112]

> Dear Tarabehn,
> About the Lathi Drill I wrote to L. that if his motive was the teaching of Gymnastics I saw no harm in Lathi Drill. Of course your argument is quite right that there being a school where the boys learn Lathi Drill, it may be superfluous. The inference then is that his persistence in teaching it is against the non-violent spirit. I have advised L. not to stay with you but to go back to Nagpur as there are all kinds of complaints against him from Nagpur and now also Betul.
>
> I would want to have you and Shantabehn with me for some time so that you could thoroughly know the customs and manners of this country. I suggest a better method. You should stay where you are and plod away single-handed during Mary's [Barr's] absence, and even if you do not get another assistant like Sumitrabehn, do whatever you can. Now that Shantabehn wishes to go somewhere for becoming an accomplished weaver what can be more proper than that she should be with me and have her training here? I am sure she would be perfectly happy. You should have no anxiety about her health.[113]

Regarding the above reference, a *lathi* is a stick or cane and "Lathi Drill" would refer to a martial art using the sticks. Often Indian police used lathis to control crowds or to punish prisoners. Polly's resistance to lathi drill is consistent with the Chesleys' intense dislike of cadet training for boys.

Barr mentioned that Gandhi sent her a note with a copy of his letter to Polly/Tara so that she would know what was happening. In other notes to Barr, Gandhi added a few more tidbits: "We have the trinity here: Mary C., Mary I. and Sumitra. Mary C. grumbles that I have put her on curds for she has a little cold.

"The Marys went on Monday with Sumitra. Mary C. and Sumitra do not get on well together. But S. is determined to finish the six months she promised."[114]

Just as Mary Barr was thinking that she needed to return to Khedi, she received a note from Gandhi urging her to get better first. A few days later he wrote that Mary Ingham was in hospital in Nagpur, and Sumitra was in Betul Hospital. "Just now the Khedi work is broken up."

As Mary Barr recounted: "Sickness produced the miracle which joint colleagueship was unable to do, and from the time of Sumitra's illness there was a very tender friendship between Sumitra and Mary C. Sumitra had been removed to Wardha Hospital as soon as she was able to bear it, so a few days after my return to Khedi, Mary C. went there to be near her.

"There was in this letter much about Sumitra. Indeed it was months before she was quite strong again. So Mary C. stayed on in Wardha week after week, tending Sumitra."[115]

The spectre of illness cast its shadow more often than not; however, the *Harijan* of July 27, 1935, gives a delightful picture of lighter moments in Gandhi's circle. It bears out what Polly herself wrote in a letter to her cousin Will Forbes around this time: "I think that so far as he lets himself get personal attachments he is quite attracted by me, partly I think because I'm more inclined to joke than most of those around him and he loves a joke. His parting words (on the first special appointment) were: 'Don't lose your sense of humor, and don't make more lines through imitation,' putting his hand on my forehead."[116]

And from the *Harijan* of July 27, 1935, Mahadev Desai, Gandhi's secretary, wrote:

A SARTORIAL SERMON

Even our humdrum life is not without its fun. We had for guests last week Miss Chesley and Miss Ingham who are keenly interested in our rural reconstruction effort and are giving their own contribution to it by settling down in a village near Betul. Miss Ingham has come only recently but Miss Chesley has been in the village for over six months. She has a keen spirit of inquiry. This pleases Gandhiji. One day during her brief stay in our midst she raised a question about the short-sleeved kurtas (shirts) and the shorts some of us are wearing. Most of us used to wear dhotis and even now do wear dhotis when off duty, but the various kinds of manual work to be done here compelled us to take this up as a convenient, easiest-washable and cheapest workman's uniform. But Miss Chesley saw something incongruous and inartistic about this and said so to Gandhiji. As the talk was informal we had capital fun out of it.

'But why do you object to it?' said Gandhiji.

'Because it is English.'

'But why should I not adopt whatever is best in English dress?'

'It is so inartistic. The English shorts go ill with the flowing Indian shirts.'

'Then I suppose you would be horrified if I asked people to wear the sola hat.'

Here Miraben took up the battle and said it would certainly shock her.[117] The sola hat was most expensive and extremely uncomfortable.

'That only shows that the hat you wore when you were in England was a misfit.'

'No, I had the best hats available in those days, but I never liked them.'

'What I feel is that the sola hat is a good protection from the sun.'

'I would any day wear an Indian pugri in preference to the hat. It does keep off the sun as well.'

'It does not.'

'Well, well. But these shorts are bad. Between the loincloth that you wear and the shorts these people wear there is all the difference between heaven and hell.'

'Oh!' said Gandhiji, astonished. 'Then you will explain why it is so shocking.'

'Perhaps I am putting it too strongly; I shall say there is all the difference that there is between day and night.'

'But that is not my reason,' said Miss Chesley, 'I simply can't stand this incongruous mixture. Your loincloth is Indian. Why should they not put on something like that? Let it be all Indian or all English.'

'Then to be all English I must go to a grogshop, too?' said Gandhiji. And all roared with laughter. 'As regards my loincloth

I know that it is far superior to the shorts. But if they all adopted it they would be laughed at for trying to look like the Mahatma.'

'But why not wear the lower part of the shirt inside the shorts?'

'Yes, that is what you do. But it is hygienically bad.'

The argument went on for a fairly long time but I had quite forgotten it, when my memory of it was revived when on the eve of her departure Miss Chesley said that she felt so strongly about the thing, that she must speak to us, the culprits.

One of [the reasons] has already been given in the talk I have narrated: "Why on earth should you discard your beautiful Indian costume and go in for this slavish imitation of the English?"

Her second argument was the very bad example we were setting to the masses: "As you have the privilege of very close association with Gandhiji, everyone looks up to you, and you must not set a bad example."

I have reproduced this interesting talk to show how jealous some English friends are of what is good and artistic in India. The talk did not leave many of us convinced, for the simple reason that we had discarded nothing Indian. The shirt and the shorts we were wearing were adopted as working men's clothes and we often discard the shirt altogether in hot weather. Much as we would love to do with the scant loincloth with which the poorest Indian contents himself, we confess our unreadiness to cut down our dress to that size. As for the bad example, I wish the people amongst whom we work copied it. For they wear much more clothing than necessary.

But we must thank Miss Chesley for her frankness and for reminding us that we are watched by people, not only in the matter of our dress but of our general behavior, and that we must not forget that we are in no way to be unworthy of the privilege of our association with Gandhiji.

Perhaps it goes without saying, but the "ji" at the end of "Gandhi" is an honorific used to show respect to elders, either male or female. As for the sola hat, or pith helmet, most people would associate it as one of the iconic symbols of British imperialism. In spite of this, Gandhi admired the hat and in *This Was Bapu*, a book of Gandhi quotations and anecdotes, we find the following: "My narrow nationalism rebels against the hat, but my secret internationalism regards the sola hat as one of the few boons from Europe. But I know that national likes and dislikes are not governed by reason. I do not expect India to take kindly to the sola hat. It is in reality an easily portable umbrella without the necessity of one hand being occupied in carrying it."[118]

The ill health that plagued Sumitra and Shanta (Mary Ingham) earlier in the year persisted. A letter dated November 13, 1935, from Gandhi to Mary Barr gives this information: "I believe that Shanta has been suffering from over-tiredness; but it was strong enough to induce fever which she seems to have got rid of. She is taking sufficient nourishment. Sumitra had a very bad night. She developed high fever, about 105°; so she had to be sent back to the hospital today. Naturally Tara is in charge.

"Tara has not been bombarding me with questions. It is only during meals that she asks a few questions. She is keeping quite well. Hitherto soya beans do not seem to have disagreed with her.

"Love, Bapu"[119]

This missive is typical of countless letters written by Gandhi over the years—full of news on the health of his friends and associates. He loved experimenting with diet himself and also trying out his dietary theories on others, some with success and others less so. He did not necessarily expect others to adhere to his dietary regime. While he was completely vegetarian, at one time, when the doctor recommended eggs for Mary Barr, Gandhi urged her to eat them. When she asked him to suggest a substitute for eggs, his answer was: "The only substitute for eggs is eggs!"[120]

~~~

Polly stayed in Wardha to help Sumitra, whose recovery was very slow. At the same time, Polly was studying Hindi and making friends in the Mahila (meaning "Women") Ashram. When four of the women planned to take a pilgrimage to the Himalayas, Polly decided to go with them. According to Mary Barr, Polly returned to Khedi in April 1936 "in order to select the necessary outfit for the pilgrimage and left again early in May."

Not long after, on May 15, Gandhi wrote to Mary Barr:

> Chi. Mary,
> I have just had a wire saying that Mary C. died at Hrishikesh. The news is stunning, unbelievable. I have no further particulars. I had warned her against the pilgrimage. But she had an iron will. I have wired for particulars. Her forgiving nature and charity had captivated me. Her belief in the goodness of human nature was beyond all praise. She has sacrificed herself for the cause she believed in. Shanta [Mary Ingham] is here and she has given Miss Blyth's address. Miss B. was her partner. You will tell me all you know and I ought to know about Tara.
>
> I am looking forward to Miss Madden's letter. I am glad she will be with you for one year. Tara wanted me to invite her to see me again. Only, she must go slowly in making changes in her life. Europeans simply cannot make some changes. You will take a lesson from Tara's life and not overdo things.[121]

Tara/Polly likely did overdo things. Gandhi viewed her as fragile, health-wise. But vulnerability was surely far from Polly's view of herself. She had always been physically active, playing sports, hiking, and bicycling. In trying to live the life of the poorest Indian villager without having a period of gradual immersion, she did not develop the immunity needed to counter the high risks of infection that India presented. She believed she was invincible.

A few brief words on Pearl Madden are in order. In the *Collected Works*, Madden is referred to as a Canadian missionary, but when I checked the denominational archives for all the churches in Canada, I found nothing about her. It turned out that Madden worked as the treasurer for an American organization, the Woman's Foreign Missionary Society of the Methodist Episcopal Church. I would never have known this had I not discovered an extant letter in the Sabarmati Archives in Ahmedabad, dated October 8, 1924, written by Madden on the society's letterhead. This was a stroke of good luck because, as previously mentioned, most of Gandhi's incoming correspondence was lost due to his tendency to recycle paper. It was obvious that Madden had great admiration for Gandhi and was one among many who hoped he would convert to Christianity. At the time of that first contact by letter, a handwritten postscript revealed her fear of association with Gandhi: "This is strictly personal and not to be made public in any way." This caveat hints at the potential trouble Madden thought might accrue if it were known that she, as a missionary, had any sympathy with Gandhi and the nationalist cause. Years later and in her retirement she chose to stay in India for a time. Finally she felt free to involve herself in Gandhi's village work. Mary Barr was more than grateful for Pearl's timely entrance on the scene. In *Bapu*, Barr wrote: "It seemed providential that she [Madden] should have appeared just at the time when Mary C. was so tragically taken. During the two years of her stay in Khedi, she quite revolutionised the spinning and weaving industry, which was hardly worthy of the name of 'industry' before her arrival. She, with her business-like brain and tireless devotion, did more for the development of the work than Mary C. and I could have done together in a much longer time. She became known to the villagers as Motibehn, for 'Moti' is the Hindi name for Pearl."[122]

Gandhi, in writing to Pearl after Polly's death, had this to say: "Tara, who is the link between us, had written to me just before she set out on her fatal pilgrimage, that I must invite you to Wardha and cultivate your acquaintance much more fully. Yes, we must meet and know each other better. For me Tara's death has made it a sacred trust. There was a time when I used to pooh-pooh Tara's reading of people. But her persistence about some people and the truth of it made me revise my opinion of her judgments. Her reading of you therefore draws me towards you."[123]

Madden's tenure in Khedi provided a productive two years of service to village uplift before she left India in 1938 at the age of sixty-two to be reunited with family in Canada. Even in Canada, she continued to promote Gandhi's cause. Using a spinning wheel designed by Gandhi, Madden, dressed in Indian clothing, demonstrated the craft

Pearl Madden, using a spinning wheel designed by Gandhi at the Canadian Handicraft Guild Exhibition, Calgary, 1939. [CALGARY HERALD]

of spinning at a Canadian Handicraft Guild exhibition in Calgary; a photo appeared in the *Calgary Herald* on January 18, 1939.

The suddenness of Polly's death caught Mary Barr, Gandhi, and all her friends off guard. The news was a terrible shock. And while Polly's life was over, there were reverberations for some time to come. Gandhi's letters to those who knew Polly reflected his feelings. The following day, May 16, in a letter to Narandas Gandhi, the son of one of his cousins, Gandhi wrote: "Yesterday I had a telegram telling me of the death at Rishikesh of a very benevolent lady, Tarabehn Chesley. She was on her way to Badri-Kedar with other women. She was a learned person, living an exceedingly simple life."

He wrote the following response to a letter from Jamnalal Bajaj, the person who donated the land for the ashram at Wardha and who first telegrammed Gandhi to tell him of Polly's death: "Tarabehn was indeed an extraordinary woman. Her single-minded devotion, firmness of mind, purity, generosity and love of India baffle description."

To another friend, Lilavati Asar, Gandhi wrote: "Tarabehn passed away on her way to Badri-Kedar. Mahadevi nursed her exceedingly well. She had a severe attack of fever."

Mirabehn (Madeleine Slade), perhaps the most well-known of Gandhi's Western women friends, herself suffering from fever at the time, received the following from Gandhi: "Tara's death has disturbed me much. She was an extraordinarily good woman, possessing great strength of mind. Her love was amazing. I have a graphic description of her death. Brave Mahadevi was by her side all the time."

And to Bajaj again: "I send herewith Gopal's letter for you to read. He seems to have been greatly shocked at Tarabehn's death."

Amrit Kaur, who became the first woman to hold a Cabinet position (as Minister of Health) in the post-Independence government and subsequently was the first woman to be elected president of the World Health Organization, was a close associate of Gandhi. In a letter written days after Polly's death, he said, "Did I tell you about Tara's death during her pilgrimage to Badri-Kedar? You will see all about this in *Harijan*. She was one of the noblest of women I had the good fortune to meet."

Mahadevi Omma was one of Polly's friends at Mahila Ashram. I could not write this book without recounting something of her life and my own story of meeting her, but first of all, Mahadevi's dramatic account of Polly's death is key to our knowing how she came to her end. The following report was sent to Gandhi, then translated from Hindi and distributed to some of Polly's friends and family:

> Concerning Mary Chesley (Taraben)
>
> Told by Mahadevi Omma
>
> May 4/36 five of us (four Indian women and Tara) set out from Wardha for a pilgrimage in the Himalayas. We went to Hardwar by train and stayed for two days. Then, each carrying a load on her back, we began our mountain climb. People were kind and full of wonder at women attempting such a journey without any man to help. They often gave us food. Our first halting place was a Sadhu's hut where we were kindly received.[124] It was

terribly hot and Tara began to get cold and a fever, so we stayed a day at our second stopping place. We suggested that we go back to Hardwar and wait until Taraben should be better, but she wanted to push on. For three days we continued climbing. Tara, on account of spasmodic fever, refused to eat but took a little milk. On the 5th day we threatened to go back and leave Tara if she would not agree to go back herself (by this time we were carrying her luggage). However, she said she wanted to get higher where it would be cooler, and that even though we all went back she would continue alone. So we set off at 4 a.m. again next morning, starting out early in order to get as much walking done as possible before the sun put out its full strength.

Tara had agreed to go on a horse so we covered twelve miles that day. She had a fever again that evening but determined to push on as there was a hospital at the next village, Dev Prayag. It was a three-day trek to reach there, but it was possible to take a short cut by crossing the river down a deep gorge, and then going by bus on the other side. I would take Tara by this quicker route and wait at Dev Prayag for the other three who would go by the ordinary pilgrim's track. Next morning we all set off. It was difficult getting Tara down the steep incline to the river even on a horse. The ferryman demanded Rs. 10 to take us across. However, on arrival at the other side, he realized Tara's weak condition and was pleased at my helping a foreigner. It was with difficulty that I persuaded him to take 6 annas. While I was paying the boatman Tara and the boy who was looking after the horse, went on ahead, and in the dark I could not find the road, so I just sat on a stone and prayed until dawn. I caught up and we were soon in a bus to Dev Prayag. Tara was getting very weak so I gave her water and made her as comfortable as possible, and then went to fetch the doctor, who came and took Tara to his little hospital on a stretcher. There for three days he looked after her with the utmost kindness, and fed me too, but refused to take any remuneration.

Dev Prayag was hotter than any place we had been to so when our friends turned up we thought it better to get Tara back to Hardwar for in spite of the great kindness of the Doctor there, the hospital was so small that we felt the heat more than we would in a larger building. We sent for a special car and I went in it with Tara, leaving the others to await our return in Dev Prayag. On the way she asked me to stop the car and write in Hindi "I leave all my property to Bapu." Then she signed it "Tara" in Hindi. She was lying with her head in my lap and kept murmuring "Mahadevi Omma" and I said, "Yes, your Mahadevi Omma is here, but keep your mind on God and not me."[125] By this time she had grown so weak that as we came into Rishikesh I determined to get the Doctor there. He came at once but when he saw her he said, "It is too late." And her life fled before we could move her out of the car. So I brought her to Hardwar and one or two friends and I laid her out in a new piece of white khaddar. Then we took her to the Gurukul and cremated her, using ghee and sweet scents.[126] The boys and young men of the Gurukul came and chanted their Vedic chants and waved incense over her pyre. I never saw a more beautiful ceremony. It was most impressive.

In a minor way, Polly's death became an international story, in large part due to her friendship with Gandhi and the fact that on her deathbed she willed her estate to him. This caused complications because it was a declaration with no witness other than Mahadevi and also because Polly had written several wills over the years.

Polly had named Lena Bachman, her old friend from Lunenburg, executor of the first will on record, written in 1925 before Polly and her father departed for England. When Lena received word of Polly's death, she began the probate process in Lunenburg County, unaware of the later wills that Polly had written (see Appendix II). News of the later wills confused matters, and Lena's lawyer in Lunenburg was in the midst of trying to discern with London lawyers the state of things when Lena Bachman herself died suddenly from a condition that had gone undiagnosed. Like Polly, who died at the age of forty-four, Lena was still a relatively young woman, so her death was equally unexpected.

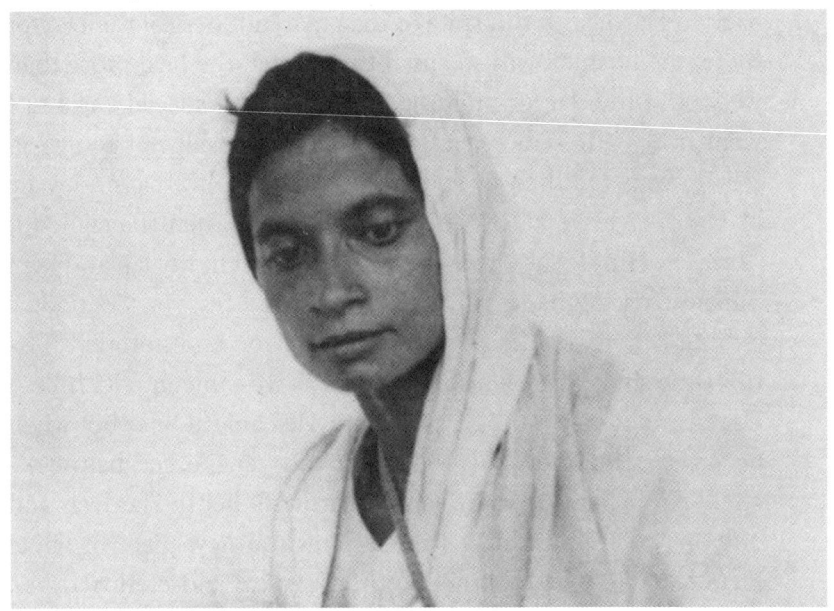

Mahadevi Omma at the time of Polly's death in May 1936.
[Murray Forbes, Mahatma Gandhi]

Trying to sort out what happened with Polly's estate has remained an unsatisfying loose end. Although I believe that Gandhi may have eventually benefitted from Polly's estate, I have not been able to establish this with absolute certainty. A number of Polly's cousins had a vested interest in the outcome of probate because she had no living siblings and no descendants. The trail of correspondence I have been able to find gives hints and leads but no conclusion to the mystery. From the letters quoted herewith, the reader will get an idea of the difficulty of settling the estate.

A letter dated July 2, 1936, and written to Polly's cousin Reverend E. W. (Will) Forbes is in response to one that he had written to Gandhi. Six weeks after Polly's death, this correspondence came from Mahadev Desai, Gandhi's personal secretary.

> Maganwadi, Wardha, India
>
> Dear Friend,
> Mr. Gandhi was delighted to have your letter of May 27th. Ever

since Miss Chesley's tragic death he has been trying to find out the names of her friends and relations. Though she was literally a member of our family we knew nothing of her material possessions and of her blood relationships. Your letter is the first from Canada to shed light.

Even as you had no intimation of her illness we also had none. We know that she was taking a risk in undertaking that pilgrimage. But she would not be deterred. She was never physically very strong and so Mr. Gandhi thought this pilgrimage would be a strain on her health. He tried to dissuade her. But there was such determination in her nature. The trek and the heat proved too much. Suddenly taken ill, she walked on until her legs refused

Nova Scotian Follower Of Gandhi Succumbs

LUNENBURG, May 24.—Miss Mary Albee Chesley, B. A., B. Sc., of Lunenburg, a Christian missionary and a follower of Mahatma Gandhi, died in India, according to a despatch from Harwar, yesterday. Her death occurred after a short illness, while she had been working with All-India Village Industries Association, near Betul. She was 41 years old.

Miss Chesley was a daughter of the late Judge Samuel Chesley, of Lunenburg and a niece of the late Hon. B. Russel, Bedford, one time Justice of the Nova Scotia Supreme Court.

She was the only living member of her immediate family, a brother, Robert, and a sister, Agnes having been drowned in Lunenburg harbor 41 years ago when a sailboat turned over. Her father died several years ago at sea while returning to this province after a trip to England.

Newspaper clipping from when Polly died in May 1936. [NOVA SCOTIA ARCHIVES]

to move. Dear friends accompanied her. One of the sisters took charge of her and tried to take her to the nearest hospital, but she passed away before they could get there. I enclose two issues of our weekly "Harijan" containing Mr. Gandhi's and my articles on her death.

Before her death she wrote in her own handwriting a couple of lines to the effect that all her property, including monies invested in banks or otherwise belonged to "Bapu." The bulk of the monies that she received from time to time from Canadian banks she passed on to Mr. Gandhi to be used for the Village Industries Association. The moment she cast in her lot with us to live in a village about a hundred miles from here, she decided on a simple villagers' life and to observe the vow of poverty. She kept little for herself, gave to other workers and passed the rest to the Village Industries Association. It is not surprising that she willed away all her possessions to Mr. Gandhi.

There is little personal property here. It consists of a bicycle, a sewing machine and a few odds and ends, but we now discover from her friends in England, the principal of whom is Miss Pat Blyth that she had some property in England and that she had some money owing to her by Miss Blyth and Cecilia Morris whose promise to repay the amount (£800) is now in Mr. Gandhi's possession.[127]

Miss Mary Barr who was her companion in the village where she worked is collecting all her papers and things. She has just passed on to Mr. Gandhi a duplicate cheque from the Canadian Government in payment of her annuity. There is another pay order dated June 11th received only a couple of days ago. Miss Barr says that there are various other papers about money matters, a receipt for an Indian Post Office Bank book and also a cheque book on Barclays Bank.

The fact that she has willed her property to Mr. Gandhi is embarrassing for him. He himself owns no property and whatever comes to him becomes a trust to be used for the welfare of the poor. He has had to undertake trusts of this kind before but the present one is of such a peculiar nature that Mr. Gandhi would appreciate any advice that you may make in the matter.

I quote here relevant paragraphs from Miss Blyth's letter to Mr. Gandhi dated June 2nd:

"Her last letter to me was written on April 29th when she was planning to leave for a pilgrimage. Can you please tell me why and how she died? I have been left in charge of her affairs here and I must ask you to send me her letters, papers and so on so that I may communicate with her relatives. I do not even know their addresses until I get these papers."

"May I thank you for the happiness your work brought to Mary who was always a lonely and little understood person here in England. Her letters from India have been full of deep spiritual peace and contentment so that I have envied her.

"I am sure that her accounts of the work in India have brought to some here at least a little more understanding of the sufferings of India and of your plans for it."

Miss Blyth's address is Potters Bar High School, Middlesex, England.

Now I have placed before you all the facts about Miss Chesley in my possession. Any more light that you could give and any suggestions that you have will be welcome.

Yours sincerely,
Mahadev Desai
Secretary of Mr. Gandhi

P.S. I am enclosing two photographs one of Miss Chesley after her death and the other of the funeral pyre.

A second letter from Mahadev Desai follows, dated July 9:

Dear Mr. Forbes,
I wrote to you last week. Mr. Gandhi has another letter from you this week. I should add a few details to my last letter.

Miss Chesley's will—if "will" it can be called—is in the Hindi language, and is naturally unattested. Perhaps the law of succession requires two witnesses and I am not sure what law will apply to Miss Chesley. In the meantime letters of administration have to be applied for, and they can be applied for only by you as her nearest heir. Will you kindly therefore enable us to submit an application to the High Court at Nagpur by signing a power of attorney in Mr. Gandhi's favour or my favour, so that we may act on your behalf?

Since writing to you I've have had two more letters from Canadian friends Mrs. Eunice Buchanan and Miss Lena Bachman, Lunenburg (N.S.)

Yours sincerely,
Mahadev Desai

The following excerpt is from one of the articles Mahadev Desai referred to, written by Gandhi for *The Harijan* soon after Polly's death:

May 23, 1936

IN MEMORIAM

Miss Mary Chesley, an Englishwoman, came to India in 1934, when the congress was in session in Bombay. As soon as she landed she came to my hut in the Congress Camp and told me she knew Mirabehn and had expected to come with her but somehow or other she had preceded her by a week. Her desire was to serve India through her villages. She did not prepossess me by her talk and I thought she would not stay in India many months. But I was wholly mistaken. She had come to know of Miss Mary Barr who had commenced village work in Betel (C.P.). Miss Barr brought Mary Chesley to Wardha and we were together for a few days. Miss Chesley showed a determination that surprised me. She began work with Mary Barr in Khedi, adopted the Indian costume and changed her name to Tarabehn and toiled at Khedi in a manner that alarmed Mary Barr. She would dig, carry baskets full of earth on her head. She simplified her food as much as to put her health in danger. She had her own income from Canada from which she kept only about Rs. 10 for herself and gave the rest to the A.I.V.I.A. [All India Village Industries Association] or to Indians with whom she came in contact and who needed some help. I came in closest touch with her. Her charity was boundless, she had great faith in the goodness of human nature. She was a devout Christian. But she had no narrowness about her. She did not believe in converting others. She was a graduate of the London School of Economics and a good teacher, having conducted together with a companion a school in London. She realized that she must learn Hindi. For being able to pick up conversational Hindi she lived in the Wardha Mahila Ashram and there formed a plan of going to Badrikedar. I had warned her against the adventure. But it was difficult to turn her from adventures when her mind was made up. Only the other day she started on her perilous pilgrimage. And I got a message on the 15th from Kankhal saying, "Tarabehn expired." In her love for India's villages she was not to be excelled. Her passion for India's Independence was equal to that of the best among us. She mixed with poor women and children with the greatest freedom. She was a self-effacing worker. May her soul rest in peace.

M. K. Gandhi

A couple of days later, on May 25, 1936, *The Scotsman*, published in Midlothian, Scotland, ran an article about Polly's death, "Miss Mary Albee Chesley, a Canadian disciple of Gandhi at Hardwar is reported to have died at Nagpur." Another notice, under the headline "Taraben Dead, Mr. Gandhi's Canadian Disciple," appeared in the *Civil & Military Gazette*, Lahore, Pakistan, on May 26, 1936.

The following week, Mahadev Desai added further news in the *Harijan*:

Saturday, May 30, 1936

Taraben Chesley

When Gandhiji wrote last week about the late Mary Chesley—better known amongst us as Taraben—we had no details of the tragic story of her death. They are now available. She was as great and good and true in her death as in her life. As Gandhiji has already said, she had an income that would enable her to spend the summer on a hill-station. But she would not think of it. She planned instead a pilgrimage to Badrikedarnath (Himalayas) with sisters from the Mahilashram, Wardha, with whom she had worked who had captured her heart. On the journey she caught a cold, the sisters pleaded with her to return but she would not listen. She insisted on walking with her own kit on her back. Deadly fever—pneumonia perhaps—laid her low. When she could not move she consented to be taken to the nearest hospital. As she was being taken there, life was ebbing away. She dictated her will. The brave sister Mahadevi who accompanied her and nursed her only knew Hindi which fortunately Miss Chesley had learnt during the last six months. These were the words she dictated: "All the property in my name, including money in Canadian banks, belongs to Bapu," and signed it in Hindi: "Taraben." She died soon after in Mahadevi's lap. The latter who adored Taraben and who knew that the deceased's love for India equaled her own, decided to cremate her. She took the corpse to Gurukula, Kangri. The Gurukula friends cremated it according to the Vedic rites. Thus closed a beautiful life full of promise. I cannot believe that her services have ended. She has left behind her comrades who have caught from her the fire of loving and selfless service.

When Mahadev Desai referred to hill-stations, he was speaking of those places at higher altitude where the British would go in the hottest months to get out of the heat. The most famous of the stations at Simla (now Shimla), in the Himalayan foothills, was a centre of imperial social life, the summer capital of the Raj.

As mentioned earlier, my first inkling that Polly went to India came from the obituary that the Friends' Archive in London sent to me. It appeared along with a covering note written by Mahadev Desai in the August 1 issue of the *Harijan*.

The following notice about the late Taraben Chesley appearing in the Quaker weekly *The Friend* will be read with interest. She was so reticent about her past career that we knew little. This brief notice shows that she had treated her life as a sacred trust and it was full, wherever she was, of the service of humanity. If in England she was a member of "The Neighbours" who restrict themselves to a maximum of the average annual income per head, here she contented herself with the average annual income of an Indian.

"Mary Chesley was born in 1891. Trained as a teacher at Mount Allison University, Canada, she also studied in London and at the Sorbonne. She was a B.A. and B.Sc. (Honours in Public Administration). Her first teaching posts were in Bridgewater, Nova Scotia; San [Diego]; and the King Edward High School at Vancouver.

About 1918 she raised a thousand pounds for Russian relief. Failing to get much response by descriptions of Russia's needs, she procured some pictures of the plight of Russians, persuaded cinemas to show these pictures, and herself stood at the door with a collecting box.

Coming to England, she had a pacifist motion put forward in one of the English annual Labour conferences. A subsequent Foreign Secretary tried hard to dissuade her, as he did not wish the executive to have the onus of turning down a pacifist motion. At the Conference she spoke in support of the motion. A subsequent Prime Minister spoke against it.

In 1926 Mary Chesley and Olive Warner conducted a small private school in Quaker Lane, Potters Bar, Mary Chesley carrying it on herself, when Olive Warner went to South Africa. She gave up the schoolwork two or three years ago to spread the practice of Christian economics, nationally and internationally. She was a member of Professor Bellerby's group, The Neighbours, who restrict their personal spending to the average wage of the country.

In the year 1931 she had joined Friends (Quakers), and was a member of Welwyn Garden City Meeting.

India seemed to her to offer the best scope for her experiments."

The notice in *The Friend* continued with quotations from Gandhi's memorial tribute. Some of the biographical details in the article were incorrect; however, it provided leads to new information.

In the September 19 edition of the *Harijan*, a further note was published.

> About Taraben Mary Chesley
>
> Almost every mail, letters are being received from the late Mary Chesley's relatives and friends extolling her virtues and telling me of the benefactions received by them from her and of promises of help made by her. Though Mahadev Desai has been giving correspondents information as he can, it is necessary to make an announcement for the benefit of all concerned that the will made by her in my favour just before her death does not appear to be valid according to the Indian Succession Act. Even if it can be proved, I have no desire to use her property, except with the concurrence of her relatives and friends, for the sake of the Indian village industries work, which was her latest and last love. If the property came into my hands, I should examine all her commitments and promises in the West and try to satisfy them before making use of anything left. I have cheques from her Bank, uncashed. My advice to her cousins is that the nearest of them should take out letters of administration and send me legal authority to part with whatever is in my hands or Miss Mary Barr's. The deceased had so reduced her personal wants in India that there is hardly anything left which can be converted into money. All she received was generally made over to me for village work. I hope this gives all concerned such information as is in my possession about the affairs of the deceased humanitarian.

With regard to her bank (Barclays), a letter dated September 2, 1936, from the bank manager of the Potters Bar branch to Reverend Forbes makes it apparent that Forbes was the cousin most intimately involved in trying to solve the estate questions.

Dear Sir,

Miss Mary Albee Chesley

We thank you for your letter of the 8th ultimo.

We have an account here in the name of Miss M. A. Chesley and we are holding certain property on her behalf.

We are much obliged to you for the information you give, but you will appreciate that if, and when, the necessary legal formalities are completed enabling a legal representative to deal with the property of the deceased, we should be compelled to comply, subject, of course, to the production of the necessary documents to satisfy us.

Yours faithfully,[128]

While the settlement of Polly's estate was of particular interest to those named in certain wills, as well as the various cousins, the story also aroused general curiosity and reverberated on the wire services internationally. In Australia, where the digitizing of newspapers has been widely carried out, at least ten journals across the country ran more or less the same story with minor variations concerning property in Bridgewater, Nova Scotia, which Gandhi had supposedly inherited from Polly and was possibly up for sale because of taxes being in arrears. New Zealand carried accounts in four of its papers. The *Bridgewater Bulletin* made great hay over this issue of Gandhi's taxes. I suppose it made newsworthy copy to think that Gandhi owned land locally and was being derelict in his duties regarding the taxes.

A much more recent article that paraded itself as a slice of history further sensationalized this story. The Halifax *Sunday Herald* of June 5, 2011, ran the story under the headline "Deadbeat Mahatma—How the town of Bridgewater ended up in a property dispute with India's father of independence," making the proverbial mountain out of a molehill. There was never any confirmation at the time that Gandhi had a legal claim to Polly's estate. In fact, Lena Bachman's lawyer, W. P. Potter, was undertaking to have the Lunenburg will probated, and according to his accounts, on November 7, 1936, he wrote to the Town Clerk of Bridgewater and enclosed a cheque for $17.84 in payment of the taxes owing.[129]

The *New York Times* of October 25, 1936, carried a Canadian Press story "Gandhi Loses a Bequest" that also appeared in the New Zealand newspaper *Evening Post* on August 11, 1937, under the title "A Loss to Gandhi." Its appearance indicates how intrigued people were with this story globally.

> A report from Bridgewater, Nova Scotia (Canada) states that Mahatma Gandhi will not receive any share of the estate of the late Miss Mary Chesley because there was only one witness instead of two to a will in which she bequeathed him property and capital. Miss Chesley, a Lunenburg woman, who went to India and became one of the Mahatma's followers, died last May in India. The estate she left to Mr. Gandhi included about ten acres of pasture lands in Canada, property in England, an interest in an estate in North Dakota, and $2,600 in bonds and other personal property. The Probate Court has ruled the will invalid, and recognized a previous one, in which the Independent Labour Party of Great Britain and relatives of Miss Chesley were named beneficiaries.

Much confusion and misinformation was afloat. Polly named the Independent Labour Party in her first will, but there were two or more later wills written in Britain in which the party was not listed as a beneficiary.

Articles concerning Polly's estate appeared in American papers as well, such as the *Nevada State Journal* (October 21, 1936), *Sheboygan Press* (Wisconsin; October 9, 1936), and the *Charleston Daily Mail* (West Virginia; November 4, 1936). Even a German newspaper, the *Alpenzeitung*, carried the story on January 1, 1937. More extensive digitizing of newspapers will inevitably reveal other accounts. An article praising Polly's life of service appeared under the title "Charity Suffereth Long And Is Very Kind: The English Quaker Who Gave Herself to India" in the July 4, 1936 edition of the *Children's Newspaper*, a British publication providing uplifting news of the world. In spite of Polly's near-disappearance from the historical record, it is clear that, at the time of her death, her story held a certain drama and was a source of curiosity internationally.

The following letters to Polly's cousin E. Will Forbes from two of Polly's friends, Lena Bachman and Pat Blyth, and another cousin, Gyrth Russell, provide different glimpses of the situation regarding the settling (and unsettling nature) of the estate. The first letter, from Lena Bachman, indicates her questioning of Gandhi's claim (and she did have something to lose if he was granted the estate) and makes reference to family correspondence that went back to the time when Mary Russell Chesley and her sister, Alma ("Aunt Am"), were still alive.

August 22, 1936

Dear Mr. Forbes,
I received your letter....
I will keep the pieces of will as you suggest and if there is any other information you can give me after you hear from Miss Blyth, I would be pleased to receive it. I understand she too is in possession of a will. I had a letter from Gandhi's secretary, and pictures like you received.

I did something, and I hope I did right. What do you think? I was worried about those letters after I said I would send them to the Miss Chesleys, and realized they were entrusted to my care for over ten years, and wondered if my dear friend would wish me to let them go, the thought bothered me so much, that I wrote to them to come and spend a few days to look them over, as I didn't feel right about letting them go out of my possession. I do feel like burying them. You took your own personal letters, and I was glad you found some which awakened fond memories, and you were like one of the Chesley family, and they seemed to belong to you, as no doubt Aunt Am and Mrs. Chesley saved them.
...
We all send best regards to you and Mrs. Forbes.

Yours sincerely,
Lena B. Bachman

Based on the fact that Lena died rather suddenly, it is unlikely she got around to destroying the letters. I imagine they are the same letters that her daughter, Natalie Corkum, disposed of only a short while before I met her. When I first talked with Natalie about Polly, she said she had held on to Chesley letters for so many years but finally decided that no one would be interested in them. Little did she know! Another conversation with Natalie led me to think that she echoed her mother in wondering whether she should share those letters with anyone. Natalie mentioned that personal letters she had saved (one from her father when she was a child and some from her husband) would be buried with her.

The letter from Pat Blyth helps to round out a picture of a generous Polly, whose sympathies for anyone in need was real and immediate.

> Potters Bar High School,
> Potters Bar, Middlesex, England
> August 23 [1936]
>
> Dear Mr. Forbes,
> Many thanks for your letter. I had heard from Mr. Gandhi that he had written to you asking you to sign the power of attorney, and, as I believe, with you, that Mary's wish was that all she had should go to his work, I wish you had felt yourself able to do so.
> He would certainly not neglect the three cousins whom you mention as being needy, and I have already mentioned Mrs. Rousse's case to him.
> The will you mention, in Mrs. Lena Bachman's possession is absolutely valueless, as there is certainly a will of 1930–31 in possession of a Mrs. McCreath in Barnet, about which some steps are being taken.[130]
> This is a complicated will, I believe, making various small bequests to friends here, but I am sure that Mary had quite forgotten its existence, or the existence of the will in Canada. She made, during the few years of my friendship with her, some three or four wills, one in favour of the Oxford Group Movement, in which she was temporarily interested, and one before that in my favour, when I was beginning the school, and was in difficulties.

She destroyed these two wills when she became interested in Gandhi's work and most certainly meant to make a new one in his favour after investigating the work for herself. She was perfectly conscious when the Hindi "will" was made, and surely had shown by her last years of life where all her interest lay.

She left me in charge of her house, of which I have the use of the downstairs schoolroom and land at the back, in return for paying all rates and taxes on the house, and keeping the garden in order, as well as looking after the house.

I let the upper flat for months to a tenant who died in Feb. of this year. Then my maid and family lived in it for 11 or 12 weeks. The first tenant's rent I banked in Mary's name at Barclays Bank. The rent from the maid I have had to use in urgent repairs to the house, which, at the back was beginning to rot and grow damp on account of the rotting balcony.

As you suggest, I have no intention of sending any money to Mr. Gandhi until the will is proved.

She lived, as you know, in a style of the utmost simplicity, possessing only the barest necessities.

Mrs. Rousse told me that Mary had written in answer to a letter of hers. She asked me for her carpet and armchair and I gave her these.

You mention Mrs. Rousse as being mentioned in the will which Mrs. Bachman has. During the last years, Mary felt shabbily treated by Mrs. Rousse, and, though she would be incapable of bearing grudges in the face of Mrs. Rousse's need, I know that she would not now have thought of her in preference to Mr. Gandhi's work. I told him about Mrs. Rousse, as in the second (Mrs. McCreath's) will, Mary left her the income from the house until 1940 (when her three daughters should be settled and able to help her). Hers is a needy case, for the next year or two, and Mr. Gandhi has said that he would consider all such cases.

What I have said about her is in strict confidence—I feel that she considers that she has some claim, and you should know the facts.

I have heard from another cousin of Mary's—Mr. Gyrth Russell, who wrote kindly offering to help me if things were difficult.

She gave me the deeds of the house, saying that she meant me to have it for my lifetime. I shall, however, not make complications by attaching importance to words spoken in the warmth of Mary's heart, when I am quite sure that—now that I am no longer in such difficult circumstances—she would prefer that Gandhi have the revenue from the house for his work.

She was more than good and generous to me. Without her help I should have had a harder fight than I could have managed.

I am sure there are many who, like myself, feel her loss more and more poignantly as time passes.

Yours sincerely
Martha ("Pat") Blyth

A letter from Gyrth Russell to his cousin Will Forbes in the fall of 1936 adds to the picture. Readers may recall that Polly wrote about spending time with Gyrth in London when she was a student there. He and Polly and Will Forbes were all first cousins, from the Russell side of the family. Will's mother was an older sister to Mary senior, whose brother Benjamin was Gyrth's father.

October 13, 1936

Dear Will,
No doubt you have had the letter from Mahadev Desai with a copy of "Harijan" in which Gandhi has made a public statement about Polly's affairs. It seems from this that I am the one indicated to take out the letters of administration. I have not done so, but I have written to ask for a Death Certificate, so that, whoever handles the matter will have something to start with.

He speaks of other wills left by her. I am advised by my bank that it is likely to be trouble to get the estate settled up by reason of being in three or four different countries, and I am not keen to undertake it if my own share is likely to be so small as to hardly pay me for the time and trouble. If it is agreed by the others that I should receive a twelfth or thirteenth (according to the exact number of cousins) I am willing to take out letters of administration here and give a legal bond for the proper disposal of the proceeds of the estate. I am advised that, should I do this, it will save a great expense and months of delay, since I am only a few hours away from the property at Potters Bar and the Air Mail to India takes but a few days.

Of course, if there is an earlier will in existence, that alters everything. In that case, when I know who the heirs are, I shall send on the Death Certificate to them and they can take the necessary action.

With kindest regards,

Yours sincerely,
Gyrth

There is no indication that Gyrth had anything further to do with this matter.

For details laid out by Polly in her wills of 1928 and 1934, see Appendix I and II. As noted in the 1934 will, Polly left much of her estate to the Inner Team of the Oxford Group. The following letters regarding the estate and the letters of administration taken out over the course of the two years following Polly's death indicate the confusion left in its wake.

On November 12, 1936, a member of the Oxford Group wrote to Will Forbes:

Dear Mr. Forbes,
I enclose a will made by your cousin Miss Mary Chesley in favour of the Oxford Group. We are giving up our claim to it entirely in favour of her family who might benefit. I have also been in touch with the Miss Blyth and Miss Morris referred to in the will, and they agree also to make no claim.

I understand that there are other wills. Which ever will turns out to be the legal one, we thought you would like to see what her wishes were for the members of her own family.

Yours sincerely, G.[?] Evans.

The fact that this will was at some point copied into the Lunenburg Will Book of the *Nova Scotia Probate Records* indicates to me that Forbes must have shared this information with the County Probate Court. The probate records include a letter from W. P. Potter of Lunenburg, the lawyer representing Lena Bachman, dated December 22, 1936, to a lawyer in England. Written over a month after the Oxford Group had sent the will to Forbes, it indicates gaps in communication between the various parties, for Potter wrote: "There are rumors of another Will which is supposed to be in the possession of a Mrs. McCreath."

In 1937, a full year after Polly's death, the question of her estate was still unresolved. Lena Bachman was no longer involved because she had died earlier in the year, on March 9. A letter dated November 13, 1937, from one of the cousins, Bernard W. Russell, to the Oxford Group further indicates a lack of communication between Forbes and his Russell cousins. Bernard Russell, who was a lawyer, was writing on behalf of his cousin Edith and some of the other Russell relatives.

> Dear Sirs:
> Some time ago Miss P. Blyth of Potters Bar School, Middlesex, delivered to you the will of Mary Albee Chesley under which she attempted to leave a bequest to you.
>
> A previous will which she made was probated in Lunenburg, and I am acting for the administratrix [Edith Russell] with the will annexed. It is apparent that the will in your favor revoked the probated will and should therefore be probated whether the bequests contained are valid or not, because if not valid there would be an intestacy which would benefit certain relatives of Miss Chesley who are much in need.
>
> Would you be kind enough to inform me whether you still possess this will and send me a copy of the same.
>
> Yours very truly,
> B. W. Russell

Here is the reply from Evans of the Oxford Group, written later that month: "With reference to the will of Miss Mary Chesley, delivered to us by Miss Blyth, we no longer have it in our possession. We sent it to the Rev. E. Forbes, one of Miss Chesley's relatives in Bermuda, so that, even if the will were not proved, he might see what were her wishes.

"I am sorry that we have not got the address of Mr. Forbes, but possibly some of the other relatives may know it. It is possible too that the Manager of Barclays Bank, Potters Bar, may be able to help you."

Based on this letter, it would appear that Forbes and the Russells were not in contact even though they were first cousins. The following year, in April 1938, the Lunenburg Will Book contained another renunciation from the Russell cousins as Bernard, the lawyer, filed for a new letter of administration. After this, the trail goes cold. I found no other references to what might have happened until a 1948 newspaper article came to my attention in the most circuitous way.

I mentioned that during the time I lived in Lunenburg, I had never heard of the Chesleys. Once I became interested in Mary Russell Chesley and subsequently became fascinated with her daughter Polly's life, I sought out older people in the community who might have known the Chesleys. Someone led me to Natalie (Bachman) Corkum, whose mother, Lena, had been a close friend of Polly's. I confess that in my first phone call with Natalie, I was nearly heartbroken when she told me that she had, only shortly before my contacting her, destroyed letters and photos regarding Polly. But when I visited Natalie, our conversation revealed many personal memories that were most helpful in my effort to understand Polly's interests and personality. Natalie also provided photographs of Polly, included in this book.

I gained further leads from Natalie in follow-up visits, but it was years later that the next major breakthrough came. Someone in Lunenburg heard about my research interest and contacted me to say that he had found an article "about that woman" (Polly) in his mother's attic. It was an article that was new to me. Undated and without the newspaper's masthead, it did, nevertheless, reveal new information, and it was clear that it had not been written immediately after Polly's death in 1936 but upon the death of Gandhi in 1948. I have since identified the date and in which paper it appeared. A portion of the *Halifax Chronicle* article of January 31, 1948, follows:

Nova Scotian was Gandhi's Associate

The sensational end of Mahatma Gandhi—shot to death by a political agent at New Delhi—recalled that one of his close associates for years was a Nova Scotia girl, Miss Mary Chesley, of Lunenburg. Gandhi adopted her as his daughter—she was known in the family as Taraben—and she died in India at the age of 41 in 1936, while on a hot weather walking pilgrimage to Badrikedar in the Himalayas, accompanied by Ashram sisters from Wardha, where she was engaged in village association work.

Miss Chesley left considerable property in England to the cause of Indian independence which she did not live to see triumphant, and which Gandhi survived by only about a year.

Typical of many newspaper articles, some of the facts are incorrect: Polly was in India less than two years, and she was forty-four at the time of her death. In addition to information already shared earlier, the article spoke of Polly's cousin, Rev. Forbes. At the time of Polly's death, he was living in Bermuda. In 1948 he was living in Dartmouth, Nova Scotia, and that information inspired me to check the Public Archives of Nova Scotia for his obituary. My hope was that he had lived at least until 1961, because from that year onward there is a record of the obituaries published in the *Chronicle Herald* and therefore available on microfilm.

By good fortune, I discovered that Will Forbes died in 1962. He was a widower with no offspring. The only lead was that the obituary mentioned the minister, a Reverend MacDonald, who had performed the funeral service.

Aware that ministers moved often to different pastorates during their career, it seemed unlikely that the minister would be in Dartmouth and, perhaps, even less likely that he was alive, considering that I was on this search almost forty years after Will Forbes's death. However, with no other option available, I searched the telephone book to see if this individual was listed. I found his name and called, preparing myself for the possibility that his widow might answer. A man answered. At this point, I realized how ludicrous it was that I was phoning a minister who had officiated a funeral service decades ago to find out...what? This gracious man accepted my query without any hint that my call was odd or unwelcome. Reverend MacDonald remembered Reverend Forbes and his wife, who was originally from Scotland, and told me the following: In the Forbes's later years, a niece had come from Scotland to take care of them. The niece had returned to Scotland after their deaths, and Reverend MacDonald expressed regret that he could only remember her last name. I was marvelling at the retired minister's remarkable memory yet was aware that the trail was getting cooler by the minute. As an afterthought, he said, "Reverend Forbes had a cousin. He's dead, but he had a son."

I realized how unlikely it was that any of this information would be of use to me, for the cousin was no relation to Polly, he being from the paternal side of Will Forbes's family, and Polly being related to Will through his mother, Mary senior's older sister. I hung up the phone knowing the name of the son of the deceased cousin of the deceased Rev. Forbes. Still, it was all I had, and like a dog with a bone, I could not let go. I found the name in the phone book and called. He answered and when I explained myself, he said, "I have some letters and photos concerning that woman." Needless to say, my heart began to race. He generously lent me the material that day. The photos that were taken at the time of Polly's death were those received by Rev. Forbes from Gandhi. Letters from India were among the treasures that he had saved all these years, some excerpts already quoted in this text.

During the course of my search for evidence of Polly's past, I had often come up against dead ends. Then I would have an unexpected and uncanny breakthrough. Call it fate, synchronicity, or serendipity—I myself have found it difficult to label why this was happening. I might never have found this Polly-related material if even one part of the chain of events leading to its uncovering had been broken. If Reverend Forbes had died a year earlier, his obituary would have been impossible to find. If the newspaper had not given the name of the minister who performed the funeral service, my search would have ended there. If I had been unable to find him in the phone book because he had moved or died, that would have ended the search. If the minister had not answered the phone, if his memory had not been as sharp, or if he had been unable to recall the name of the son of the cousin, I would have hit the end of the trail there. If either the minister or the Forbes relative had not been home that day, would I have had the temerity or audacity to call another day, considering how unlikely it was that anything would come of this line of inquiry?

The following story is another small miracle of synchronicity. Years ago, I had discovered that Gandhi's personal secretary, Mahadev Desai, who died in prison in 1942 at the age of fifty, had a son. Born in 1924, Narayan Desai had a distinguished career in India, promoting, teaching, and writing about non-violence. Narayan would have been a boy when Polly was alive, so I wanted to find out if he had ever known her or Mahadevi Omma, Polly's companion in whose arms she died on the way to the Himalayas. I found an email address and wrote to him. I heard nothing. I subsequently found another email address and tried once more. Nothing. Finally, I found a postal address and eventually received word from him. He stated that he had not known Polly but thought that I might be looking for Mahadevi *Tai* (meaning grandmother). He gave me an address in Bangalore for her. Over the next three years, I wrote three letters to that address, unwilling to accept the possibility that I would never hear anything. My persistence was ultimately rewarded when on March 12, 2002, I received the following email from her great-nephew:

> Respected Sharon,
> This is Siddharth Sharma from Bangalore, India. Let me introduce myself. I live in the same ashram as Mahadevi Tai. You can safely term her as my grandmother. She is now 97 years old and resultantly has some memory lapses. But these are lapses of short-term memory. She remembers vividly past occurrences. She remembered instantly Taraben and her companionship even before she was shown the photograph sent by you. Her English is not fluent but people here will help overcome this difficulty. Tai is a living legend in India. Not many people of that generation of freedom fighters who helped liberate India with the weapon of Ahimsa [non-violence] are alive today.
>
> Looking forward to an extended session of correspondence.

Perhaps, dear reader, you can appreciate how excited I was to receive this email. I do not even know why I had continued to send letters into the ether when I had not received any responses with the first two attempts. I suppose I was unwilling to believe that the lead Narayan Desai had given would serve no purpose.

In 2003, I had the great privilege of meeting both Mahadevi Tai and Narayan Desai in India. Mahadevi Tai lived in an ashram that she had established in 1963 for orphans. When I visited, it was also a place for the elderly. Not long after arriving in New Delhi, I flew to Bangalore to meet Mahadevi. Because of her age, the visit was a priority. As it turned out, Mahadevi Tai would live for another few years. She died in 2006 at the age of one hundred.

I had two visits with Mahadevi. To meet the last person in the world to see Polly alive and one of the last alive to have known her at all was a special privilege. Siddharth served as our translator with patience, love, and respect for his elderly relative. Mahadevi's short-term memory was very restricted, but when I showed her the photograph taken when Polly died, she immediately welled up with emotion and while wiping away her tears, said (in Hindi), "She was my *didi* (older sister)" and recounted the story of Polly's last days. It was as though the event had just occurred. However, ten minutes later, looking at the picture again, she went through a similar reaction, remembering anew what had happened sixty-seven years earlier but not what had happened ten minutes prior.

Mahadevi's past tells a distinctly Indian story. She came from a high caste family in Karnataka and, like other girls in India at that time, was betrothed when a child. The person to whom she was betrothed died, and she became a child widow before any consummation of the marriage. Those who have seen the 2005 film *Water* by Canadian filmmaker Deepa Mehta, which tells the story of a child widow forced to live with other outcast widows, will know that the life of a girl or woman was worth little once a victim of such fate. In theory, it was legally permissible to remarry, but in custom, this rarely happened.

When Gandhi was on one of his tours around the country, he stayed with Mahadevi's family. Mahadevi was inspired by Gandhi's independence movement and felt that she could lead a useful life if she

Mahadevi Tai and the author meeting in 2003. [Bill Plaskett]

were to join the cause. As a young widow with limited opportunities, she had nothing to lose. Because of Gandhi's adoption of *brahmacharya*, which included sexual abstinence, he gave encouragement to men and women to lead celibate lives and serve the greater good. Mahadevi asked to go live in Wardha. She became like a daughter to Vinoba Bhave, who was both a follower of and a spiritual inspiration to Gandhi. After Gandhi's death, Vinoba Bhave initiated the Bhoodan (Land Gift) Movement in the 1950s whereby wealthy landowners were encouraged to give land for use to landless people. He walked thousands of miles around India, accompanied by Mahadevi and others. These *padayatras* (journeys by foot) attracted countless pilgrims. Vinoba was a celibate man with no children, and when he died in 1982, he specified that Mahadevi was to light his funeral pyre, an honour that almost universally went to a male member of a family. When Mahadevi turned one hundred, she was "felicitated" and referred to as the "grand old lady of Karnataka and noted Sarvodaya leader" (*The Hindu*, January 11, 2006).

She had gone to jail three times during the freedom struggle. When I visited Mahadevi, she told a story of being in prison. Mahadevi stood up and bowed as she described how she had informed the prison guard that she would bow in respect to him as a person but that she could not bow in submission. The fire and fervency of the Indian independence cause was still evident in her eyes and voice as she recalled this story.

On my second visit, she sensed rather than knew that we had met before. She expressed the hope that she had been welcoming. Even with her limited mobility, she was determined to come to the veranda when it was time to say farewell. In a final photo, she insisted on not having her cane in the picture. Walking away, I turned several times to see her standing there, knowing the unlikelihood of ever seeing her again. It was as though she was equally aware of this fact, remaining on the porch until we disappeared from view.

~~~

Polly's life ended in May of 1936. She had a peripatetic life and a restless, seeking mind and heart. She was generous (to a fault, as Gandhi had put it) and had engaged passionately with various political, social, and spiritual enthusiasms over the years. Because of her several wills and the circumstances of her death, her story momentarily captured the attention and curiosity of people across the globe. There were those with a vested interest in her estate, so her monetary legacy held their attention for a few years. Nevertheless, it is in the words of a few friends in the time following her untimely death that we gain further insight into the person that Polly was.

The *Harijan* of July 18, 1936, contains a touching report from Gandhi regarding the veranda Polly had built and its continued use:

> A Villager's Humanity
>
> The reader will be glad to see the following pictures sent by Miss Mary Barr of Khedi of what I have called "A Villager's Humanity."
> Barr wrote: "Yesterday I found an old woman sitting in the wet with her calf. I asked her why she did not sit in the verandah

with the rest of her party and keep dry. (They were some wandering people who had asked leave to camp for 24 hours on the verandah.) She replied, 'I am sitting by this calf. Its mother is dead.'

"This afternoon I found two donkeys had come to the verandah out of the rain and my first instinct was to 'shoo' them off as they would spoil the floor. They obediently 'shooed' and I immediately felt ashamed remembering yesterday's old woman and invited them back. They came!

"I am sure Tara would be glad to know that HER verandah is sheltering all kinds of men and beasts during these wet days."

The reference to Tara, i.e., the late Mary Chesley, entirely bears out what I knew of her, and now that her numerous intimate friends have come to know about her premature and unexpected death, I have been receiving touching letters about the qualities of her heart and head. From those I copy the following:

"Polly (Miss Chesley) was built of the stuff from which martyrs are made. She never knew fear. She was a keen pacifist and persuaded me to take the post left vacant at her mother's death as Superintendent of Peace and Arbitration in the W.C.T.U. for Canada. Polly and I worked together to gather money for the Russian and Chinese famines, getting ten thousand dollars. We also collected one thousand for German children's relief."

This last quotation was from Eunice Buchanan, Polly's friend in Berwick. Following Polly's death, a small notice in the *Berwick Register* on June 3, 1936, revealed something new—a hint of Polly's projected plans: "A recent dispatch from India conveys the sad tidings of the death of Miss Mary Chesley, B.A., B.Sc., after a brief illness. Miss Chesley had been a frequent visitor with Eunice Buchanan, South Berwick. Three days after the news of her death had been received, Mrs. Buchanan received a long letter from Miss Chesley in which she said she was well and happy in her All India Village Industry work and was planning a lecture trip around the world and a chance to see her old friends in Canada."

This is the only clue available as to Polly's possible next adventure. The idea of Polly doing a lecture trip around to world to tell of what was happening in India is entirely in character. Whatever cause Polly took on, she did it with complete enthusiasm and passion. Speaking out on social and political issues seemed to be built into her DNA. While she was very much her mother's daughter, perhaps one of the ways in which she differed was that she seemed a restless soul and needed to be continually on the move. It is only from her English friend Pat Blyth that we get a hint that Polly might have been a lonely soul. It is perhaps not surprising that she, with no immediate family, a better than average intellect, and a propensity to completely commit to causes, might have been "little understood," as Blyth said. It does seem as though she found a spiritual home in India and a community of like-minded workers who appreciated her. Even so, the idea that she might have travelled, yet again, to share her story of India and Gandhi's work suggests that Polly, had she lived, would not have remained in any one place for long. Would she have returned to India after a world tour? Before discovering the small article in the *Berwick Register* suggesting she was planning a tour, I had imagined that Polly might have found enough contentment that she would have remained in India indefinitely. Now I am not so sure. Like the uncertainty of what happened to Polly's estate, Polly's potential future, had she lived, is also one of mystery.

In July 2014, I travelled to Britain to make one last attempt to find out what happened to Polly's estate. I thought I might not find the answer to that question, but at the very least, I could put the question to rest. That is what I had to settle for. For some reason, 1938 was the last date of deeds available for Middlesex County, which included Potters Bar where Polly had a house, and also the last date of records of probate in India (I had already determined that no will had been probated in England). It is highly possible that such records were lost during the Second World War bombings in London. Because Polly's Russell cousins had taken out letters of administration in Canada in 1938, I knew that resolution of the estate had not been completed by that time. Earlier newspaper articles reporting that Gandhi would not be the recipient of Polly's estate may have been premature. The

1948 article referred to earlier implies that Polly's estate did benefit the Indian cause, and because of the references in that article to letters written by Polly to her cousin Will Forbes, I feel sure that he provided the newspaper with this information.

This niggling question regarding the estate ultimately had little to do with Polly's life story, but it was one of those mysteries I wanted to solve. If, in fact, her estate did go to Gandhi's cause, it means that her deathbed wish was honoured. Small compensation for dying so young, perhaps, but obviously Polly knew at the time that her life was coming to an end, and she used her last breath to articulate her wishes for India and its struggle for independence. An economist to the very end, she wanted her good financial fortune to be of benefit for work she believed in.

CHAPTER 9
Celebrating Voices of Dissent

MARY CHESLEY AND HER DAUGHTER POLLY COMMITTED THEIR lives to social justice and peace. Mary worked in Lunenburg, reaching out to the world through her reading and writing. Whether she travelled much outside of her native province is unknown; however, through her prodigious reading, she kept informed on international affairs. She, in turn, reported on both local and international news, keeping members of the WCTU and the general public informed through articles and WCTU department reports. As an initiator of one of the earliest chapters of the Women's International League for Peace and Freedom in Canada, she reached well beyond the scope of the Woman's Christian Temperance Union, encouraging her "sisters" in the organization to do the same.

Mary and her husband, Samuel, paved the way for their daughter Polly to reach out further. Polly undoubtedly showed her intelligence and sense of adventure very early on, and her parents had the wisdom to give her the freedom to pursue an independent life. This was all the more admirable when one considers their loss of their two older children to a tragic boating accident.

Mary Russell Chesley was a white, middle-class woman who likely had little exposure or contact with either Indigenous or African Nova

Scotian people, particularly while living in Lunenburg. To what extent she had thoughts on race or class is only hinted at in some of her writings. In her article supporting the position of the radical suffragists (suffragettes) of England, she spoke sympathetically of John Brown who was committed to the abolishment of slavery. She also spoke of support for working-class women in her rebuttal to Attorney General Longley in 1895. Her involvement with the Women's International League for Peace and Freedom spoke to her interest in global peace.

Polly, because of her broader exposure in Britain and France to international students, cultivated friendships with people from across the globe. I believe that her interest in learning other languages—French, Esperanto, and Hindi—indicated her willingness to engage with and embrace cultures other than her own. Her commitment to labour politics and her joining a group like The Neighbours, where members gave away any money they had beyond what a working-class person in Britain could earn, spoke to her desire to use her privilege for the betterment of others. In India, essentially taking a vow of poverty and living like the poorest of villagers, Polly lived her politics in the most concrete of ways.

Through my research on women involved in social and political activism internationally, I have seen that activist individuals and groups were well-connected, through personal letters and group circulars. Today, the Internet allows for easy access to communication and information-sharing; one hundred years ago, while everything would have been slower, there were still great efforts made to keep connected and informed. One finds that the activists on the world stage were friends, colleagues, and allies, even though miles and continents kept them physically apart. We know from Polly's letters to her parents that she knew prominent people in social movements in Britain long before going to India.

One example of interconnectedness between people spanning continents is the fact that Olive Warner, Polly's first partner in running the school in Potters Bar, became a friend and colleague of Polly's friend in India, Mary Barr. Barr and Warner met in South Africa. It is unclear whether Olive was born in Britain or South Africa. It may be that when she and Polly established their school in 1926, she was only sojourning in Britain for a few years; there is evidence from a letter she wrote in 1919 to the African American writer and civil rights activist W. E. B. Du Bois that she was living in South Africa at that time.[131] She was publishing a pacifist newsletter, *The Ambassador*, and was writing to Du Bois to see about exchanging that and other relevant material about South Africa for issues of *The Crisis*, a newsletter that Du Bois edited.[132] Exactly when she went to England is unknown, but she returned to South Africa in 1930. She initiated schools for Indian and Zulu children and for a time lived in Phoenix Settlement, first established by Gandhi in 1904 and subsequently run by Manilal Gandhi, the son who remained in South Africa. Olive Warner taught one or more of Gandhi's grandchildren. A Quaker, she was active in the international peace movement and supported civil rights.

Mary Barr, also a Quaker, first went to South Africa in 1940 to live with her widowed father, who had relocated there from Britain. She, too, became friends with Gandhi's son Manilal, and it was during her time in South Africa that she began writing her book *Bapu: Conversations and Correspondence with Mahatma Gandhi*, which was such a rich source of information about Polly's time in India. Barr's first visit to South Africa was brief, but in 1943, she returned to resume care of her father and remained there until after his death in 1950. For a time, Olive Warner and Mary Barr lived together and both supported the struggle for civil rights in South Africa. Barr even went to prison for her participation in the resistance movement in 1946.[133] Barr eventually made her way back to India where she lived in Kotagiri, near other close friends and activists who also had strong international ties with peace workers across the globe.[134]

Mary and Polly Chesley were part of that international circle, and as a voice for peace, Mary Chesley's analysis and prophetic writings leading up to, during, and after the First World War remain pertinent. Polly followed in her mother's footsteps and attempted to convince the British Labour Party to take a stand for total disarmament. While the majority of people pay lip service to the idea of peace, only a minority will actually stand up and declare themselves true pacifists. Peace and reconciliation with those considered the enemy rather than armed détente or outright war is an ideal that few can truly accept.

The Chesley mother and daughter dedicated their lives to promote their principles. Some may believe that such work is in vain; however, the determination to strive for a better world is as much a part of the human condition as the opposite inclination to make the world a darker place through baser ambitions and war.

One example of the dismissive way government and affiliated associations speak about pacifism could be seen in the Canadian War Museum's travelling exhibition ironically titled "Peace—the Exhibition," which was on display at the Canadian Museum of Immigration, Pier 21, from May to October 2014. The presentation glossed over the truth in significant ways, particularly in its treatment of Treaty history with First Nations, painting a false picture of harmonious relations between the British and Indigenous people. Nor did the exhibit give much attention to alternative voices to the prevailing nationalist rhetoric that was so strongly supported by the Conservative government, in power at that time.

Of particular pertinence was the curious juxtaposition on one panel concerning the First World War, which held a quotation by a woman named Agnes Chesley, followed by a brief mention of the WCTU Peace and Arbitration Department.

> "While hoping and praying for peace we should prepare for war."
>
> Agnes Chesley
> Military conference report
> 11 March 1913
>
> The W.C.T.U. established a Peace and Arbitration Department in the 1890s to convince Canadians that arbitration and reconciliation were better than war. Most of these women were not pacifists. They later supported wholeheartedly Canada's participation in the First World War.

I experienced surprise and annoyance that these two items should be paired together on the same panel. First of all, had researchers done their work, the panel would have included a quote from Mary

Chesley, rather than the one from Agnes Chesley (no relation). Agnes Chesley, a journalist, art critic, and suffragist, served as women's editor for the *Montreal Star* and wrote columns for other publications covering art exhibitions in Montreal.

James Wood, in his book *Militia Myths: Ideas of the Canadian Citizen Soldier, 1896–1921*, more fully quoted Agnes Chesley, selecting an excerpt from her article "Canadian Women and War," which appeared in the *Montreal Sunday Herald* and was subsequently printed in the October 14, 1913, edition of *Canadian Military Gazette*. "The day has not yet come when war will be abolished, and in the meantime it is our duty to train our men to play their parts like men, should the occasion arise. While hoping and praying for peace we should prepare for war. This preparation does not mean any hastening of the awful day of war. It simply means that that our husbands and sons are trained and able to be of service should their services be needed."[135]

Readers will recall that Mary referred to the military conference to which the WCTU had been invited. When General Sam Hughes, Minister of Militia and Defence from October 1911 to November 1916, organized this military conference in February of 1913, he had the brilliant foresight to invite women's groups to send delegates. Keen on the mass development of cadet training, Hughes recognized that the support of wives and mothers would be invaluable to the success of his agenda. It is clear that Agnes Chesley believed in the ethos of "manliness," as did Ida Powell Starr, the WCTU member in direct opposition to Mary Chesley and her critique of militarism. Starr, in all probability, attended this same conference.

The "Peace" exhibition's statement about the Peace and Arbitration Department of the WCTU is both facile and inaccurate when considering Mary Chesley's strong writings. That Agnes Chesley should be quoted here rather than Mary Chesley, who gave years of her life as the provincial and national Superintendent of the Department of Peace and Arbitration, is a grave disservice to history. While I would not pretend that Mary's position on cadet training was universally accepted within the WCTU, there certainly were others within the organization that held similar views to Mary (Anna E. Gordon, quoted in chapter 4, being one obvious example). Recognizing that attitudes changed as the possibility of war loomed ever closer and when hostilities eventually broke out, it was still an incorrect assumption that WCTU women "wholeheartedly" supported Canada's participation in the First World War. This is simply untrue.

Voices of dissent are censored and silenced, especially during times of war, and, more often than not, do not get recorded for posterity. I will not address the difficult territory of defining patriotism here, but women and other marginalized groups, such as First Nations, African Canadians, traditional peace churches, and naturalized Canadians from "enemy countries" might have felt quite differently about war. [136]

The deep chasm that exists between those who feel that war is a necessary evil and those who believe that nothing justifies the taking of any human life has not narrowed over the centuries. Wars continue, but we need the courageous voices of those who advocate non-violence—the voices of conscience. Most people want to live in peace, but the question of how we get to that state is still up for fierce and, often, bloody debate.

The Chesley story is just one of innumerable stories that have been forgotten or lost. The focus of historians has too long been on white male military and political figures and their exploits. That is changing and the histories of women, people of colour, and the LBTGQ+ community have become ever more expansive and dynamic fields of study. While it is more challenging to find primary source documents for these groups, the excitement of the detective work involved in such endeavours makes it well worth the effort. To bring forward a hitherto untold story is satisfying for the historian, and such revelations enrich our understanding of the past. Hidden "everyday" heroes are revealed.

The Chesleys deserve recognition for commitment to ideals that were not universally popular. They were guided by faith in what they considered right and just. Even readers who do not hold the same political views as the Chesleys might appreciate their bravery for voicing such thoughts at a time when women were often silenced. Their courage has been inspirational. This biography is my gift to them, posthumously.

ACKNOWLEDGEMENTS

SOME OF THE PEOPLE I HAVE TO ACKNOWLEDGE WITH THANKS are no longer alive. However, they contributed a great deal to my knowledge of the Chesleys. I am indebted to the late Natalie Corkum (1915–2017) and her son, Hugh Corkum, for stories and photos that allowed me to flesh out the Chesley family personalities. Audrey Oldershaw, a distant Chesley relative, got in touch with me because of my other writings about the Chesleys, and she generously shared family photos. Murray Forbes had miraculously saved and shared photos and correspondence that his father's cousin had received from Polly as well as Gandhi. The most generous Narayan Desai (1924–2015), son of Gandhi's beloved secretary, led me to Mahadevi Tai (1906–2006), the last person to see Polly alive. Mahadevi's great-nephew, Siddharth Sharma, made it possible for me to have such a rich time with Mahadevi in Bangalore.

Several people read early versions of this manuscript, and their comments encouraged me to continue with this project. Many thanks to Dr. Gail Campbell, Jessica Tellez, Danuta Snyder, and Bill Plaskett.

Research takes one to various archives, and I would be remiss not to acknowledge the debt I owe to numerous collections (they're listed in the bibliography); however, the Nova Scotia Archives, the Friends Library in London, England, and the Mount Allison University Archives have been most valuable. David Mawhinney at Mount Allison University was particularly helpful, providing photographs of Polly's years at the school.

I am indebted to Nimbus Publishing and especially Angela Mombourquette for believing in this project. Marianne Ward was a meticulous editor and endured my challenges with tracking edits in Microsoft Word. A heartfelt thank you.

My children, Joel and Anna Plaskett, their spouses Rebecca Kraatz and Tyler Cameron, and my grandchildren, Xianing Plaskett and Elsie Cameron, are true blessings in my life, and I am grateful to all my extended family for their very existence. I dare not go into naming all the dear friends who have cheered me on for fear of missing someone, but I hope you know who you are and know that your friendship means so much to me.

Appendix I:

FIRST WILL MADE BY MARY ALBEE CHESLEY

The will of Mary Albee Chesley, written the 26th day of October 192[5] in the town of Lunenburg, Nova Scotia.[137]

I hereby bequeath all my personal property with the exception of my Grandfather's clock and a chest of drawers made by Sir Samuel Cunard both at present in the home of Mr. Arthur Russell but including a mahogany table Japanese Cabinet and small old fashioned mirror in the same house to my friend Mrs. Lena Zinck Bachman. Said chest of drawers and clock I bequeath to my cousin Rev. E. W. Forbes for his life should he wish them, on his death the same go to my cousin Frances Russell or her heirs. Should he not desire them, to go immediately to the same Frances Russell.

A five hundred dollar and one hundred dollar Victory Bond registered in my name I bequeath to my friend Lena Bachman the interest of same to be forwarded by her to the Independent Labour Party of Great Britain, on maturity the sum to be reinvested and interest sent as before to the British I.L.P. Should my friend however, through sickness or other serious misfortune be in need of interest or capital she shall be free to use it. If on her death any capital is left the same shall go to the British I.L.P.

The two one thousand dollar Victory Bonds in my name shall be disposed of as required by my father in his will.

I hereby make my friend Lena Zinck Bachman the sole executrix of my estate.

Appendix II:

LAST WILL MADE BY MARY ALBEE CHESLEY BEFORE SHE LEFT FOR INDIA

This is the last Will and Testament of one Mary Albee Chesley of 21 Quaker Lane, Potters Bar in the county of Middlesex made this second day of October 1934.[138]

I hereby revoke all wills made by me at any time heretofore. I appoint those persons who may be decided upon by the body known as the "Inner Team" of the Oxford Group to be my Executors and direct that all my debts and funeral expenses shall be paid as soon as conveniently may be after my decease, the second to be kept to the lowest possible figure and to be carried out according to the usages of the Society of Friends [Quakers].

I give and bequeath unto the Inner Team of the Oxford Group all of which I am possessed with to be used as they under guidance may see fit. The following important qualifications to the above are however to be noted. (1) The property known as 21 Quaker Lane, Potters Bar, shall not be sold as long as Miss Blyth and Miss Morris require to use the house (or lower) part together with the garden for their school. They shall pay a rent agreed upon under guidance between themselves and the executors. (2) The mortgage for eight hundred pounds held by me on the property known as Anthorn[e] School shall never be foreclosed as long as the property is in the hands of the present owners. Interest at the rate of 3 3/4% shall be paid to the executors. Should the present owners any year be unable to pay all this interest it shall be decided after a frank talk with the executors what part if any of the interest shall be paid that year. If any year any of the following friends should need financial help to supply the necessities of life they shall notify the executors and money from the interest on the mortgage shall be used to help them. If more is needed and Miss Blyth and Miss Morris are able to do so they shall pay the money needed and the sum as paid above the interest shall be regarded as payment on the mortgage. The following are the friends referred to in the above and they shall be sent a copy of the clause of this will referring to them—Mrs. Lena Bachman, Lunenburg, Nova Scotia; Mrs. Eunice Buchanan, Waterville, Kings Co., Nova Scotia; Mrs. Cora Hirshberg [apparently a distant cousin on the Chesley side] 7011-60th Ave., Seattle, Washington, USA, or any of my cousins Edith, Bell or Helen Russell, Dahlia St., Dartmouth, Nova Scotia. No proof of their want is required other than a letter by them stating that they are in need of the necessities of life. Should Miss Blyth or Miss Morris sell Anthorn[e] and should their position be such that they cannot reasonably hope to supply their needs during the rest of their lives the executors shall upon an examination of the facts and under guidance allow them such part of the mortgage still unpaid as they seem likely to need to keep them in the necessities of life for the rest of their lives. They on their parts will only keep this fund separate and only use it when absolutely necessary and in their wills will provide for the return of any part that may be left after the death of both.

[signed by the witnesses]

To the Inner Team of the Oxford Group,

My furniture and clothing I also bequest to the Inner Team of the Oxford Group with the following reservations. The painting above the fireplace shall go to Nancy Russell, 29 Keildon Rd., Battersea Rise, London. My friends, Miss Mary Carpenter, 100 [or 10a] Peabody Estate, Horbrand [or Herbrand or Harbrand], London and Mrs. Dorey, Potters Bar shall be free to take any one article they may wish as a keepsake. My friend Miss Blyth shall take any number of articles she may wish.

Endnotes

1. Report of Peace and Arbitration, WCTU Records, MG 20, vol. 356, #8, WCTU Convention 1908.
2. See Sharon M. H. MacDonald, "Hidden Costs, Hidden Labours: Women in Nova Scotia During Two World Wars," master's thesis, Saint Mary's University, 1999.
3. Quoted from Terry Crowley's paper on Ada Mary Brown Courtice in Thomas P. Socknat, *Witness Against War: Pacifism in Canada 1900–1945* (University of Toronto Press, 1987), 35.
4. Marjorie Sykes, *An Indian Tapestry* (Sessions Book Trust, 1997), 261.
5. Catherine Cleverdon, *The Woman Suffrage Movement in Canada* (University of Toronto Press, 1950) and Sharon M. H. MacDonald, "A Passionate Voice for Equality, Justice, and Peace: Nova Scotia's Mary Russell Chesley," in Janet Guildford and Suzanne Morton, eds., *Making up the State: Women in 20th-Century Atlantic Canada* (Acadiensis Press, 2010), 45–55.
6. From Benjamin Russell, *Autobiography of Benjamin Russell* (The Royal Print & Litho Ltd., 1932), 15.
7. Nathaniel Russell and Mary Hibbert were married by a Reverend Sandeman in Boston. Sandeman headed up a sect of Christianity that originated with his father-in-law, John Glas, who had been a minister in the Church of Scotland. Sandeman came to Boston from Glasgow in 1764. In some ways, the Sandemanians, as they were called, held similar values and beliefs to Quakers. Ministerial authority was absent in the church, and they upheld pacifism in the conflict between Britain and the colonies. Hence, there were those who remained faithful to the Crown and subsequently moved to Nova Scotia.
8. I only discovered while doing other research that Polly is commonly a familiar form for Mary.
9. "Nathaniel Russell (Senior)—What is known," MG 100, vol. 262, #8, NSA.
10. A dramatic account of this murder can be found in Mrs. William Lawson's *History of the Townships of Dartmouth, Preston and Lawrencetown* (Morton & Co., 1893), 125–9.
11. For one account of the history of Quakers in Dartmouth, see Maida Barton Follini's "A Quaker Odyssey: The Migration of Quaker Whalers from Nantucket, Massachusetts to Dartmouth, Nova Scotia and Milford Haven, Wales," *Canadian Quaker History Journal* 71 (2006): 1–21.
12. Dartmouth Nova Scotia Preparative Meeting, Society of Friends Minutes, 1786–1798, 105 (original copy in Nantucket Historical Association Collection).
13. Russell, *Autobiography*, 9–10.
14. Russell, *Autobiography*, 28.
15. *Halifax Chronicle*, September 19, 1935.
16. "Howard Russell Drowned," *Dartmouth Patriot*, September 17, 1901; "Drowned While Bathing," *Morning Chronicle*, September 19, 1901; "Howard Russell Drowned," *Halifax Herald*, September 19, 1901.
17. freepages.rootsweb.com/~coleharbour/genealogy/Bissett/d1.htm#i136.
18. In historical records, the middle name Ainsley is variously spelled Ansley, Annesley, and Ainslie.
19. *Catholic World* 63, 378 (September 1896): 787.
20. *Acadian Recorder*, October 18, 1895.

21. Published online in the *Lunenburg Barnacle*, July 13, 2023, by editor-at-large Sal Falk. thebarnacle.ca/time-machine-mahone-bay-by-tricycle/.
22. "Vote of Sympathy to Judge Chesley," *The Wesleyan*, November 13, 1895.
23. *The Argosy* 25, 2 (November 1895): 9. According to David Mawhinney, archivist, Mount Allison University, Elizabeth "Bessie" Alcorn (1865–1921) was a graduate of the MtA Ladies' College and taught art there from 1891 to 1896.
24. "History of the Chesley Family" is no longer available online. There is reference to the document at campbellsport.govoffice.com/vertical/sites/%7B247D4AC2-95B0-44CE-8C93-8CEAB868D151%7D/uploads/%7BD122978B-34AA-4CCA-A212-829AD551C-85B%7D.PDF.
25. Thank you to Dr. Gail Campbell for this information.
26. MG vol. 3542 WCTU includes both the Lunenburg and the Western Nova Scotia District minutes, 1892–1894.
27. Maria Angwin became the first licensed female doctor in Nova Scotia in 1884. Lois Kernaghan, "Angwin, Maria Louisa," *Dictionary of Canadian Biography*, biographi.ca/en/bio/angwin_maria_louisa_12E.html. Maria Angwin and Mary Chesley were close in age, both had lived in Dartmouth, and both were active in the WCTU and the suffrage cause.
28. In 1905, the union presented a resolution to the Lunenburg municipal council recommending that prisoners in the jail be provided with an occupation. Natalie Corkum, whose mother had been Polly's good friend, recalls having visited the prison to play music and sing on a regular basis. She told of a prisoner who gave her a violin he had made while incarcerated.
29. The one notable exception is an essay by Marilyn Färdig Whiteley, "Mary Russell Chesley, 'Controversialist,'" published in *Touchstone*, 24, 2 (May 2006): 48–57. Whitely covers some of the same territory as is included here. She also referred to Mary and Samuel in her book *Canadian Methodist Women, 1766–1925* (Wilfrid Laurier University Press, 2003). For my essay, see "A Passionate Voice for Equality, Justice and Peace: Nova Scotia's Mary Russell Chesley," *Making up the State: Women in 20th-Century Atlantic Canada*, Janet Guildford and Suzanne Morton, eds. (Acadiensis Press, 2010), 45–55.
30. Petition for the Enfranchisement of Women. Nova Scotia Archives (NSA) RG5 "P," vol. 21A, #38.
31. NSA, MG 20, vol. 356, 5th Annual Report, 1900.
32. NSA, MG 20, vol. 356, 12th Annual Convention, 1907.
33. NSA, MG 20, vol. 357, 69, WCTU, 13th Annual Maritime Report, 1895; 1st Annual Nova Scotia WCTU Report, 1896, 55–57; vol. 356, 4th Annual NS Report ,1899, 91. The *Halifax Herald* published a woman's supplement on October 1, 1895, which included an article written by McKay, "When Men Shall Learn War No More."
34. NSA, WCTU MG 20, vol. 356, #8, Convention 1908, 67–69.
35. NSA, MG 20, vol. 356, #9, WCTU Convention 1909, 71.
36. Courtice Family Papers, Archival and Special Collections, University of Guelph Library.
37. Hugh Corkum, an avid collector of "Lunenburgiana" and the son of Natalie Corkum (daughter of a close friend of Polly's), is in possession of the extensive Chesley correspondence concerning the purchase of land, the design of the building, and all that was entailed in bringing the Lunenburg Opera House project to fruition.
38. While the word *College* is written here, she in fact was registered at the university.
39. *Argosy*, April 1908, 302.
40. digital.lib.sfu.ca/ceww-941/musgrave-fanny-wood. I have also seen the manuscript of an unpublished novel, held in private hands, found in the attic of a house where Fanny spent her last years.

41. See F. W. Musgrave, "The Dark Side and Bright Side of Woman's Franchise" (Register print, 1911), available at Acadia University and in microfiche at Dalhousie University.

42. Catherine Cleverdon, in her seminal work *The Woman Suffrage Movement in Canada*, relied on Ella Murray, a relative newcomer in the 1910s to the Halifax suffrage scene, who did not have a grasp of the work done outside of Halifax (for Murray's feeling regarding Chesley, see E. M. Murray to Catherine Cleverdon, July 30, 1946, Catherine Cleverdon Papers, Library and Archives Canada. Thanks to Dr. Suzanne Morton and Dr. Janet Guildford for this reference). Carol Bacchi's work, *Liberation Deferred? The Ideas of English Canadian Suffragists, 1877–1918* (University of Toronto Press, 1983) was even more removed from considering the Maritime region at all. For a critique of Bacchi's work, see Ernest Forbes's article in *Atlantis* 10, 2 (Spr. 1985): 119–26.

43. Fanny Musgrave's less orthodox thinking is also indicated by a notice in the *Daily Echo* (Halifax), October 10, 1912, in which it is reported that she gave a talk advocating a vegetarian diet at a WCTU convention.

44. *Montreal Daily Witness*, April 13, 1912.

45. NSA, MG 20, vol. 356, #11, WCTU Convention, 1911.

46. NSA, MG 20, vol. 356, #12, WCTU Convention, 1912.

47. The Imperial Order of the Daughters of the Empire (IODE), a patriotic and pro-military women's group formed in 1900 at the time of the South African (Boer) War, also supported war efforts during both world wars.

48. Archives of Ontario, Canadian WCTU fonds, Micro MS 885.

49. NSA, MG 20, vol. 357, 1st Annual WCTU Report, 1896, 57.

50. Archives of Ontario, MV 8464.14, WCTU, *White Ribbon Bulletin*, June 1913.

51. "Muscular Christianity" as a philosophical movement or cultural trend held sway during this time.

52. When I was carrying out research on wartime relief work, I came across stunning statistics. In the case of American soldiers (remember that the Americans only joined in 1917, close to war's end), "in the 33 months from April 1, 1917, to December 31, 1919, there were 96,657 men with psychiatric disorders admitted to military hospitals and probably as many more with milder degrees of disability not hospitalized. Even at the time of Pearl Harbour over half of all patients in veterans' hospitals had psychiatric disorders; the overwhelming majority represent mental casualties from the last war." George K. Pratt, *Soldier to Civilian: Problems of Readjustment* (McGraw-Hill Book Company, 1944), 16.

53. Jo Vellacott, "Anti-War Suffragists," *History*, 62 (1977): 411–25.

54. See, among others, Janet Kitz, *Shattered City: The Halifax Explosion and the Road to Recovery* (Nimbus Publishing, 1989) and Ken Cuthbertson, *The Halifax Explosion: Canada's Worst Disaster* (HarperCollins Publishers, 2017). One of the most well-known fictional accounts is Hugh MacLennan's *Barometer Rising* (Duell, Sloan and Pearce, 1941).

55. NSA, MG 20, vol. 356, 23rd Annual Convention, 1918.

56. In 1918, only women who had a certain amount of real or personal property or earnings were eligible to vote. In 1920, these requirements were eliminated and universal suffrage was established (which nevertheless excluded certain minority groups, such as Indigenous women). "History of Voting in Nova Scotia": nslegislature.ca/about/history/history-voting-nova-scotia.

57. NSA, MG 20, vol. 356, 24th Annual Convention, 1919.

58. Jean Barman's *Sojourning Sisters: The Lives and Letters of Jessie and Annie McQueen* (University of Toronto Press, 2003) provides a revealing look at a pattern of teachers migrating west that began in the nineteenth century and continued through the decades. Thanks to Dr. Gail Campbell for alerting me to this book.

59 The 1914 *San Diego City Directory* lists Mary A. Chesley, teacher La Jolla Public School, renting at Waverly Lane, La Jolla.

60 Mark Guy Pearse (1842–1939) was an internationally renowned preacher, lecturer, and author. His book *Daniel Quorm and his Religious Notions* sold several hundred thousand copies in multiple languages.

61 Haddon Hall dates back to the eleventh century. The Vernon family acquired the manor in the early thirteenth century, and it was home to the reputedly beautiful Dorothy Vernon who, legend has it, eloped with John Manners in the 1500s. Numerous dramas and literary works have romanticized the story, perhaps the most famous being *Dorothy Vernon of Haddon Hall*, a bestselling novel by Charles Major that was published in 1902. Haddon Hall has also been the setting for several present-day film and television productions and is still owned by the Manners family.

62 John Wesley (1703–1791) was a theologian and founder of Methodism.

63 Polly would have been familiar with William Wordsworth's poem "Lines Composed a Few Miles above Tintern Abbey."

64 Edward Burne-Jones was an English painter and designer who worked closely with William Morris as part of the Arts and Crafts movement of the late nineteenth century.

65 Polly is likely referring to a Miss Scott-Moncrieff (rather than McCrief). Scott-Moncrieff was a prominent name in British literary and legal circles.

66 The Radcliffe Camera (which includes the Upper and Lower Camera sections) is a part of the Bodleian Library at Oxford.

67 Sharon M. H. MacDonald, "Neither Memsahibs nor Missionaries: Western Women who Supported the Indian Independence Movement," PhD dissertation, University of New Brunswick, 2010.

68 Polly would have been interested in noting these particular names because Meisner, Bachman, and Diehl were all familiar Lunenburg County names. In fact, Polly's closest friend in Lunenburg was Lena Bachman.

69 While Polly must have had financial help from her parents, presumably she tutored to pay for some of her expenses.

70 In 1914, Sylvia split from her mother and sister over their positions on the war, and Sylvia began the newspaper *Woman's Dreadnought* (which eventually became the *Workers' Dreadnought*). In the July 3, 1915, issue, on page 4 under "Gratefully Acknowledged," Mary Chesley is listed as a donor to the paper. Source: LSE Digital Library.

71 Vancouver School Board Teachers' Record Book Series 330 56-A-5, Vancouver City Archives.

72 Since COVID-19, one can find numerous articles concerning Vancouver and the Spanish flu epidemic online.

73 A British group formed in 1914 to press for more responsive foreign policy and which was opposed to military influence in government. Polly was one of its earliest members.

74 LSE, WILPF Files 4/2.

75 See Jo Vellacott, "Anti-War Suffragists," *History* 62 (1977): 411–25.

76 Susan Lewthwaite, "Ethelbert Lionel Cross: Toronto's First Black Lawyer," in *The African Canadian Legal Odyssey: Historical Essays*, edited by Walker Barrington (University of Toronto Press, 2012), 49–83.

77 Held annually at the Southeastern Yearly Meeting of the Religious Society of Friends, Lakewood Retreat Center, Brookside, Florida.

78 NSA, Miller Family Fonds, MG 1, vols. 582–695, Micro Reel 10, 906.

79 Available online through the Nova Scotia Archives: novascotia.ca/archives/Lunenburg/archives.asp?ID=19.

80 *The Morning Chronicle*, October 2, 1924.
81 Phone conversation with Elizabeth Hebb, June 28, 2001.
82 Taped conversation with Natalie Corkum, May 1, 1998.
83 Charles H. Mercer Fonds MS-2-659, Dalhousie University Archives.
84 The Misses Chesley (Sarah and Lucy) and Mrs. John McCormick (Annie Louisa Chesley) were sisters. Lucy, a single woman, lived on the old Chesley homestead in Upper Granville. Fortuitously, a great-niece of hers, Audrey Florence Chesley Oldershaw, discovered my interest in the family through a reference online to my master's thesis and contacted me. Apart from one image of the Chesleys in front of their house, I had no photos of Mary Russell Chesley. Audrey furnished me with another photograph of the Chesley family at their cottage, one that likely came from her great-aunt Lucy.
85 British Newspaper Archives, *Norwood News*, Friday, July 27, 1928, p. 5. Polly may have been furnishing her mother with No More War Movement articles earlier on, because periodic news was republished in the *Progress Enterprise*.
86 Such rationale is still much in play when it comes to either military or industrial activity. Environmentalists argue that jobs in the oil industry could be converted to jobs that produce more ecologically sound choices for power. Necessity can push innovation as we saw during the COVID-19 pandemic. Manufacturing plants were willing and able to quickly convert their production lines to make health and safety equipment instead of their regular products. If the Black Lives Matter movement has any lasting impact on society, it may mean that the huge budgets spent on policing might be better used to provide more social programs, counselling, and housing—preemptive solutions to the problems of poverty—and reduce the punitive measures that our society overuses. Loss of jobs in one sector could open up jobs in another.
87 *The Labour Party Report, 29th Annual Conference*, Brighton, October 1929. Labour Party Reports, Dalhousie University Microfilm, HD8395 L2 1901, p. 215. A brief mention was made to Polly's "emotional speech" in Kenneth E. Miller's *Socialism and Foreign Policy: Theory and Practice in Britain to 1931* (Marinus Nijhoff, 1968), 221.
88 *Labour Party Report*, 215–6.
89 Hertfordshire Archives and Local Studies, Welwyn Garden City Preparative Meeting, NQ9.
90 British Library, IOR: L/P&J/12/428.
91 ukunitarians.org.uk/chatham/history.htm
92 *The Rise of Labour and the Fall of Empire: The Memoirs of William Hare, Fifth Earl of Listowel*, edited by H. Kumarasingham (Cambridge University Press, 2019), 45–47. Thank you to Harshan Kumarsingham for permission to quote the following passage.
93 J. R. Bellerby, *A Contributive Society* (Education Services, 1988), xv.
94 M. E. Frances Bellerby, quoted by J. O. Jones, introduction to John Rotherford Bellarby, *A Contributive Society*, xiv.
95 With thanks to Jessie Tellez for discovering an updated internet entry for Open Charities in which Education Services 2010 is listed as a charity. Further information is available at find-and-update.company-information.service.gov.uk/company/07697173/filing-history in which one can read about the organization, the annual reports, and donations that are still being given to worthwhile projects.
96 The Oxford Group, a Christian organization founded by American Lutheran minister Frank Buchman, was very popular in England among Christians of numerous denominations.
97 rove.nla.gov.au/
98 Here are the results of a search for "Mary Chesley" on Gallica, the digital library of the Bibliothèque nationale de France: gallica.bnf.fr/services/engine/search/sru?operation=searchRetrieve&version=1.2&query=%28gallica%20adj%20%22Mary%20Chesley%22%29&suggest=0#resultat-id-2.

99 Polly's cousin Reverend Will Forbes received this letter, which was shared among a number of Polly's friends, as per her request.

100 Jack C. Winslow, *Why I Believe in the Oxford Group* (Hodder and Stoughton, 1934).

101 Minnie Hewitt was a well-respected and long-serving teacher in Lunenburg.

102 The Gonds were a tribal group, considered to be part of what are now called the "scheduled castes."

103 F. Mary Barr, *Bapu: Conversations and Correspondence with Mahatma Gandhi*, 2nd ed. (International Book House Ltd, 1956), 108.

104 Barr, 110.

105 Barr, 1.

106 gandhiserve.net/about-mahatma-gandhi/collected-works-of-mahatma-gandhi/.

107 Barr, 116–23.

108 Barr, 128, 135–6.

109 Barr, 137–8.

110 Barr, 140.

111 Barr, 140.

112 When exactly Mary Chesley took on or was given the name Tarabehn is unclear. Mary Ingham became known as Shantabehn (Shanti meaning "peace").

113 Barr, 148.

114 Barr, 149.

115 Barr, 150–1.

116 Quoted in "Nova Scotian was Gandhi's Associate," *Halifax Chronicle*, January 31, 1948, p. 3.

117 Miraben was probably the most famous of Gandhi's British friends. Madeleine Slade (1892–1982) was the daughter of an English admiral and joined Gandhi in 1925. Thinking of her merely as a devotee, I initially was somewhat dismissive of her, yet while I was in India, someone convinced me to reassess her, and the result of that reassessment was a chapter on her in my dissertation.

118 R. K. Prabhu, *This Was Bapu* (Navajivan Trust, 1954), 69.

119 *CWMG*, vol. LXII, 130. Letter to F. Mary Barr, November 13, 1935, 114.

120 Barr, 144.

121 *CWMG*, vol. LXII, 472. Letter to F. Mary Barr, May 15, 1936, 404–5.

122 Barr, 152–3.

123 Barr, 154–5.

124 A sadhu is a religious ascetic.

125 Omma is another honorific, meaning "mother." Although Mahadevi was younger than Polly and had never been a mother, she had been married or betrothed, therefore was referred to as "mother" rather than "sister."

126 The Gurukul (literal meaning: community of the guru) Kangri was an experimental educational institution run by the Arya Samaj, a Hindu social reform and social service organization. In March 2010, historian Carey Watt, who participated as a reader and examiner at my dissertation, informed me that Gandhi had visited the Gurukul a number of times since returning to India; he commented that "it is significant that Chesley was cremated there because it highlights Gandhi's ongoing connections to the Arya Samaj and their common interest in social service and innovative educational initiatives."

127 I presume Cecilia Morris is a friend of Polly's.

128. Received through my correspondence with Barclays Bank.
129. Nova Scotia, County of Lunenburg, Court of Probate, In the Estate of Mary Albee Chesley, deceased. Solicitor's Costs, Nov 7, 1936, p. 3.
130. This will, in fact, was dated December 17, 1932. Lena Bachman's lawyer had obtained a copy of it, but its contents remain unknown.
131. Letter dated August 27, 1919, "To the Editor of The Crisis," W. E. B. Du Bois Papers, Series 1, Corres. University of Massachusetts Amherst Libraries Special Collections and University Archives.
132. Vera Brittain, *The Rebel Passion: A Short History of Some Pioneer Peace-Makers* (George Allen and Unwin Ltd., 1964), 195.
133. "Frances Mary Barr (1895–1968): A Memoir," supplement to *The Friendly Way*, 87 (April 1969), 8. Marjorie Sykes, one of Mary Barr's close friends and associates, wrote this memorial.
134. For a collective biography of like-minded women living in India during this time, see my dissertation, "Neither Memsahibs nor Missionaries: Western Women who Supported the Indian Independence Movement," University of New Brunswick, 2010.
135. See James Wood, *Militia Myths: Ideas of the Canadian Citizen Soldier, 1896–1921* (UBC Press, 2010), 183–5, 314.
136. See Sharon M. H. MacDonald, "Hidden Costs, Hidden Labours: Women in Nova Scotia During Two World Wars," master's thesis, Saint Mary's University, March 1999, particularly chapter 2, "Alternative Voices: Peace as a Feminist Issue" and chapter 3, "Patriotism and Propaganda in their Gendered Dimensions." collectionscanada.gc.ca/obj/s4/f2/dsk2/ftp01/MQ40353.pdf.
137. The original will was dated 1925. When it was copied into the Will Book at a later time, the date was mistakenly recorded as 1928. Nova Scotia Probate Records, Lunenburg Will Book, Micro 19837, 495.
138. Nova Scotia Probate Records, Lunenburg Will Book, Micro 19837, 582.

Bibliography

PRIMARY SOURCES

Australia Newspaper Archives

Bibliothèque nationale de France

British Newspaper Archives

Canadian Peace and Arbitration Society files, Courtice Family Papers, Archival and Special Collections, University of Guelph Library.

Canadian WCTU fonds, Archives of Ontario.

Dartmouth Nova Scotia Preparative Meeting, Society of Friends Minutes, 1786–1798 Nantucket Historical Association Collection

Gandhi papers, National Gandhi Museum Library, New Delhi, India

Gandhi papers, Sabarmati Ashram Archives, Ahmedabad, India

India Office Records, British Library, London

McGrigor-Miller Collection, Nova Scotia Archives (NSA), Halifax.

New Zealand Newspaper Archives

Nova Scotia House of Assembly Proceedings and Debates

Pearl Madden papers, United Methodist Church (US) Archives, Madison, NJ

W. E. B. Du Bois Papers, University of Massachusetts, Amherst Libraries Special Collections

Will and Probate Records, Lunenburg County Probate Office and NSA microfilm

Woman's Christian Temperance Union papers, Nova Scotia Archives, Halifax

Women's International League for Peace and Freedom records, London School of Economics, London

SECONDARY SOURCES

Bacchi, Carol. *Liberation Deferred? The Ideas of the English-Canadian Suffragists, 1877–1918*. Toronto: University of Toronto Press, 1983.

Barr, F. Mary. *Bapu: Conversations & Correspondence with Mahatma Gandhi*. India: International Book House, 1956.

Bellerby, John Rotherford. *A Contributive Society*. London: Education Services, 1931 (reprinted in 1988).

Brittain, Vera. *The Rebel Passion: A Short History of Some Pioneer Peace-Makers*. UK: George Allen and Unwin Ltd, 1964.

Calnek, W. A. *History of the County of Annapolis, Nova Scotia: Including Old Port Royal & Acadia*, Local Histories Collection, Libraries and Cultural Resources Digital Collections (CU16080885), University of Calgary, 1999.

Chesley, S. A. "Reporting Disease in Cattle in Lunenburg County." National Archives of Canada.

Cleverdon, Catherine. *The Woman Suffrage Movement in Canada*. Toronto: University of Toronto Press, 1950.

Färdig Whiteley, Marilyn. *Canadian Methodist Women, 1766–1925*. Waterloo: Wilfrid Laurier University Press, 2003.

Färdig Whiteley, Marilyn. "Mary Russell Chesley, 'Controversialist,'" *Touchstone* 24, 2 (May 2006): 48–57.

Follini, Maida Barton. "A Quaker Odyssey: The Migration of Quaker Whalers from Nantucket, Massachusetts to Dartmouth, Nova Scotia and Milford Haven," *Canadian Quaker History Journal* 71 (2006): 1–21.

Forbes, Ernest. "The Ideas of Carol Bacchi and The Suffragists of Halifax: A Review Essay on *Liberation Deffered? The Ideas of the English Canadian Suffragists, 1877–1918. Atlantis* 10, 2 (Spring 1985): 119–26.

Foremothers in Equality, Some Early Nova Scotia Suffragists. Nova Scotia Advisory Council on the Status of Women, 2000.

"Frances Mary Barr (1895–1968): A Memoir." Supplement to *The Friendly Way* 87 (April 1969).

Gandhi, Mahatma. *Collected Works of Mahatma Gandhi*. Publications Division, Ministry of Information and Broadcasting, Government of India, 1958–84.

Kumarasingham, H., ed. *The Rise of Labour and the Fall of Empire: The Memoirs of William Hare, Earl of Listowel*. Cambridge, UK: Cambridge University Press, 2019.

Lawson, Mrs. William. *History of the Townships of Dartmouth, Preston and Lawrencetown*. Englewood, Co: Morton & Co., 1893.

Leonard, John William, ed. *Woman's Who's Who of America, 1914–1915*. The American Commonwealth Co., 1914.

Letson, W. A. *Lunenburg By the Sea*, c. 1896.

Lewthwaite, Susan. "Ethelbert Lionel Cross: Toronto's First Black Lawyer." In *The African Canadian Legal Odyssey: Historical Essays*, edited by Walker Barrington. Toronto: University of Toronto Press, 2012.

MacDonald, Sharon M. H. "Hidden Costs, Hidden Labours: Women in Nova Scotia During Two World Wars." Master's thesis, Saint Mary's University, 1999.

MacDonald, Sharon M. H. "Neither Memsahibs nor Missionaries: Western Women who Supported the Indian Independence Movement." PhD dissertation, University of New Brunswick, 2010.

MacDonald, Sharon M. H. "A Passionate Voice for Equality, Justice and Peace: Nova Scotia's Mary Russell Chesley." In *Making Up the State: Women in 20th-Century Atlantic Canada*, edited by Janet Guildford and Suzanne Morton. Fredericton: Acadiensis Press, 2010.

Miller, Kenneth E. *Socialism and Foreign Policy: Theory and Practice in Britain to 1931*. Leiden, The Netherlands: Marinus Nijhoff, 1968.

Morgan, Henry James. *The Canadian Men and Women of the Time: A Hand-Book of Canadian Biography*. William Briggs, 1898.

Musgrave, F. W. "The Dark Side and Bright Side of Woman's Franchise." Register Print, 1911.

O'Hagan, Thomas. "Some Canadian Women Writers." *Catholic World* 63, 378 (September 1896): 787.

Pratt, George K. Soldier to Civilian: Problems of Readjustment. New York: McGraw-Hill Book Company, 1944.

Roberts, Barbara. *"Why Do Women Do Nothing to End War?": Canadian Feminist-Pacifists and the Great War*. CRIAW/ICREF, 1985.

Russell, Benjamin. *Autobiography of Benjamin Russell*. Royal Print & Litho Ltd, 1932.

Socknat, Thomas P. *Witness Against War: Pacifism in Canada 1900–1945*. Toronto: University of Toronto Press, 1987.

Sykes, Marjorie. *An Indian Tapestry*. Sessions Book Trust, 1997.

The Labour Party Report, 28th Annual Conference. Birmingham. October 1928.

Vellacott, Jo. "Anti-War Suffragists." *History* 62 (1977): 411–25.

Wood, James. *Militia Myths: Ideas of the Canadian Citizen Soldier, 1896–1921*. Vancouver: UBC Press, 2010.

Index

A

Abell, Walter 125
Aberdovey, Wales 85
Aberystwyth, Wales 85
Acadian Recorder 10, 11, 28, 128
Acadia University 125
A Contributive Society 162
Advocate of Peace 39
ahimsa 176
Ahmedabad, India 194
Aitkens, Mrs. 108, 109
Albee, Hannah Elizabeth 6
Allen, Major-General Henry T. 137
All India Village Industries Association (AIVIA) 177, 204, 224
Allisonia 41, 43, 45
Alpenzeitung 210
Alpha Beta Society 42–47
Ambassador 229
Ambleside, England 79
American Friends' Service Committee (AFSC) 124
American Revolution 2
Andrews, C. F. (Charlie) 172
Angell, Norman 64
Anglican Church 172
Annapolis Valley, NS 135
Anthorn[e] School 237, 238
Archibald, Edith 19, 20, 66
Argosy 41, 43, 45, 46, 71, 72, 110, 120
Argus 128
Arnold, Mathew 80
Asar, Lilavati 197
Ashley House 90
Asquith, Mr. 136
Australia 209

B

Bachman, Lena 72, 75, 140, 156, 170, 199, 204, 209, 211–216, 235,–238
Badri-Kedar 196, 197
Bagi 168, 171
Bajaj, Jamnalal 196
Bangalore, India 220, 221, 233
Bapu: Conversations and Correspondence with Mahatma Gandhi 174, 229
Bapu (*also see* Gandhi, Mohandas) 169–171, 175, 185, 186, 188, 193, 199, 202, 206
Barclays Bank 202, 208, 213, 217

Barmouth, Wales 80
Barr, F. Mary 169, 174–179, 183, 186–196, 202, 204, 223, 228, 229, 245, 246
Battery Point 10
Beddgelert, Wales 83
Behn, Aphra xv
Behn, Tara xv
Bell, Dr. Jane Heartz 116
Bellerby, John (Jack) Rotherford 160–163
Bellerby, M. E. Frances (Parker) 163
Bembridge, Thomas 1
Bennet, Grace 82
Bermuda 148, 217, 218
Berwick Register 122, 134, 224, 225
Betul Hospital 190
Bhave, Vinoba 222
Bhoodan (Land Gift) Movement 222
Bibi 167–171
Birmingham Mail 151
Bissett, Agnes Davidson 2, 9
Black, Mrs. George 116
Blake, Lillie Devereaux 25
Bloch, Jean de 64
Blue Bird, The 104
Blue Rocks, NS 141
Blyth, Martha (Pat) 157, 160, 202, 211–214, 225, 237, 238
Bois de Boulogne 101
Bombay, India 168, 169, 204
Boone, Gladys 125
Borden, Sir Robert 118
Boston, MA 1, 25, 97
Bracey, Bertha 159
brahmacharya 184, 222
Breton, Miss 105
Bridge of Alexander 98
Bridges, Monica Waterhouse 106
Bridges, Robert 106
Bridgetown Monitor 157
Bridgetown, NS 148
Bridgetown Spectator 148
Bridgewater Bulletin 128, 209
Bridgewater High School 71
Bridgewater, NS 126, 140, 207, 209, 210
Bright, John 36
Britain xv, 2, 34, 40, 50, 63, 64, 74, 77, 97, 119, 125, 135, 136, 148, 149, 153, 158, 160, 164, 165, 167, 172, 210, 225, 228, 229, 235

British Council of the World Alliance for Promoting Friendship through the Churches 135
British Newspaper Archive 165
Brooklyn, NY 61
Brown, John (Osawatomie) 52, 228
Bryn Mawr 126
Buchanan, Eunice 134, 135, 137, 146, 169, 204, 224, 238
Buchanan, John 134
Buchman, Frank 164, 172
Bunyip 164
Burbidge, Mr. Justice Wheelock 156
Buxton, England 81

C

Calgary Herald 196
Cameron, Elsie 234
Cameron Highlander 92
Cameron, Tyler 234
Campbell, Dr. Gail 240, 241
Campbell, May 90
Canadian Cadet Service 35, 39, 55–58, 61, 62, 143, 145, 189, 231
Canadian Defence League 55
Canadian Fisher 148
Canadian Horticulturist 135
Canadian Men and Women of the Time, 8, 9, 34, 132
Canadian Military Gazette 231
Canadian Museum of Immigration 230
Canadian Peace and Arbitration Society 40
Canadian War Museum 230
Canadian White Ribbon Tidings 129, 130
Carpenter, Mary 238
Catholic World 8
Charleston Daily Mail 210
Chesley, Agnes 8, 10–14, 230, 231
Chesley and Geldert 156
Chesley, Hannah 6
Chesley, James 7, 72, 73
Chesley, John Beecham 6
Chesley, Judge Samuel Ainsley viii, 5, 7, 8, 15–18, 31, 40, 41, 49, 73, 113, 115, 122, 129–131, 140, 141, 146–148, 153–157, 227
Chesley, Mary Albee (Polly) viii, ix, xiv, 8, 15–18, 41–49, 69, 71– 80, 84, 86–100, 103, 105–107, 110–127, 131–159, 164–167, 171–210, 214–219, 223–229, 235, 237
Chesley, Mary Russell vii–xiv, 3, 8, 9, 15–38, 49–71, 91, 110, 114, 119, 128–132, 217, 227, 229, 231

Chesley, Reverend Robert Ainsley 6,–12
Chester Basin, NS 140
Chester, England 77, 83
Chester, NS 140
Chicago, Illinois 40
Children's Newspaper 210
Christa Seva Sangha Ashram 169, 171
Christian Guardian 51
Christian Inquirer 121
Christmas 101, 127, 128, 131
Chronicle Herald 218
Civil & Military Gazette 205
Cleverdon, Catherine x, 239, 241
Close, Henry E. 125
Coleridge, Samuel Taylor 80
Collected Works of Mahatma Gandhi (CWMG), The 186, 178
Columbia University 125
Committee for Relief of German Children 4, 134–138, 143, 144, 224
Committee on Social-Industrial Relations 125
Congress Camp 204
conscientious objectors 2, 35, 87, 124
Constantine 36
Contagious Diseases Act 117, 171
Copenhagen, Denmark 54
Corkum, Hugh 16, 233, 240
Corkum, Lena 142
Corkum, Natalie (Bachman) 5, 16, 140, 141, 142, 156, 212, 217, 233
Corkum, Peter 10
Corkum's Island 10
Courtice, Ada May Brown viii
Courtice, Andrew Cory viii
Courtney, Leonard 94
Courtney (Potter), Catherine (Kate) (Lady Courtney) 94, 95, 119
COVID-19 111
Crisis 229
Cross, Ethelbert Lionel 121

D

Daily Echo 12, 22
Dalhousie University 114, 145
Dalhousie University Archives 145
Dandi, India 176
Dartmouth, NS xiii, 1, 2, 4, 5–7, 16, 218
Daventry, England 94
Dawes Report 139
Defence of the Realm Act 87, 90
Delhi, India 183–185
Delny, Scotland 92

Department of Christian Citizenship, WCTU vii, 69, 114
Department of Franchise vii, 30, 50, 67
Department of Militia and Defence 55, 57, 60, 231
Department of Peace and Arbitration, WCTU viii, 34, 53, 58, 114, 128, 131, 132, 143, 146, 230, 231
Depression, the 134
Desai, Mahadev 190, 203–208, 214, 220
Desai, Narayan 220, 221, 233
DesBrisay, Dr. 10
Dev Prayag, India 198, 199
Diehl, Miss 105
Digby, NS 71
disarmament 115–118, 122, 134, 149–153, 165, 229
Dix, Otto 118
Dolgelly (Dolgelau), Wales 81, 85
Dominion Superintendent of Militia, WCTU 57
Dominion Superintendent of Peace and Arbitration 142
Dorey, Mrs. 238
Doyle, Christine 125
Du Bois, W. E. B. 229
Durham, Mr. 89

E

Eckstein, Anna B. 54
Edinburgh Evening News 164
Edinburgh, Scotland 91
Education Services 163
Eiffel Tower 104
Elliot, Alma (Jonathan) 1
Elphinstone, Marjorie 90
enfranchisement vii, 8, 9, 18, 20–22, 26, 27, 30–34, 49, 50, 53, 65, 69, 114, 122, 127, 131, 132
England viii, 37, 233
Episcopal Peace Fellowship 124
Equal Suffrage League 67
Esperanto 141, 228
Evans, Edward 124
Evans, Harold 125
Evening Echo 122
Evening Mail 26, 115, 157
Evening Post 210

F

Fabian Society 95
Fargo, ND 72
Fellowship of Reconciliation 124, 135

Fight the Famine Committee 94
First Baptist Church 137
First World War viii, 90, 121, 151, 229, 230, 232
Firth of Forth 91
Fontainebleau 102
Forbes, Reverend E. W. (William) 5–7, 11, 190, 200, 208, 211, 214,–219, 226, 235
Forest of Dean 86
Foyer des Étudiants 95, 99
France 37, 40, 53, 74, 77, 95, 97, 105, 106, 115, 118, 125, 142, 150, 158, 228
Franchise Bill 9
Franchise Department 69
Free Religious Movement 159
Friends Library and Archives 164, 233
Friends of India Society 106, 148, 158–160
Friend, The ix, 110, 148, 206, 208
Future of War, The 64

G

Gabrielle Amethyst 50
Gallerie La Fayette 100
Gandhi, Mohandas (Mahatma) ix, 148, 158, 164, 169–233
Gandhi, Narandas 196
Garty Farm 90
George, Lloyd 136, 138
German Distress Relief Fund 135
Germany 37, 40, 121, 124, 134–139, 143, 153, 159
Glasgow, Scotland 93
Gloria, Miss 88, 89, 90
Gloucester, England 77, 86
God of War, The 59
Gokhale, Gopal Krishna 175
Gordon, Anna E. 61, 231
Gordon, General 38
Gounod, Charles 101
Grace Methodist Church 6
Graham, Rev. E. E. 116
Grasmere, England 80
Graves, Robert 118
Great Illusion, The 64
Grierson, Frank 120
Grunland, Rev. 12
Gurukul 199, 206, 244

H

Habeas Corpus Act 87
Haddon Hall 81, 242
Hague Conference 54, 116

INDEX 251

Hague, The 64, 118, 119
Halifax, NS xiii, xv, 20, 27, 68, 72, 97, 115, 122, 128, 129, 132, 144, 146, 148, 171, 209
Halifax Chronicle 217
Halifax Citizen 156
Halifax Explosion 65, 68
Halifax Herald 10, 22, 29, 140
Hall, Elizabeth (Bessie) 126, 127, 140, 170
Hardwar (Haridwar), India 197–199
Hare, William Francis 160
Harijans 183
Harijan, The 185, 190, 202, 204–208, 223
Harijan Training Colony 183
Harrison, Frederic 37
Haslam, Rev. 12
Hathaway, Mrs. W. Frank 118
Hayes, Rev. Will 159, 160
Hebb, Elizabeth 140
Hebb, Marion (Holder) 140
Henderson, Arthur 152
Hereford College 89
Hertfordshire Archives 158
Hewitt, Miss 170
Hibbert, Mary 1, 239
Hillcrest Cemetery 15
Himalayas 193, 197, 206, 220
Hindi 193, 199, 205, 213, 228
Hinduism 168, 172, 181, 184, 185
Hindu, The 222
Hirshberg, Cora 238
Hitler, Adolf 121
Holmes, Dr. Jesse 124
Hotel des Invalides 98
House of Commons 94
Housman, Laurence 159
Hrishikesh, India 194, 196, 199
Hughes, General Sam 231
Hughes, Laura viii, 119
Hull, Dr. William I. 124
human rights 52, 53, 160
Hyde Park 146, 147, 153

I

Independent Labour Party of Great Britain 106, 149, 150, 210, 229, 235
Independent Order of Odd Fellows (IOOF) 41
India ix, 90, 93, 116, 117, 158, 159, 164, 167, 170–178, 187, 193, 195, 200, 204–207, 220–229, 237
Indian National Congress 171, 177
Indian Post Office Bank 202

Indian Succession Act 208
India Office Records (IOR) 158
Industrial and Provident Societies Act 161
Ingham, Mary 188, 190, 193, 194
Inverness, Scotland 92
Irenaeus of Lyons 36
Islam 181, 182
Itarsi, India 169

J

Jones, Bishop Paul 123, 124
Jones, Burne 88
Jones, Dr. Stanley 175
Jones, J. O. 162
Jones, Rachel T. 125
Journal of Education 39

K

Kamlani, Atma 159
Kankhal, India 205
Kaur, Amrit 197
Kentville, NS 140, 144
Keynes, John Maynard 116
khadder 178
Khedi, India 178, 188, 189, 194, 195, 204
Kibworth, England 77
King Edward High School 110
Kinney, Julia (Chesley) 72
Kipling, Rudyard 37

L

La Chapelle de la Reine 102
Lady Courtney 94
La Fontaine 105
Lahore, India 205
La Jolla, California 72, 74, 80, 242
Lambeth, Miss 104
Lansbury, George 150
Lathi Drill 189
Lay Down Your Arms 39
League of Nations 122, 150
League of Nations Society 145
Lester, Muriel 147, 148
Letson, W. A. 128
Lewthwaite, Susan 121
Libby, Frederick 124
Library of the Society of Friends ix
Llangollen, Wales 83
Local Council of Women of Halifax 68
Lodi News-Sentinel 72
London, England 74, 77, 93, 94, 148, 150, 164, 225

London School of Economics 74, 95, 119, 158, 205
London University 105, 115, 122
Longley, Attorney General James Wilberforce 21–27, 65, 228
Longstreth, Walter 124
Louvre 98
Lucknow, India 168
Lunenburg by the Sea 128
Lunenburg County Times 11
Lunenburg County Women's Group (LCWG) xiii, xiv
Lunenburg, NS ix, xiii, xiv, 5, 8, 10, 12, 15, 16, 19, 74, 106, 118, 119, 121–134, 140, 145–148, 199, 209, 210, 216, 218, 227, 228
Lunenburg Opera House 41
Lunenburg Will Book 216, 217

M

MacDonald, Ramsay 94, 136, 149, 151
MacDonald, Reverend 219
MacKay, J. D. 139
Madden, Pearl 194–196
Mahila Ashram 193, 197
Mahone Bay, NS 11, 96
Malesherbes, France 103
Manchester, England 82
Martyr, Justin 36
Marybehn. *See* Barr, F. Mary
Mary, Queen of Scots 91
Mawhinney, David 233
McCormick, Mrs. John 148
McCreath, Mrs. 213
McCrief, Miss Scott 88
McGillivray, Rev. 12
McKay, Margaret B. 35, 58
McNaughton, Violet viii
Meerut, India 170
Melun, France 102
Memoirs of Earl of Listowel, The 160
Mercer, Charles H. 145
Methodist Church 2, 4, 7, 12, 31, 43, 177
Middleton, NS 39
Midlothian, Scotland 205
Militia Myths: Ideas of the Canadian Citizen Soldier 231
Mirabehn. *See* Slade, Madeleine
Monmouth, Wales 85
Montreal Star 52, 231
Montreal Sunday Herald 231
Montreal Witness 51, 170, 172
Moral Damage of War, The 39

Morash, Benj. 10
Morgan, Henry James 8
Morgan, Miss 104
Morning Chronicle 5, 11, 65, 105, 128
Morris, Cecilia 202, 237, 238
Mosley, John 37
Motherwell Times 164
Motibehn. *See* Pearl Madden
Mount Allison Ladies' Academy 5, 7, 13, 41
Mount Allison University 5, 18, 41, 45–48, 71, 138, 156, 207
Mount Allison University Archives 233
Mount Saint Vincent University xv
Murray, Ella x
Murray, E. M. 68
Musgrave, Amy 49
Musgrave, Fanny 49, 50, 51
Muslim (Moslem) 168, 172

N

Nab Cottage 79
Nagpur, India 190, 204, 205
Nantucket, MA 2
National Indian Congress 177
National Labour Party 149
Neighbours, The 159–163, 207, 228
Nevada State Journal 210
New Brunswick 6, 7
New Delhi, India 218, 221
New England 1
Newfoundland 6, 7, 156
New Outlook 146, 147
New Ross, NS 140
New York, NY 61
New York Times 210
New Zealand 209, 210
Nobel Peace Prize 152
Normal College 71
North Dakota 72
Norwood News 149
Notre Dame 96
Nova Scotia 71, 207, 209, 210, 218
Nova Scotia Archives vii, 218, 233
Nova Scotia Law Reports 7
Nova Scotia Probate Records 216
Nova Scotia Provincial Union 131
Nova Scotia Reports, Vol. 40: Containing Reports of Cases Argued and Determined in the Supreme Court of Nova Scotia 7
Nova Scotia Writers' Federation xv
Nugent, Alex 174

O

O'Hagan, Thomas 8
Oldershaw, Audrey 233
Olmsted, Allen 125
Olmsted, Mildred Scott 125
Orbita, SS 146
Order of the Great Companions 160
Overton, Miss 77, 81, 90
Owens, Wilfred 118
Oxford, England 77, 87, 89
Oxford Group 159, 164, 169, 172, 212–217, 237, 238
Oxner, Mary 127

P

pacifism viii, 93, 94, 124, 207
padayatras 222
Pakistan 205
Palace Theater 120
Pankhurst, Christabel 106
Pankhurst, Dr. Richard 106
Pankhurst, Emmeline 106
Pankhurst suffragettes 147
Pankhurst, Sylvia 105, 106, 148, 159
Paris Conference 94
Paris, France 95, 96, 98, 102–106
Payne, Richenda 159
peace advocacy x, 3, 9, 18, 31, 34, 39, 40, 49, 52, 54, 57, 59, 61–71, 106, 114–134, 140–153, 178, 224, 227–231
Peace and Arbitration Department. *See* Department of Peace and Arbitration, WCTU
Peace Congress of the United States 40
Peace Testimony 2
Pearse, Mark Guy 81
Pendle Hill 123
Pennland, SS 155
Perth, Scotland 92
Petitcodiac, NB 6
Petition for the Enfranchisement of Women 21, 66
Philadelphia, Pennsylvania 123, 126–133
Philadelphia Record 123
Phoenix Settlement, South Africa 229
Pier 21 230
Pilsna, SS 178
pith helmet 192
Place de la Concorde 98
Pleasant Street Methodist Church 137
Plynlimon, Wales 77
Poona, India 169

Poor Law 87
Porter, Lulu DeBlois 144
Potters Bar, England 148, 149, 207, 208, 212–217, 228, 237
Potter, W. P. 209, 216
Powell, General Baden 38
Powers, Ada L. 131
Princes Inlet, NS 5, 140, 141
Progress Enterprise 10, 30, 72–79, 87, 90, 93, 95, 98, 100, 106, 110, 120, 123, 128, 133, 146, 155
prohibition 9, 134
Provincial Wesleyan 7

Q

Quaker Mission 169
Quakers. *See* Religious Society of Friends

R

Rafkin, Rev. 12
Raikes, Robert 86
Rajah of Barampur 168
Raymond, Mrs. 118
Regent's Park 96
Register 135, 137
Religious Society of Friends (Quakers) viii, ix, xv, 1, 2, 4, 9, 94–97, 100, 123–129, 135, 158, 159, 163, 183, 188, 206, 207, 229, 237
Reynolds, A. R. 129
Reynolds, Reginald 158
Rhayader, Wales 85
Riley, James Whitcomb 16
Rishikesh, India. *See* Hrishikesh, India
Ritcey's Cove, NS 10
Ritchie, Dr. Eliza 20, 67
Robert, Henri 105
Rochdale, England 82
Rousse, Mrs. 213
Ruhr occupation 121
Russell, Agnes (Bissett) 1, 5
Russell, Alma (Aunt Am) 2, 4, 19, 20, 129, 141, 146, 211
Russell, Arthur 235
Russell, Bell 238
Russell, Bernard W. 216
Russell, Bertrand 159
Russell, Edith 169, 216, 238
Russell, Frances 235
Russell, Gyrth 96, 97, 211–214, 215
Russell, Helen 238
Russell, Howard 2, 5

Russell, John 2, 5, 16
Russell, Judge Benjamin 2–7, 40, 97, 126
Russell, Mary (Polly) 2, 4
Russell, Mary Rebecca 1, 2, 5
Russell, Nancy 238
Russell, Nathaniel 1, 4, 9, 239
Russia 37, 40, 118, 120, 153, 207, 224
Russian famine relief 135
Rydal, England 79
Rypons, Mr. 89

S

Sabarmati Archives 194
Sabarmati Ashram 176–178
Sabarmati, India 176
Sahib, Khan 182
Saint Augustine 179
Saint Francis 179
Saint John Standard 117
Saint Saëns 105
Salt March 176
San Diego, California 72, 207
Sangnier, Marc 147
Sassoon, Siegfried 118
satyagraha 176
Satyagraha Ashram 176
Save the Children 94, 119, 120, 135
Scandia 149
Scotland 90, 205
Scotsman 205
Second Peninsula, NS 96
Second Round Table Conference 177
Second World War 124, 225
Seine, the 102
Shanta (Mary Ingham) 193
Sharma, Siddharth 220, 221, 233
Shaw, George Bernard 64
Sheboygan Press 210
Sibly (Libby), Frederick 123
Silver, Capt. S. 10
Sixth International Democratic Peace Conference 146
Slade, Madeleine 197, 204, 244
Smith, D. 149
Smith, Elma 16
Snowdon, Wales 77, 83
socialism 53, 54, 106
sola hat 192
Sorbonne, the 95, 99, 105, 207
South Africa 157, 175, 207, 228, 229
Speakers' Corner 147, 153
Spencer, Herbert 37
Spindler, Israel 10

St. Albans, England 78
St. Andrews, NB 91
Starr, Ida Powell 57, 60, 62
St. Giles Cathedral 91
St. John's, NL 6, 7, 156
Students' Christian Association 101
Students' Hostel 101, 102, 104
suffrage x, xiv, 20, 21, 28, 30, 34, 71, 129
suffragettes 34, 96, 147, 228
suffragists viii, 94, 106, 228, 231
Sumitra 188, 189, 190, 193
Sunday Herald 209
Sunday School Movement 86
Superintendent of Peace and Arbitration 224
Suttner, Baroness Bertha von 39
swadeshi 176
Swanwick, England 77
Swarthmore College 124, 125
Sydney Record 119
Sykes, Marjorie ix

T

Tagore, Rabindranath 172
Tai (Omma), Mahadevi 197, 199, 200, 206, 220–223, 233
tapasya 176
Tarabehn (Taraben, Tara) 183, 189, 196–206, 220
Tatian 36
Teesdale Mercury 164, 167
Tertullian 36
This Was Bapu 193
Tikey, Mr. 90
Tintern Abbey 77, 85
Tolstoy, Leo 36
Toronto Star 121
Trafalgar Square 96
Treaty of Versailles 121
Truro Daily News 137, 139
Tuileries, the 98
Two Orphans, The 104

U

Union of Democratic Control 95, 117, 122
United Church of Canada 146, 156
Universities Relief Committee 135
University of London 74, 75
University of Pennsylvania 124
untouchables 183
US Congress 53

V

Vancouver 110–119, 207
Vancouver School Board 110
Vancouver Sun 111
Vane, Maynard 116
Van Merle, Miss 94
Vernon, Dorothy 81
Versailles Peace Conference 116
Victory Bond 235
Vienna, Austria 159
Village Industries Association 202
Voltaire 105

W

Walsh, Reverend Walter 39
Walton, Bernard 125
Wardha Hospital 190
Wardha, India 170, 171, 183, 184, 193, 197, 200, 204, 206
Wardha Mahila Ashram 205
Ward-Whate, Rev. F. C. 121
Warner, Olive 148, 157, 207, 228, 229
War Resisters' International 178
Washington Disarmament Conference 118
Webb, Beatrice (Potter) 95
Webb, Sidney 95
Weekly Monitor 148
Wells, H. G. 64
Welwyn Garden City Meeting 158, 207
Wesleyan Academy 7
Wesleyan Church 83, 169
Wesleyan 12, 16, 35, 43, 47, 113, 129, 147
West Coast Sentinel 164
West Indies 134
Westralian Worker 164
White Ribbon Bulletin 35, 54, 56, 57, 60, 61, 63
Whitney, Janet Payne 124
Who's Who in America 8
Whynacht, Samuel 10
Willard, Frances xiv
Willis, E. J. 26
Winslow, Jack 169, 172
Woburn, England 78
Woman's Christian Temperance Union (WCTU) vii, xiv, 8, 9, 15, 19, 20, 25, 30–69, 87, 114, 119, 128, 130–134, 142, 144, 146, 224, 227, 230–232
Woman's Foreign Missionary Society of the Methodist Episcopal Church 194
Woman's Journal 25

Women's Social and Political Union (WSPU). *See* suffragettes
Women's Council House 115
Women's Institute 120
Women's International League for Peace and Freedom (WILPF) 64, 116–124, 141, 227, 228
Women's International Peace Conference 64, 119
Women's Social and Political Union 106
Women's Who's Who in America 9, 132
Wood, James 231
Wordsworth, William 80
World Health Organization 197
Wright, Sara Rowell 130

Y

Yarmouth, NS 39
Young, Austin 10
Young, Mrs. E. A. 118

Z

Zangwill, Israel 59
Zola, Émile 37